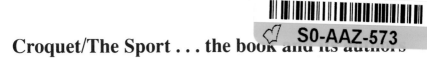

Croquet/The Sport . . . the book and its authors

Over the past thirty years, the game of croquet that millions of Americans remember from childhood, has changed dramatically . . . and for the better. From the countless bumpy backyards of yesteryear a newer, more challenging version (which has been described as a combination of chess on grass, billiards, golf and war), is now being played on smoother and faster lawns by increasing numbers of intelligent, fun loving, discriminating people. They have been drawn to the one sport where youth has no advantage over age, nor male over female, and have discovered the social, recreational and competitive rewards of the SPORT of Croquet.

"CROQUET/The Sport" is the only book to offer the beginner and expert alike, the authoritative presentation of croquet basics: grips, stances, stalking, swings and shot-making. Added to this, are over 295 photos and diagrams, valuable tactical and strategic direction, tips on practice, customs and etiquette, appropriate equipment, clothing and accessories, tournament formats, a brief history of croquet, up-to-date USCA records and a list of USCA clubs.

All of this, and the only complete printing of the Official Rules of the United States Croquet Association Six Wicket and Nine Wicket and Golf Croquet, outside of the pocket version issued by the USCA, make "CROQUET/The Sport," the most comprehensive book on the sport published to date.

Jack R. Osborn

. . . founded the United States Croquet Association, codified the original official rules in 1976 and is widely credited for the dramatic growth of the sport in America.

Dubbed "Mr. Croquet" by Town & Country Magazine, Jack Osborn has competed in over two hundred tournaments since picking up his first Jaques mallet in 1960, winning a record 80 events, including seven USCA National Titles. As captain of the U.S. National Team for eight years, he has represented America in International matches in England, Scotland, Ireland, South Africa, Australia and Bermuda.

In 1983, Osborn co-authored (with Jesse Kornbluth) "Winning Croquet—From Backyard to Greensward" (Simon & Schuster), which has been heralded as the definitive book on the sport and has served as the textbook for USCA schools and clinics.

Also author of countless articles on the sport, including the croquet section of the New World Encyclopedia, Jack has been editor and publisher of the official USCA magazine, "U.S. Croquet Gazette" since it began publication in 1979.

Based in Palm Beach Gardens, Florida, now headquarters of the USCA, Jack can be frequently found on the five championship courts at the PGA National Resort practicing his favorite sport.

John C. Osborn

. . . has played croquet since age seven, collecting dozens of major tournament titles including the 1987 USCA National Singles Championship. A member of the USA's International Team since 1983, John resides in New York City where he teaches at the NYCC's courts in Central Park.

CROQUET
THE SPORT

by
Jack R. Osborn
Founder, President Emeritus
United States Croquet Association

Incorporating
"Winning Croquet—From Backyard to Greensward"
with
Jesse Kornbluth

and
John C. Osborn
and
Dr. Carlton H. Mabee

Forward by
Herbert Bayard Swope, Jr.

Instructional Photographs by William Powers and Lucien Capehart
Illustrations by Allen Scheuch and Diane Ristuccia

FARSIGHT COMMUNICATIONS, INC. / Palm Beach Gardens, Florida

Published by Farsight Communications, Inc.
7100-24 Fairway Drive
Palm Beach Gardens, Florida 33418

Designed by Diane Ristuccia

Manufactured in the United States of America

1 2 3 4 5 6 7 8 9 10

Library of Congress Cataloging in Publications Data

Osborn, Jack R.
Croquet, The Sport

**Library of Congress Catalogue Card Number
89-91583**

**ISBN 0-9624568-0-2 cloth
ISBN 0-9624568-1-0 paper**

CONTENTS

FOREWORD

The subtitle of this book might well be "A Story of Reincarnation," for croquet (pronounced now and forevermore "cro-KAY") was buried in the backyards of our country for years. Now it has reemerged, not only hale and hearty but even in white flannels (where obtainable) on the greenswards of more than three hundred eager clubs from Maine to California and Florida to Puget Sound.

As this book and its predecessor "Winning Croquet" reveals, the "backyard" or "garden" set game was not the only version of play in America during the past half-century. The first rumble of heavy-mallet, iron-wicket croquet grew to a roar on Long Island in the 1920s, when my father, then executive editor of the late *New York World*, organized weekend games on our lawn in Great Neck. Here, an egocentric and emotional group of nonathletes who mostly comprised the Algonquin Round Table and Thanatopsis Literary and Inside Straight Poker Club—Alexander Woollcott, Dorothy Parker, George and Beatrice Kaufman, *New Yorker* publisher Raoul Fleischmann, Heywood Broun, Marc Connelly, and many others—waged deadly combat.

Although the game was, in those happy, less trying times, played with the same English-made equipment as now, it was not quite croquet as we now know it. The principal difference was the size of the court; at my father's house, croquet balls could be driven with impunity down the sloping drive toward Manhasset Bay. Later, at Sands Point, where Margaret Emerson had a magnificent course, the roots of her trees provided deep snares and impenetrable barriers from which it might take more than one stroke to return one's ball into action.

It was on Mrs. Emerson's lawn that tournament play really began, with Averell Harriman, George Abbott, Howard Dietz, Ogden Phipps and Richard and Dorothy Rodgers, among others, competing every summer until the mid-1950s. Meanwhile, thanks to Darryl Zanuck and Samuel

Goldwyn, the game was progressing in parallel manner on the West Coast. Zanuck's challenging but unorthodox course in Palm Springs—there was a fountain in the middle—and Goldwyn's two manicured lawns in Beverly Hills saw a whole new group of croquet talents arise—George Sanders, Jean Negulesco, Cesare Danova, Gig Young, Bill and Howard Hawks, Richard Zanuck, Mike Romanoff and Louis Jourdan.

Although this book touches reverently on that era, its principal emphasis is on the present and the promising future of the sport. The teaching techniques set forth have proven highly effective over the past decade and with study and practice will be of invaluable help to beginner and expert alike.

Because the unlimited playing areas to be found on the courts of the past have shrunk, like the dollar, the game now demands more accuracy than ever. It continues to be chess played on your feet. And the limited boundaries make it more viable for what was once called "the weaker sex."

Skills that once took years to master (mostly by osmosis) are being acquired in months by neophytes who avail themselves of the competitive joys of club tournaments, which are now played under the same rules across the country.

With the persistence of Jack Osborn, who made the United States Croquet Association come alive, plus the knowledge of the game to be gotten from this definitive book, there seems little doubt that USCA members will be playing a major role on courts around the globe as charter members of the newly formed World Croquet Federation.

Herbert Bayard Swope, Jr.
President, Croquet Foundation of America
Member, U.S. Croquet Hall of Fame
Palm Beach, Florida
1989

ACKNOWLEDGMENTS

To those of you possessing a copy of "Winning Croquet—From Back yard to Greensward" (Simon & Schuster, 1983), much of what you will read herein may have a familiar ring to it. This is not by accident.

When, in 1987, the remainder of the initial run of copies was nearly exhausted by the growing USCA membership and others coming into the sport at the rate of one new club a week, a decision as to whether to reprint the original, or to write a new book had to be made.

Since it had become the preferred "text" book of USCA school and clinic programs, because of the basic instructional sections dealing with grips, stances and swings, along with other fundamentals of shot-making and play, the temptation to simply reprint "Winning Croquet" was the initial choice. After recognizing that not only had the rules and records of the USCA gone through several evolutionary changes and updates, but that new teaching techniques by our small, but growing number of American professional instructors, such as Teddy Prentis, Peyton Ballenger, Bill Hoy, Bob Kroeger and Johnny Osborn, had also evolved since my co-author, Jesse Kornbluth and I had written "Winning Croquet" back in 1982, clearly suggested that more than reprinting was in order.

John C. Osborn's record as the top player in the USCA's Grand Prix rankings from 1984 through 1987, along with a well-earned reputation as an instructor at his home club in New York and with the faculty of the USCA National School since 1982, fully justifies his father's choice of him to contribute to the instructional chapters of this book.

Similarly, the choice of Dr. Carlton Mabee to share his knowledge and passion for croquet court construction and maintenance in the revised chapter "Lust for Lawns" can only make this new book more useful to readers seeking help in this important area in the development of the sport.

What we also recognized, however, in reviewing the contents of "Winning Croquet," was the considerable contribution that Jesse Kornbluth's warmth, wit and skill had brought to the "backyard" viewpoint which had made our book so enjoyably readable by countless people who have praised its "balance" over the years.

For that reason, and with his permission, we have kept his chapter on the "backyard," as well as other prose which readers have told us they have found helpful in introducing them to the fun and challenge of the sport.

Our thanks, as well, to Jane Berentson for shopping with Jesse for that now historic backyard croquet set.

Also for their contribution to the success of "Winning Croquet" and this sequel, we are grateful to Willie Espada, Alan Scheuch and William Powers for their instructional graphics and photos. "CROQUET/The Sport" has doubled the number of photos and drawings through the talented camera work of Robert Phillips, Ken Nelson, Lucien Capehart, Roy DeFillipis along with many others and the computer graphics wizardry of Bill Hoy and Art Director, Diane Ristuccia.

Our ongoing gratitude to those good friends who have made both of these books possible is extended to G. Nigel Aspinall, Cesare Danova, Bernard Neal, Libby Newell, William Ormerod, Eula Osborn (Spectator of the century), Herbert B. Swope, Jr., Cathy Tankoos and the late S. Joseph Tankoos, John W. Solomon and the croquet associations of England, Scotland, Ireland, Australia, South Africa and newly formed Croquet Canada. Special thanks are extended to the President's of the last two, Ian Gillespie and Bill Langstroth, whose dedication to the betterment of the sport is unparallelled.

To the entire membership of the United States Croquet Association and the members of the Croquet Foundation of America's U.S. Croquet Hall of Fame current (and future), the USCA Executive Committee led now by Rudulph (Foxy) Carter, Dan Shepherd and Anne Frost, our thanks for the roles you have all played in making the title of this book come true.

Lastly, although first in our appreciation, are those who have suffered through the creative and publishing process here at Farsight. Jean Arrington, Al Hollender, Carolyn Shores, Tricia Hickory, Kathy Weaber, Lou Fusco with an able assist by Frank Maradie, the copy editing of Betty Taylor and the glue who put it all together, Diane Ristuccia. Bless you all.

INTRODUCTION

" Croquet? You've got to be kidding!"

While I still hear this occasionally, it was the standard exclamation of folks when told what the USCA blazer badge I was wearing at the "21" Club bar a dozen years ago represented. Today, one of my favorite retired Jaques mallets hangs over the end of that famed bar, and the wonderment at the explanation has waned significantly as a spark of respectful recognition has replaced amused disbelief. Still, if this were a word association test and this examiner suddenly uttered the word "croquet," Americans would have one of three responses.

One has to do with a game played in Edwardian England by the very rich at great country houses. From these houses, on languid summer afternoons, come men in high collars, ties and wool jackets. On the lawn, they encounter women who still favor petticoats, long dresses, hats and gloves. Together, they have sport: he taps the ball, then she does. Finally it's time for tea. Oh, what a lovely afternoon! A triumph, in fact. No ungentlemanly displays of temper. No unladylike manifestations of competitive zeal and, best of all, no perspiration.

Another, shared by countless millions of Americans, is the childhood memory of a hazy afternoon in gentler times at grandmother's house with all the family, but mostly the kids, knocking little striped balls through wide mouthed wire wickets with unbridled abandonment.

The other mental picture is also American, and it has nothing to do with gentility. In this vision of croquet, the game is simply a polite form of war. Let's hear no blather about "family entertainment"—this is hand-to-hand combat in suburban backyards. Teeth gritted, sweat escaping every pore, the players stalk one another, trading insults, disputing every shot. What are they waiting for? The moment when they can send their opponent's ball rolling in the general direction of Mongolia. Why are the mallet heads covered with plastic? So the skull of any player who gets bashed won't be mortally wounded. Will they be friends when the game's over? Not if they can avoid it.

It is the aim of this book to banish all these misleading images and replace them with what we know to be the truth about modern croquet: it's the one amateur sport that millions of Americans can play with pleasure all their lives.

Yes, the ultra-chic *do* knock croquet balls around on pristine green-swards at the world's most exclusive watering holes.

And yes, croquet *can* be a vicious game that turns pleasant afternoons into emotional battlefields.

But croquet is much more than a way to achieve status or to vent pent-up hostility. Considered simply as a game, croquet is uniquely satisfying because it never fails to provide the kind of competition that excites, challenges—and enlightens—its devotees. Just when you think you've mastered it, the muse of croquet lands on your shoulder, whispers in your ear, imparts yet another hidden truth about strokes or tactics—and your game makes a quantum stride forward.

Best of all, the pleasure of growing better at croquet isn't limited to any age group or reserved for either sex. One of the better croquet players in America first took mallet in hand when he was ten; won a national title at fourteen; now that he is in his early twenties, he's competing against world class veterans who were clearing wickets before he was born. And because there's no physical contact and the mallet's relatively light, women can play as well as—or even better than—their male opponents. "You may strain a muscle below the elbow playing croquet," one wit has remarked, "but there's nothing about this game that a drink can't fix."

The pleasures of croquet are not unknown in America: each year, manufacturers say, almost 300,000 croquet sets are sold in this country. Ninety-five percent of those 300,000 sets have short-handled, plastic-tipped mallets, two stakes, small wooden balls and wide-mouthed wickets whose metal uprights are about as sturdy as wire coat hangers. In the backyards where this equipment is used, it's not unusual for balls to be ricocheted off tree trunks or for the endless paraphernalia of suburban life—swimming pools, driveways, barbecue pits and the like—to be incorporated into the game. With as many as eight players competing on these free-form courts, it's no wonder that matches sometimes seem like European bicycle races: speed contests in which sideswiping opponents is the key to victory.

We know those pleasures. We first encountered croquet in the form of one of those inexpensive backyard sets. We played croquet exclusively with that equipment for years. But these days, when we talk about croquet, we aren't referring to toy mallets, skinny wickets, caroming shots off trees, "take-overs" and arguments that rend friendships. By croquet, we don't mean the game, we mean the *sport* of croquet.

In the sport of croquet—or, as we sometimes say, *real* croquet—the court is more often 84 by 105 feet and clipped as flat as a putting green. The mallets are longer and heavier and are made of specially selected hardwoods. The composition balls are shockingly large—their diameter is only $^3/_8$ inch smaller than the cast-iron wickets they must pass through. There are fewer wickets for those balls to clear and only one stake for them to hit.

But the differences between 9-wicket backyard croquet and 6-wicket croquet are as much tactical as they are physical. In 6-wicket games, players scarcely ever seem to shoot for their next wicket. Their intention, instead, appears defensive—to protect their balls from any possible attack while setting up a controlled offense. As a result, the winner is often a player who's so far behind that he's seemingly out of the game; then hesitation dissolves into brilliantly aggressive shooting, and he suddenly roars out of the backcourt to complete the course and claim the victory.

In 1977, when a small but hopeful group of croquet fanatics founded the United States Croquet Association, very few Americans played the sport of croquet. Considering how expensive it can be to play this variety of the game, it's a miracle that even 80 people made up the five founding clubs—a set of English-made equipment might cost upwards of $1,500, and the brave soul who decides to create a real court on his back lawn is looking at a potentially hefty contractor's bill.

If croquet were only a game for the very rich, it would have remained the best-kept secret in amateur sports. But this has not been the case. As of this writing, more than 350 clubs have affiliated with the USCA—and so many members that the USCA office has had to computerize the national rankings. This 7,000 percent increase in membership since 1977 has made USCA croquet one of the fastest-growing participant sports in the country.

One reason for our conviction that this growth is but the tip of the iceberg is that American equipment manufacturers have recently introduced sets of sports-level mallets, balls and wickets that cost around $200. At this price, potential purchasers of croquet equipment are thinking twice before plunking down $30 to $85 for a set of toy-backyard equipment. Their considered decision—to buy the USCA approved equipment—is bringing serious croquet to thousands of families who'd never describe themselves as wealthy.

Another reason is that newcomers to USCA croquet no longer have to create their own greenswards. Resorts, hotels and inns, along with country, tennis and sports clubs, capitalizing on their maintenance capabilities, are installing courts, with a few even taking up the tennis nets on some of their grass courts and introducing croquet wickets onto those lawns. Colleges have added croquet to their sports schedules. And retirement communities and a score of cities have allocated funds for serious croquet courts.

But the most important reason so many people are playing the sport of croquet these days is even more basic than cost and availability. It is, simply, that USCA croquet has it all over the backyard game.

The layout of the USCA game may look funny at first. The equipment may feel uncomfortable. The rules may sound impossibly complicated. And the players—some of them, anyway—may seem not-to-be-believed. If we can only get you to step onto a court and start to play, however, you'll soon see how little any of that matters. For on the greensward, as afternoon shadows darken the lawn and the faint sound of ice tinkling in frosted pitchers punctuates the steady *thonk* of croquet balls, it will all become clear to you: this is not only a beautiful game, it is terrific *fun*.

The compelling advantage USCA croquet has over backyard croquet is that the 6-wicket game is much more involving. In the 9-wicket backyard game, a highly developed propensity for whacking every ball that ventures near yours is often the factor that decides the match. Real croquet requires much more from you: cunning, patience, courage, skill and a good sense of humor.

Theater critic and Algonquin wit Alexander Woollcott once remarked that serious croquet is "no game for the soft of sinew and gentle of spirit." It is also, as he neglected to add, not a game for the slow-witted or unimaginative. For croquet isn't just a form of war; it's also chess and billiards. And so, along with mastering the technical aspects of the sport—how to hold the mallet, and so on—it is essential that you master croquet strategy.

According to movie mogul and croquet fanatic Darryl Zanuck, "You can learn to hit the ball very easily, but to learn the strategy takes a minimum of two years." If, however, you are taught in such a way that you start playing croquet with strategy in mind—if, the first day you take mallet in hand, you can be made to understand that victory consists in making many wickets in one turn, not one in every turn—we believe that you will be playing good strategic croquet within just a few months. By the end of the season, with some practice and guidance, you may well be playing impressive "B"-level USCA croquet. In two years you could be in the finals of the USCA national championships—as happened in 1982 to an Arizonan after less than a year of play—or regularly beating everyone in your zip code.

But can you *really* learn how to play winning croquet from a book?

Historically, the answer is yes. Some of the most brilliant players—many of them women—in turn-of-the-century England learned to play entirely from books, and diligent study of those out-of-print texts would give you a strong sense of the basics. But if you stepped onto a modern greensward and used the strategy you'd learned from those books, you'd have a problem; the game they describe is very different from the sport as it's played today in America and in a growing number of other neighboring countries.

This book is specifically written for today's players—from beginners to experts. If you've never held a mallet before and have just started to consider the idea of investing a few bob for a backyard croquet set, we feel confident that we will soon have you playing that game with verve and style. If you're presently a backyard player who's wondering why your neighbors are suddenly buying new equipment and arranging their wickets in a different way, we'll show you how to beat them. Even if you are already a member of the USCA and are even now mastering four-ball breaks, take-offs and peels, this book can be a handy reminder of the most basic truths of croquet.

All we ask in return is that none of you drop this book at our feet after you've thoroughly trounced us on the greensward.

CROQUET.

AS PLAYED BY

THE NEWPORT CROQUET CLUB.

BY

ONE OF THE MEMBERS.

Sic ludus animo debet aliquando dari
Ad cogitandum melior ut redeat tibi.
PHŒD., Lib. iii, Fab. 4.

NEW YORK:
SHELDON & COMPANY
498 & 500 BROADWAY.
1865.

*Early American
Croquet Rule Books
from 1865 and 1871.*

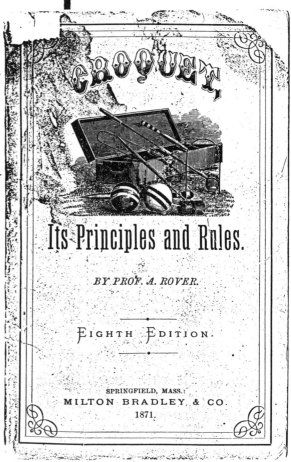

CROQUET

Its Principles and Rules.

BY PROF. A. ROVER.

EIGHTH EDITION.

SPRINGFIELD, MASS.:
MILTON BRADLEY & CO.
1871.

1

IN THE BEGINNING . . .

(where Croquet came from,
where it's been and where it's going)

In spite of considerable and exhaustive research by English chroniclers of the game of croquet, its origins remain clouded in obscurity. The only consensus discernible to this writer is that the sport as we know it today traveled from Ireland to England in 1850 where an ivory-turner named John Jaques II produced croquet equipment, introduced the game at the Great Exhibition of 1851 and received a Gold Medal for his efforts.

The late D. M. C. Prichard, in his extraordinary comprehensive "History of Croquet," dismisses the long held theory that croquet descended from the stick and ball game known as Pall Mall, played by Charles II in the 1660s, by suggesting that while they "both probably derived from the primitive human instinct to have some fun by hitting a round object as far or as accurately as possible," if Pall Mall were an "ancestor of anything, it was golf."

As for the name Croquet itself, earlier examinations leave us to choose between the French word "crochet," a small hook; croche, "a shepherd crook," or as having derived from the Irish "cluiche," meaning play, which in modern pronunciations sounds like croquet. While I personally favor the latter (having been born on St. Patrick's Day), it's best to press on to more compelling issues, such as how this "new" game was played.

It has been suggested that a Mr. Spratt did publish some rules for croquet around 1851 which had, together with a crude set, been given to him by a Miss McNaughton. These rules, which showed a court setting of two stakes and ten "arches" placed seven or eight feet apart, making it possible to run up to three wickets in one stroke, bear a remarkable likeness to the American "backyard" game as we know it today.

"Players strike their balls alternately: but when a player sends his ball through an arch he is entitled to another stroke, and also when he 'roquets' his adversary, he gets another stroke. 'Roquet' is produced when a player strikes his opponent's ball with his own; he should then put his ball quite close to his opponent's and, placing his foot firmly on his own ball, strike his opponent's ball, and send it as far as possible in an unfavorable direction; his opponent has to play from that point, and his own ball remains steady; then he also gets another stroke."

As you will recognize the practice of putting one's foot on the ball, which became known as a "tight croquet," dates back to the very beginning and although it is no longer allowed in the Association game, its memory lingers on in some "backyard" variations.

Mr. Spratt, after making nothing of it, is said to have passed the game on to John Jaques II (whose firm had been in the games business since 1795), who after making the equipment for some years noted that croquet had "won a popularity which has almost revolutionized our outdoor social life." He went on to bemoan the vast number of variations of the game and "that there are hardly no lawns in England where the game is played in the same manner in every respect."

Jaques' frustration has since been mirrored on both sides of the Atlantic and, as we will learn, was the motivation for the creation of the national governing associations in England and in the United States, albeit a century apart.

John Jaques II, credited with introducing the game in England in the early 1850s.

As A. E. Gill puts it in his book "Croquet, The Complete Guide," "It is certainly fair to say that John Jaques II was the first man to rationalize the rules of the game ... and one must accord him a sense of altruism (since) he certainly didn't need to regulate the rules of the game to promote sales of croquet equipment—sales were booming despite the lack of any hard-and-fast rules. Some measure of the success of his rules, however, is that they were published annually from 1864-1870 and ran into tens of thousands of copies. They are recognizably close to the modern game, at least in embryo, and form the basis for later refinement by early avatars of the (British) Croquet Association."

Jaques was as happy to sell croquet sets to women as he was to men, and so, by 1866, croquet had become a fashionable excuse for England's Victorian hostesses to give extravagant lawn parties. At these events, women wore anti-Aeolians—wire cages to hold their skirts in trim during their turns. Despite the skill of some women, they were somewhat patronized by their male opponents, who tended to hold their mallets with only one hand to give the ladies a sporting chance.

Eighteen sixty-seven was a landmark year for croquet, not only because almost every English hostess seemed to be send-

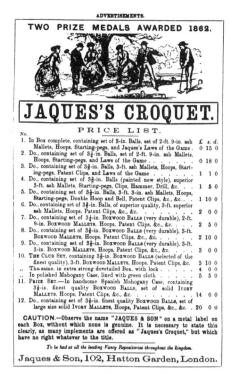

A Jaques price list from the 1860s (courtesy of John Jaques & Son Ltd.).

ing out invitations with crossed mallets and croquet balls engraved on them, but because, in that year, Walter Jones Whitmore blazed onto the scene.

A young man of considerable breeding but little reliability, Whitmore decided the surest way to create an income for himself was to sponsor England's first croquet tournament. He produced this event at Evesham, on 45-by-60-foot courts that had wickets eight inches wide. To his great good fortune, he won the tournament, thereby giving him legitimate reason to represent himself as England's first croquet champion.

Whitmore had a knack for making enemies, and by 1869 he had alienated both the sporting press and the fledgling croquet establishment, including the All-England Croquet Club he had helped launch. But Whitmore could smell success and money in croquet, and he wasn't about to let a little opposition get in his way. Barred from the AECC he founded the National Croquet Club. Blacklisted by certain sportswriters, he decided to hold a tournament that no one could ignore.

Winslow Homer painted this "Croquet Scene" in the 1860s (courtesy, Art Institute of Chicago).

As it turned out, Whitmore's 1871 extravaganza was the most remarkable tournament that croquet has ever known. Seventeen thousand troops paraded around the courts. There was a full-dress ball. Bands played without pause, and the spectators were packed five deep. Whitmore placed second, but as Prichard tells us "it was croquet as Whitmore visualized it—the pomp and splendor, the extravagance, the dazzling entertainment, the brilliant and aristocratic company and the martial music—and he, Walter Jones Whitmore, at the center, the cynosure of every eye."

It was Whitmore's greatest victory. It was also his last. The following year he was ill, and his tournament had only three players and eight spectators. A year and a half after he made all England pay attention to croquet, he was dead.

Even if Whitmore had lived, the croquet vogue could not have been sustained, for the 1870s marked the introduction of lawn tennis in England—and lawn tennis came on even stronger than croquet had. By 1887 croquet had fallen into such disrepute that the directors of the All-England Croquet and Lawn Tennis Club at Wimbledon decided that the placards inscribed with the names of the club's croquet champions should be taken down and thrown into the Thames. Fortunately a groundsman, with a better sense of history than his employers, hid them.

But while croquet was on the decline in England, it was becoming the latest rage in America. Not surprisingly, the rich were the first to take up the game, but clubs and civic groups were quick to follow their lead. Even Rutherford B. Hayes committed $6 of the taxpayers' money for a set of "fancy boxwood balls," an expenditure that enraged the Democratic opposition but allowed the President and his friends to play a higher-quality game on the White House lawn.

Why did croquet sweep a country that had, unlike England, no hierarchical class system? As a Milton Bradley handbook from 1871 suggests, it was because croquet uniquely matched the spirit of a young, aggressive, achievement-minded nation. "When we work or fight, we work and fight harder than any other people," the author noted. "We should be as enthusiastic in our play." The author of the 1865 handbook of the Newport (Rhode Island) Croquet Club saw the attraction of the game in less overtly populist terms: "Whist exercises the memory and the power of calculating probabilities, chess the imagination and the faculty of abstract reasoning, but croquet, though it taxes these mental capacities less, combines them with the delights of out-of-doors exercise and social enjoyment, fresh air and friendship—two things which are of all others most effective for promoting happiness."

INTRODUCTION.

The necessity for a uniform Code of Rules governing Croquet Players throughout the country, has, for a long time been apparent. During the Fall of 1882, players from New York City, Boston, Philadelphia, and Norwich, Ct., joined in a call for a CONVENTION to organize a national association, and adopt national rules. This call was sent to about twenty-five clubs, and on Oct. 4th, 1882, the convention met on the grounds of the New York Croquet Club, 127th Street and 5th Avenue, New York, when the following rules were adopted.

Introduction to the rules adopted at the 1882 croquet convention.

For some players, the absence of a uniform set of rules for this new game wasn't a problem. "Croquet seems to have evolved," the anonymous Newport author rhapsodized, "by some process of nature, as a crystal forms or a flower grows—perfect, in accordance with eternal laws." Cooler heads, sensing that a universally agreed-upon code of rules would encourage better play, met on the grounds of the New York Croquet Club at 127th Street and Fifth Avenue in order to form a national association and adopt national rules. On October 4, 1882, that convention, with twenty-five local clubs participating, formed the National American Croquet Association, and the last stumbling block to croquet's ascendancy seemed to have been overcome.

Unfortunately for croquet, bluenoses were discovering that the higher virtues were not all that croquet promoted. As a noncontact lawn sport, it afforded players ample opportunity to consume the dreaded alcohol between turns and for others to gamble on the outcome of the games. And then there was the issue of fine young Christian ladies besporting themselves in the open air; though their costumes and stances seem chaste in the extreme to us now, in the 1880s they apparently encouraged men to think of those ladies in terrible and unchristian ways. "The game is the gaping jaw of Hades," a right-thinking magazine editorialized in 1898. "It would be well if the enthusiasm of the clergy and laity were enlisted for suppressing the immoral practice of croquet."

Nowhere was the clergy more inclined to do just that than in Boston. Once Boston banned the game, other municipalities began to hide their croquet equipment.

As Americans struggled to cope with this moral dilemma, the English rediscovered croquet. In 1896 the United All-England Croquet Association was formed; known now as the Croquet Association, it still rules the game in England. Three years later, the sport and the name—All England Lawn Tennis and Croquet Club (now in reverse of the original order), and the roster of champions were restored to their rightful prominence at Wimbledon, where they remain to this day.

In the late 1890s a handful of players came upon the scene who were so dazzling in their shooting and in their persons that croquet once again became worthy of widespread public notice.

Of particular importance to croquet's claim to sexual equality was Lily Gower, a tall, blond twenty-one-year-old, who'd never seen a tournament and learned all her croquet from books. In 1898 she beat the previous year's winner at Budleigh Salterton. The following year, she won the national women's championship. After two more successive victories in that annual match, she took on a field of England's best male players—and won the gold medal.

Another was Cyril Corbally, who came over from Ireland with Duff Matthews and Leslie O. Callaghan in 1901. These Irish Terrors were said to be brilliant shooters and superb tacticians, but nothing about their game was more extraordinary to their English audiences than the way they held their mallets. Unlike every English player in the annals of croquet, Corbally and his friends didn't stroke the ball as if they were playing golf, they faced the ball directly and held the mallet between their legs. In 1902, in his first appearance in England, Corbally won the Open; in the six other championship matches he entered during the next decade, he lost only twice.

Finally, there was Lord Tollemache. Constitutionally irascible, he sought no mentor. Instead, he decided to perfect the game through daily practice and sheer determination. Although he never attained the skill of Corbally or Matthews, he did become croquet's premier instructor; as one commentator has written, "Those ready to learn from him on his own terms never had reason to regret it." Happily for us, he published his findings, as *Croquet*, in 1914. This book, with its inspired picture-and-text approach, has helped generations of English players improve their game.

But celebrated players were not the only reason for croquet's second ascendancy in England. Economics also were a major factor. For the Edwardian era was a time—for the rich and titled, anyway—of country houses with scores of servants, week-long tournaments and no pressing work. Even King Edward fell victim to the croquet craze; when he traveled to Germany for his annual cure, he brought his croquet set along. By the height of croquet's golden age, there were 170 English croquet clubs, with 120 annual tournaments—not including those held during the winter on the Riviera.

By the turn of the century the game had reached its zenith with hundreds of thousands of people playing basically the same version on both sides of the Atlantic. Croquet was introduced as an Olympic sport in the 1900 Paris games.

In the first decade of this century, however, some American croquet leaders, disagreeing with newly adopted British rules (which outlawed mallets with heads made of rubber, and introduced a 6-wicket court layout), opted to retain their 9-wicket version and a short handled mallet with heads of metal on one face and rubber on the other. They introduced their version of the 9-wicket sport in the 1904 Olympics in St. Louis where it was won by an American and thereafter never played in an Olympics again.

This variation of croquet, later known as "roque" (to distinguish it from the English version by removing the "C" and the "T" from the name) sparked the manufacture of countless variations of croquet sets. These were produced, together with their own often conflicting interpretation of the rules, by a large number of American toy and game makers and inevitably led to the dilution of the game as an organized sport in the USA.

At first, World War I had no effect on the game in England. On August 4, 1914, there were nine tournaments. That a war had begun at this time couldn't be determined from the next issue of *Croquet Gazette*; all the news was of players and matches. By September, however, it was clear that croquet would be suspended for the duration of the war.

In 1919, as England's croquet players regrouped, it became apparent that 20 clubs had been so decimated by the war they couldn't reopen. Although international competition between England and Australia was initiated in 1925, overseas interest in croquet was on the wane. Fortunately, America once again took up the slack.

Herbert Bayard Swope, Jr. (left), and his father, the executive editor of the "New York World," discuss croquet strategy on Margaret Emerson's court in the thirties.

W. Averell Harriman sets up on Margaret Emerson's court in Great Neck, a favorite of "The New Yorker" crowd during the 1930s.

The spark of America's croquet renaissance was ignited in the 1920s when Herbert Bayard Swope, the executive editor of the *New York World*, and Alexander Woollcott discovered their mutual passion for the game. As luck would have it, Swope owned a Long Island estate whose greatest asset—in Woollcott's view—was a lawn suitable for a croquet court. It was here that Woollcott introduced dramatist George S. Kaufman and poet Dorothy Parker, as well as others of the Round Table set, to the glories of croquet.

This was not the kind of mild-mannered, highly skilled game the English played but a brand of argumentative, vituperative, highly skilled croquet that Woollcott, more than the others, thrived on. "My doctor forbids me to play unless I win," he announced, and so determined was he to triumph in every match he played that his friends made a film in which he was burned at the stake for kicking his croquet partner. Inevitably, Woollcott and Swope had words over many things and Woollcott retired to his Vermont island and for seven years refused to speak to Swope. Swope was to play more often with Averell Harriman, the diplomat, who is remembered more in croquet circles for his exceptional patience and shooting skills than for any of his many accomplishments at the conference table.

On the West Coast, croquet was taken up by movie moguls Darryl Zanuck and Samuel Goldwyn. It is hard to say whose courts were more extraordinary—Zanuck's greensward in Palm Springs had a fountain in the center as an obstacle, but Goldwyn had two tournament-quality lawns on his Beverly Hills estate. Goldwyn had built these courts when he could no longer play golf, and on hot Los Angeles Sunday afternoons, he would often stay away from the games until he had finished his nap. "Then, when we were in the middle of a game, we'd hear the door slam and Sam would be among us," a veteran of those matches recalls. "Who's winning?" he'd ask, and then promptly demand to play with the probable winner. He was formidable because he had a shot called "Sam's crush"—a way of pushing the ball through a wicket. No one complained. It was his court.

Croquet became the weekend passion of Harpo Marx, Louis Jourdan, Mike Romanoff, Jean Negulesco, Cesare Danova, Howard and Bill Hawks, Tyrone Power, George Sanders, Gig Young and a myriad of other movie people. Gambling was commonplace—with bets of $10,000 on a single match—but so was "A"-level play. Jourdan, in particular, had a

Darryl Zanuck (right) makes a tactical point to director Howard Hawks as stars Cesar Romero (left) and Tyrone Power wait for their turn in 1946 Hollywood match.

Jean Negulesco lines up a shot on one of Samuel Goldwyn's Beverly Hills courts as Prince Michael Romanoff and Goldwyn kibbitz.

mastery of croquet technique that was equaled only by his splendid self-assurance. Before his opening shot, he would light a cigarette, inhale deeply, and then walk over to the finishing stake. Depositing his lighted cigarette there, he would turn to the starting line and make the first wicket. From here on, he was unstoppable, taking his ball all around the court and back in time to pick up that same cigarette and take one final, satisfying drag before relinquishing his turn.

When Zanuck retired from active competition, Goldwyn's court became the only West Coast greensward of note. Then Goldwyn became ill, his wife turned the water off, and the greensward became, in one player's phrase, "as dry as the Sahara." Diehards produced a sign announcing the Beverly Hills Croquet Club, planted it on Water Department property off Sunset Boulevard and played there for a year without incident, but the spirit had gone out of the game. By the mid-1950s, the majority of people playing croquet in the USA were doing so on suburban lawns with rubber-tipped mallets, thin wickets, two stakes, and undersized croquet balls, using rules disseminated by a half dozen American set makers that would have made any self-respecting croquet player consider emigrating to England.

Seen at the historic 1960 Westhampton Mallet Club flag raising ceremony are (top) John David Griffin, Harriet and Walter Marqulies, Betty White, Dupratt White Taylor and (below) E. A. Prentis, III, Alice Stapleton, Jack and Irene Osborn.

But in the early 1960s, croquet caught on in a serious way with two groups of weekenders in the Hamptons, on Long Island. Ten men founded the Westhampton Mallet Club in 1960 while 15 miles away on several Southampton estates others wielded Jaques mallets on pristine lawns. By 1967 thirty gentlemen comprising a cross section of croquet enthusiasts, whose home or business found them frequently in Manhattan, met at the New York Athletic Club to found the New York Croquet Club.

Represented among these gentlemen were the leading players from Long Island, Connecticut, New Jersey's shore, Palm Beach and the West Coast, including veterans of the Hollywood wars. Playing the 9-wicket, 2-stake game, they set up a court in a rambling bumpy glade on the east side of Central Park. By 1969 there were eighty players, and they had begun to experiment with blending the 6-wicket court setting and the basic American rules. In January of that year, the NYCC accepted the challenge of S. Joseph Tankoos, chairman of the fledgling Palm Beach Croquet Club, and the first 6-wicket tournament was held at his Colony Hotel poolside lawn. For historical accuracy, however, it should be noted that some of the matches were held on Mrs. Ogden (Lil) Phipps' rolling 9-wicket lawn and that the finals were postponed for a day so that the competitors could go down to Miami to see Joe Namath and the New York Jets upset the Baltimore Colts in the Super Bowl. This interruption provided the New Yorkers with something to celebrate, for they went on to lose to Palm Beach the next day.

Over the next few years, teams from the Westhampton Mallet Club, the Green Gables Croquet Club of Spring Lake, New Jersey, and the Croquet Club of Bermuda entered the fray in both Palm Beach and New York. Once all of these clubs were able to agree to a code of play and set forth rules for both the 9-wicket and the 6-wicket American game, they became the founding members of the USCA.

With the formation of the United States Croquet Association, in 1977, the game reached a level where it was, at last, poised to make a serious assault on the American sporting scene. Though its aims were ultimately as large as Walter Jones Whitmore's had been a century earlier, the USCA's initial goal was extremely modest—to encourage the formation of enough American clubs to justify a national championship tournament. As Jack Osborn and his associates at the USCA had long hoped, players nationwide came forth, and gathered together in clubs, and multiplied.

Some clubs consisted of only one family. Some were imaginatively designed to fit specific needs, such as the Chicago Croquet Club, which got its start with the use of artificial grass in an indoor garage. Others were equally creative: a colorful Texan and his friends started the Aerie Croquet Club on the carpeted twelfth floor of a bank building in Amarillo to avoid the hot summer sun and cold winds of winter and, perhaps, because they feared that if they let the floor lie fallow, they'd eventually divide it into offices and get overly involved in business.

And still other clubs were so wildly improbable that only truly dedicated players would believe in their existence without direct visual observation, such as the Puget Sound Croquet Club, where Seattle Seahawk owner Ned Skinner had pulled his own end-around play by installing three full-sized courts on his football team's practice field.

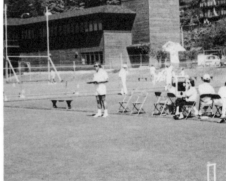

Puget Sound Croquet Club's courts at the Seattle Seahawks practice field during USCA Regional Championships in 1983.

US Croquet Hall of Famers Herbert B. Swope, Jr., Cathy Tankoos, Louis Jourdan, Libby Newell and Jack R. Osborn during a match at the Breakers Hotel.

Not all of the over 350 clubs that joined the USCA in its first twelve years have stayed the course. Death, divorce and displacement in our mobile society have taken their understandable toll but with new clubs joining at the rate of over one club a week over the past few years, growth has far outstripped attrition.

With this diverse but impassioned audience for croquet as a base, the USCA found itself growing at a rate that would warm the heart of any corporation president and caused the USCA to accelerate its plans for the game's gradual expansion.

By 1986, with nine USCA national championships having been held on the New York Croquet Clubs Central Park's four undersized courts (on the two Lawn bowling greens they share with the local bowling club), the need to provide for a growing staff in its cramped Park Avenue offices set the stage for the move of the USCA headquarters to the more spacious and friendly climate of Florida. Palm Beach County, which boasts 15 USCA clubs, including Palm Beach Polo and Country Club, The Breakers, The Beach Club and The Everglades Club, was a natural choice.

Now in residence at the 2,400 acre PGA National Resort in Palm Beach Gardens, surrounded by five full size international level croquet courts, the USCA can offer year round instructional schools and expanded national and international tournaments and events to members and newcomers to the sport.

Regional USCA Championships now feed top qualifiers to National Tournaments which have been played in California, Illinois, New York and Newport, Rhode Island, as well as Florida.

USCA State Championships have been growing in numbers yearly and sanctioned Invitational and Club Championships continue to swell the ranks of players now included in the annual USCA National Grand Prix Rankings, which was launched in 1983. (See page 259)

Of major importance has been the development of a national handicapping system which now enables USCA members across the country to compete with one another just as they would in golf. (See Chapter 13)

While many of the new clubs are still family based, the promising trend of country, tennis and sports clubs, along with well known resorts, hotels and country inns, to add croquet to their menu of sports offerings, bodes well for at-large members of the USCA and people seeking to find first class courts and facilities where they can learn and play the sport.

All of these recent developments have not been lost on the media, both here and abroad, and the coverage they have given the sport in print and TV has fueled the interest of corporate advertisers and sponsors. They have recognized that the unique "upscale" nature of the sport and the demographics (see page 209) of the USCA membership offer attractive marketing opportunities.

USCA National Headquarters at PGA National Resort in Palm Beach Gardens, Florida.

A number of leading national sponsors, from Abercrombie & Fitch to Rolex Watch, USA, have backed USCA tournaments which in 1988 offered prize money for its Open Singles Championship heralding a new professional level for the sport.

While the USCA views "play for pay" sanctioned events as a necessary further inducement in attracting more top players into fill-

Sponsor Rolex ad (US Croquet Gazette)

ing the growing need for "professional" instructors, its primary thrust is in expanding the base of amateur participants. This, of course, points to the parallel between croquet's future and those of tennis and golf, for until croquet reaches the critical mass of those more widely played (and understood) sports, income from ticket sales or TV rights will not support high stakes promotionally driven events. In planning, however, is a USCA sanctioned tour combining pro schools, cable TV, competitions and benefit supporting social activities.

Clearly, there is an opportunity here for a balanced approach to further growth of this challenging, rewarding, life extending and fun sport and it is the authors' hope that this book will help our readers to join us in making this latest chapter of croquet's history the longest and most spectacular of all.

2

BACKYARD CROQUET

by Jesse Kornbluth (from *Winning Croquet*)

In the summer of 1979, I packed up my typewriter, gathered a few books and a lot of paper, and moved my life to Southampton, New York. The idea was to improve my chances of producing a novel about high society as fine as *The Great Gatsby* by spending a summer diligently researching the ways of the old and the new rich. As a member of neither group, I told myself, I had no reason to fear I'd abandon my research in order to become a participant in either old rich or new rich activities.

It is a law of life that resort communities are blissfully sunny from Monday through Friday—and rain-drenched until the weekenders leave on Sunday night. That is how, one wet Saturday morning in June, a friend and I found ourselves at a garage sale examining household artifacts from another era. As rain beat against the garage, we imagined, as best we could, that we were in an attic, hunting for old treasures; in that spirit, we quickly decided to buy a child's blackboard ($2) and a knocked-together Fellini-blue worktable ($5). And then we saw the mallets of an ancient croquet set sticking out of a grocery bag.

This set was $4, so we bought it. We didn't have much of a backyard—a 20-by-30-foot lawn at one side of which grew a tree whose roots bulged like muscles just below the surface of the grass—but a croquet set seemed like something every house in Southampton should have, even if the dwelling in question was a small farmhouse on the fringes of an estate area. Having done our civic duty, we put our mallets, balls, stakes and wickets on the front porch. Then we forgot all about them.

Forty days or so later, when the heavens cleared, we dragged our new toys out back and laid out the court. Or, rather, we improvised, for we measured nothing. Boundaries? We had no need of them; if a ball went under a bush or car or couldn't be hit, a player was to move the ball a mallet's length away from the obstacle. Where to put the wickets? We just stuck them in the ground in a pattern that vaguely resembled the diamond-wicket layout of the game we'd played in our youth. Preparing the lawn? Why, we'd had the grass cut just a week before.

With this devil-may-care attitude, we weren't distressed to learn that our set came with only eight wickets. Like thousands of backyard croquet players before us, we improvised a solution: I took pliers in hand and cut a wire hanger to make the 9th wicket.

It goes without saying that we had no rulebook. But in backyard croquet, the absence of a rulebook is no great disadvantage: there are always at least two players who know *exactly* how the game is to be played. As we were sharing this summer house with four other experts, there was never any danger that we would all agree about the rules, and so a great deal of pre-game time was spent discussing such technicalities as take-overs, the penalty, if any, for hitting the ball twice or just pushing the ball along, and the number of shots you have if you hit another player's ball just before or after your ball clears a wicket. These disputes some-times lasted even longer than our games—but no matter how much we argued with one another, a situation inevitably arose in the first few minutes of the match which had not been covered in the rules conference.

Eventually, we hammered out a set of "house rules" and settled down to play croquet. Or our version of it, anyway. You may recognize some of our most cherished precepts from your own backyard experience. They included:

1) No matter how many players there are in the game, each player shoots with only one ball.

2) If you hit another ball, you get two shots. The first shot can be taken two ways. One way has you setting your ball next to the ball you've hit, planting your foot firmly on your ball, and smashing your opponent far away. The alternative is to place your ball a mallet head away from the ball you've hit, and shoot your own ball toward the wicket or another ball.

3) Because most of the men who eventually competed on our court had some experience playing in active sports and most of the women were lifelong smokers, women were allowed as many take-over shots as they liked. In particular, women were encouraged to take the opening shot of our backyard game—the shot through the first and second wickets—as many times as they needed to clear both wickets in a single shot, thus giving them two shots to make the third wicket. Men, on the other hand, were allowed no take-overs at any time. Worse, men with demonstrated proficiency at croquet were required to take an unspecified percentage of

their shots with their mallets held in one hand.

True to the psychology of croquet players everywhere, my friends and I believed that the rules we played under were, simply, *the* rules. To us, all regulations not used on our lawn were bogus and not to be discussed. Because we were so vociferous—and because it was our lawn, our equipment, and our iced tea—we were able to convince all the people who played with us that the sport we regularly beat them at was croquet.

If any of those people are reading this, my apologies.

For what we were playing was not croquet—it was a form of tag played with mallets and balls. At first we didn't understand this, so great was our enthusiasm for whacking the balls around. But as we got a sense of the rhythm of our game, we began to see that every

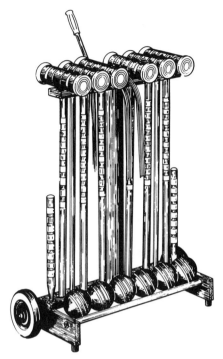

Backyard croquet sets like this have been mainstays of summers in America for generations (courtesy, Forster Manufacturing Company, Wilton, Me.).

game was fundamentally alike: one player invariably took an early lead with his single ball, and the rest of us chased after him. Late in the game, when someone was ahead by a large margin, we would band together against him and try to prevent his victory with desperate cross-court smashes. Other than that, our only applications of strategic thinking consisted of a more or less knee-jerk application of the Hobbesian view of life—that every man is at war with every other man.

Despite the predictability of our games, we played croquet so fanatically that all thought of writing *The Great Gatsby* passed from my consciousness, and I commenced to live a modest version of it. The farmhouse was now "Airedale," the tiny lawn became "the greensward." It was only a matter of time before my friends and I would decide to sponsor a tournament and call it the "Airedale Invitational."

Acquiring appropriate prizes was no problem; we bought inexpensive "gold," "bronze" and "silver" medals at an athletic-supply store and threaded red, white and blue ribbons through them. Arranging the tournament itself, however, was more of a challenge. One of our more sophisticated players suggested we contact the New York Croquet Club, on the theory that croquet was such an undeveloped sport in America its officers would help even us. Which was exactly what happened: once Jack Osborn finished laughing at the idea of a tournament on a bumpy backyard, he not only gave good advice, he offered to drop in for a few moments.

At the time, I had no idea this was an offer of any significance. Only later would Osborn confess that he long ago pledged to have nothing to do with backyard croquet—the concept of the game, the equipment or the strategy. This is not an inconvenient oath: it enables him now to avert his glance while this backyard-bred writer attempts to make a case for the beauties of the backyard game.

On the afternoon of the Airedale Invitational, though, Osborn showed up like the Johnny Appleseed of croquet. Unlike the rest of us, he wore a white shirt, white shorts and white Tretorn sneakers. He owned his own mallet, a full-sized English thing endorsed by someone named John Solomon. Clearly, if correctly importuned, he was willing to give a demonstration of the sort of croquet we had seen only in English movies.

With Osborn's appearance, both the matches and the arguments ceased, and twenty ordinarily verbal people lined up quietly behind the chalked baseline to watch a master at work. Osborn did not disappoint. He stroked his ball smoothly, controlling his shots even on our joke of a greensward. But he didn't shoot for the wicket; instead, he seemed to want to be sure he hit every other ball on the court before he went through. And having cleared one puny wire hoop, he moved all the other balls around some more, leaving himself an easy shot at the next wicket.

So deft was Osborn's shooting that one of the more knowing among us shouted, "Jump shot! Jump shot!" Osborn looked up and smiled. Then he picked up a ball and set it a foot from the next wicket. "I'm 'dead' on this ball," he announced. "If I hit it with the ball I'm going to shoot, I'll lose my turn." With that, he positioned another ball—the ball he intended to strike—two feet from the wicket. And then, hitting the ball at an angle that suggested he wanted it to burrow through the Southampton dirt and emerge in China, he got the sphere to fly over the "dead" ball and sail through the wicket. We were, without exception, amazed.

Osborn left soon after, and the Airedale Invitational resumed, but his aura lingered, for a few of us, anyway, and we resolved to upgrade our game. This is a resolution that millions of backyard croquet players have undoubtedly made over the years, but we had one great advantage: we knew how to reach Jack Osborn. For Osborn, zealot that he is, cannot disguise his hope that any player sufficiently curious about the backyard game to want to play it better just might be prodded to take up the Association game. As a result, Osborn has—albeit indirectly—given me a number of hints that have made our backyard games much more like the game he loves.

If he has not yet been able to get us playing "real" croquet, there are reasons. For one thing, when my friends and I want to play croquet, we aren't able to do so on tournament-quality courts or even, for that matter, on full-sized 105-by-84-foot lawns. Not until the recent introduction of affordable English-style equipment, were we able to use mallets, balls and wickets that were appreciably better than the $4 set that first lured me to croquet. Finally, the only guide we had to backyard croquet was the pamphlet that came with our backyard set; though admirable for its brevity, it offered no suggestions for improving the strategic level of our play.

But with this book and perhaps some upgraded equipment in your possession, you should be able to play a more interesting game of backyard croquet—and play it better—than those of us who have been duffing around backyards for years. If you are now bracing yourself for a long lecture about a complicated game with hundreds of things to remember, relax: there are few apparent differences between the backyard game you may now be playing and the USCA version. What you will soon understand, to what will probably be your great surprise, is how radically those few changes will affect your game.

How many aspects of your current version of backyard croquet would the USCA like to change?

Just three.

In order of importance, they are:

1) You must learn to "take croquet" after you've hit your ball against another. To understand what's called for here, you must forget about your cherished custom of setting your ball a mallet head away from the ball you've hit—or, as croquet players say, *the roqueted ball*—and then taking two shots. Similarly, you must banish from your mind all thoughts of placing your ball against the roqueted ball, putting your foot on your ball, and whacking away. Instead, as we explain more fully below and on page 120, you must *place your ball against the roqueted ball and "take croquet."*

What does this mean? Merely that the first shot of the two shots you've earned for hitting another ball should be—must be—a *two-ball* stroke.

You move your ball next to the ball you just hit, and without the help of a controlling foot, you hit your ball and move it and the other ball. Thus, you'll have a dual intention for this shot. First, you want your ball to go to a spot where you can do something useful with it on your second shot—like clearing a wicket or hitting another ball. Second, you want the roqueted ball to go to a spot where you can, in the near future, use it again.

The ability to send those two balls where you'd like on the croquet stroke is the essence of good croquet on both backyard courts and tournament-quality greenswards. As we will tell you time and time again in these pages, making a single wicket is nothing—making them all is *everything*. The way you do this is to move your opponents' balls to places where you can use them again as steppingstones for the rapid completion of the course. In short, you must master the croquet stroke.

To say more about the croquet stroke here would be overly technical and unnecessarily confusing. But after you've finished this chapter and have set up your backyard court, take this book outside with you and turn to "Breaks" on page 148. Once you have grasped the concept of break-making and learned one shot—the split shot, described on page 124—you will have mastered the single most important strategic principle of high-quality croquet. Should you decide, at some later time, to move up to "Association" croquet, you'll already be well-practiced in the kind of shot-making that is the hallmark of that game.

2) The kind of backyard contest in which each player uses one ball and as many as six players are on the court at any one time is also to be forgotten. *When you're playing against one opponent, each of you will use two balls; only when you're playing doubles—with four players on the court—are you responsible for a single ball.*

At first, this may be confusing for you. Not because you'll have trouble remembering the correct order of play—that's easy enough—but because of the concept of "deadness." As those who have played croquet before will recall, you're "dead" on a ball after you've struck it with your own. The only way to remove that "deadness" is to send your ball through its next wicket. Otherwise, if your ball hits the "dead" ball again, your turn ends and both balls are replaced.

In a six player game when you're playing with only one ball on a court that's littered with balls, it's easy to accumulate "deadness" on as many as five balls—but it's also relatively easy to clear yourself of "deadness" by going through your next wicket on the same turn. With only four balls in play and two balls to think about, however, it's less likely that you'll rid yourself of "deadness" in a single turn—and far less likely that you'll remember which of your balls are "dead" one or two turns down the line. In order to keep disputes about "deadness" from ruining your games, you will either have to acquire a "deadness board" (see page 70) or keep a pen and notebook with you on the court in order to make a running account of the game.

3) The shafts of backyard mallets are so short that there's not much reason for owners of backyard equipment to study the chapters in this book about grips and stances. And because the balls used in backyard sets are proportional to the rubber-tipped heads of those mallets, you'll have to use them. But you can do something about the wickets, and, if it's at all possible, *you're advised to buy nine of the white "winter wickets"—or, as they're sometimes called, challenge hoops—that are used in Association croquet (see page 64) and replace the wider, thinner wickets that came in your backyard set with them.*

Because it's more challenging to shoot for a smaller target, these wickets will reduce the likelihood that a lucky shot will determine the outcome of the game. In an idealized setting—a lawn of putting-green texture, with equipment of the best quality—nature and technology have been so manicured and perfected that luck scarcely plays any part. Obviously, on a bumpy backyard lawn that probably isn't even regulation-sized, you can't hope to control the variables to the degree possible on a greensward. But you can, by substituting Association wickets for backyard ones, establish a level of play which rewards the steady shooter who can execute the fundamentals properly. And should you choose to play Association croquet at some point in the future, not only will you not be intimidated by the narrowness of Association wickets, but you'll have mastered them.

And that's really all you need to change in order to play a better, more authentic game of backyard croquet.

Yes, you could set up your backyard wickets in a 6-wicket, 1-stake configuration so your game is a miniaturized version of true Association croquet. But, as I've learned the hard way, those who are unfamiliar with that setup may be too intimidated by it to enjoy the game—or you may find yourself coaching your untutored opponents so constantly that your own game suffers. Just as people who have learned to ride a bike don't immediately jump on a racing bicycle, those who have just developed an affection for backyard croquet don't necessarily want to abandon it for what seems like a more intellectual, challenging game. They may eventually come to see that the seemingly slower, seemingly more intellectual 6-wicket Association game is, in fact, much faster and livelier than 9-wicket backyard croquet, but in order to reach that point, it's usually necessary for them to satisfy their appetite for aggressive, shoot-first-and-ask-questions-later play.

If you are one of those players who are attracted to the 9-wicket, 2-stake game because it's a socially acceptable form of warfare, it's entirely possible that you'll never get past this stage. That's fine with us. But I would make one small recommendation to you as you rush out to play the game that's more fun than any book—in addition to reading the few pages about breaks, croquet strokes and deadness boards, which I've urged you to take to heart, turn to page 241 and read the United States Croquet Association's rules for 9-wicket croquet. True, your backyard set might still come with a pamphlet which seems to tell you—in less than a page—all you'll need to know about the regulations of backyard croquet but in 1986 America's largest croquet set maker, Forster Mfg., introduced Jack Osborn's modified USCA based rules in all their backyard sets. These rules are now also being included in other quality U.S. makers sets. In fact, as you'll soon find out, disputes occur over points too obscure to be covered by the rules included in any pamphlet. You need not memorize the official USCA rules, but you should be familiar with them so that, in the heat of play, you can find the relevant rule at a moment's notice and authoritatively—and correctly—cite croquet writ.

All Forster backyard sets now include USCA approved rules.

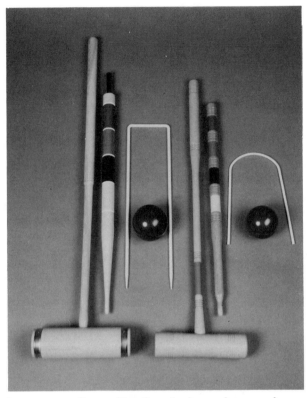

*In recent years Forster Manufacturing has made very real prog-
ress in upgrading the quality and scale of their "backyard" sets.
The "Challenge" set (above left) with 36 inch shafts and 3⁵/₈ inch
balls has received a USCA "C" classification. The "Stratford"
set on the right is the first class "D" set approved by the USCA.*

Finally, you may discover that a summer-long obsession with backyard
croquet leaves you with no desire to pick up a mallet again. Don't blame
croquet—blame your equipment. Disenchantment with the backyard
game is the first sign that you're ready to move up to Association
equipment. You may want to use this equipment on a 9-wicket backyard
course, or you may want to try your hand on an actual croquet court. No
matter. The important thing is that backyard croquet, having provided you
with a season of fun and good fellowship, has performed its ultimate
service; it has led you to discover the very real rewards to be derived from
croquet in its most authentic form.

John Solomon, the perennial captain of the English national team and, since 1981, the President of The Croquet Association, now holds more than 50 international titles. Shown here at USCA's PGA National courts as captain of the 1988 US / International Challenge Cup Team.

3

ON TO THE GREENSWARD:

An Introduction to American 6-Wicket Croquet

by Jack R. Osborn

Like those of almost all American croquet players, my roots are deeply embedded in the backyard game. Even now, having played thousands of times on some of the finest Association courts in the United Kingdom, South Africa, Australia and America and having delivered my sermon about "real" croquet at uncountable clinics and tournaments, I still have precise and affectionate memories of playing 9-wicket, 2-stake croquet on warm summer afternoons. There I am calculating the best angle to hit an opponent's ball on the Westhampton, Long Island backyard that sloped down to Beaver Dam Creek; here I am smashing my ball over the bumpy grass with rubber-tipped mallets, coat hanger wickets and spirited debates—yes, I've known those joys.

It was, in fact, because of backyard croquet that I first encountered the man who would serve as the inspirational force for my eventual dedication to the sport of croquet. His name is John Solomon, and when I met him in 1967, he was on his way to amassing 50 international and national titles, a record no other player in the world has come close to matching.

John had come to New York as the captain of a visiting team from London's Hurlingham Club. This team was to compete in the second meeting between the venerable English club and our group of American upstarts who made up the Westhampton Mallet Club. The first match, a year earlier, had been played in England under English rules; this time, the British would be playing 9-wicket, 2-stake croquet on our turf.

It goes without saying that the Westhamptonites had not fared well in England in that first contest. But playing on our 2-inch grass and using our rules and court layout, we felt we'd do much better this time. So confident were we that we might even emerge victorious that we generously provided our visitors with advisers to help them with our rules.

The New York Times headline "Croquet on Long Island Baffles Britons" will give you an idea how well our advisers did. Our players did somewhat better, achieving a 3-3 tie after three days of play in a steady downpour that might well have been imported from England.

It would be pleasant to report that this tie was the result of brilliant shot-making and superb strategic thinking by every American player, this correspondent included. Alas, the truth is more complex. For, although we did play decently, our biggest asset in those matches was probably our guests' dependence on their "advisers." Those advisers, being American duffers who were not sophisticated about the intricacies of croquet shot-making, didn't realize how much more advanced the visitors were—and because the advisers couldn't make certain shots, they never suggested them to the British.

After the first day of play, however, Solomon and his gang didn't rely so much on their advisers. Incorporating the niceties of English croquet strategy into our game, they began taking shots none of us had ever seen before. Full rolls, pass rolls, long split drives—these remarkable shots were used to start three- and four-ball breaks. Clearly, this was a level of croquet we Americans had no knowledge of.

The following year, when our team traveled to England for the third match in this evolving international series, the English thoughtfully offered us some advisers. We jumped at the chance to use them: far from disadvantaging us, I felt these players could help us advance our game to our hosts' level.

I arrived in England a full week before the matches were scheduled to begin and went directly to Hurlingham, the Mecca of world croquet. There, under the tutelage of my English mentor, the late Ian Bailleau, and John Solomon's lovely mother, I practiced until some of those advanced shots and a few of the British Association's laws began to sink in. By tournament time, I was primed for the event.

Of the thousands of croquet matches I've played over the years, there are a few whose memory I particularly treasure. That game at Hurlingham was one of them.

That I would lose was a foregone conclusion: my opponent was John Solomon. That I would score what was for me a very impressive 8 points to Solomon's 26 was less predictable. But even more than those 8 wickets, I savored being on the same court as Solomon and watching, firsthand, his masterful display of shooting. For despite my week of practice and my

The Hurlingham Club of London has, since 1959, been the headquarters of the Croquet Association (English). The courts in the foreground are more than eighty years old.

diligent reading of English croquet texts, I had no idea how large an arsenal of shots there are or how precisely a truly skilled player could place a croquet ball.

No American fared better than I did that day, and the final score was 8-0. Far from feeling humiliated by the defeat, I felt exhilarated by the possibilities it suggested. As I left the court, I was determined to learn all I could about the game as Solomon and his teammates were playing it.

In an article he wrote for the British *Croquet Gazette* after these matches, Solomon was as generous as he'd been throughout the contest. "I think only two things are needed for America to become a serious threat to English croquet," he wrote. "One is an English-type lawn; the other is the formation of an American Association for the purposes of reaching agreement between clubs on the rules of their own game as a preliminary to scrapping them altogether in favor of our own."

In the twenty years since Solomon made those suggestions, there have been great strides toward achieving all but the last. Over the course of the first decade, enthusiasts from all across the country met frequently on greenswards and in smoke-filled conference rooms to hammer out the first set of rules for 6-wicket, 1-stake American croquet. As a result of those gatherings, the United States Croquet Association was established, giving American croquet players an Association that allows them to compete locally, regionally and nationally under rules they all share. With that encouragement, English-style croquet lawns have sprouted up on American soil; there are now more than 300, with as many more being readied for play.

Of these many accomplishments, none impresses me more than the adoption of a single set of rules. Each of the framers of these rules brought to the debate the certainty that theirs was the only game to play. Reaching agreement was, therefore, a painful task. On one thing, though, there was surprising unanimity: no one felt we should, as Solomon suggested, scrap American rules in favor of the laws of the British Association.

There were several reasons for this unanimity.

While we conceded that the 6-wicket, 1-stake course was a more challenging test of shot-making, we felt that many of the other British idiosyncrasies couldn't be introduced here without permanently alienating most of the Americans who were the backbone of our young Association. We decided, instead, to keep the essence of the American backyard game and join its fast-paced, "go-for-the-wicket" spirit with the international court layout. The resulting game, we discovered, was not only more challenging to play than backyard croquet; it was, we sensed, more interactive and fun to watch than the English game.

Interestingly, our international friends have also found that American croquet now has what they'd probably describe as a certain charm. Although they remain wedded to their own conservative game and their own laws, they have now played the USCA game often enough on our courts to take it home and try it out. In several instances, they have even introduced it as a tournament event on their own courts.

Ideally, of course, croquet players the world over would play the same game according to the same rules. It is hard to imagine what would have to take place in order for that to happen. The British laws remain the closest thing to the world standard, more by tradition than by strength of numbers. If growth is considered a factor, the American game would clearly predominate. If numbers alone were to matter, however, we would all play according to Japanese rules, for two to three million Japanese are now playing a game they call "gateball" with as many as ten players on the court at any one time.

The most important developments on the international scene, for the present, is the increasing frequency of international matches and the formation of a World Croquet Federation. In 1972, as the result of another of John Solomon's suggestions, we invited a young Englishman to come to the United States and give lessons to the members of the New York Croquet Club, the better to prepare them for international competition.

G. Nigel Aspinall, England's gift to American croquet, during one of his frequent visits to the USA demonstrates his skills on the Palm Beach Polo & Country Club's courts in West Palm Beach.

G. Nigel Aspinall, then twenty-six years old, had already distinguished himself by beating John Solomon several times; he would go on to win ten President's Cups in England, which is like saying he won the world's singles championship ten times. But more important for American players, he has crossed the Atlantic many times during the past fifteen years, each time giving those fortunate enough to learn from him more insights about croquet than they would have acquired in years of unsupervised play.

By 1981, American croquet had advanced to the point where it made sense to establish U.S. International Challenge Cup matches between the top American players and their counterparts from other English-speaking countries. The success of these matches was assured when England agreed to send a team to Palm Beach and play half of its games under English laws and half under USCA rules. And what a team England sent! John Solomon, who came out of semiretirement, captained the foursome, with Professor Bernard Neal, Dr. William Ormerod and Nigel Aspinall himself filling out the group.

Against this awesome squad of multi-titled internationals—all of whom had represented their country against Australia and New Zealand in the MacRobertson Shield International competition—the United States fielded three-time U.S. Singles champion J. Archie Peck, two-time doubles

47

champion E. A. (Teddy) Prentis IV, Teddy's father, E. A. (Ned) Prentis III, who was a veteran of the 1968 Hurlingham matches, and this writer.

It would be sweet to report that after fifteen years of instruction from our English friends, we finally had parity with the English team, or, better yet, that we routed them, but neither of these dreams became reality. In spite of our much-improved play, the record book shows the score as England 15, USA 1.

That one victory? Modesty gives way to pride here. It was another of my most memorable matches. I beat John Solomon, 26-5 under American rules.

Aside from the undeniable pleasure this win gave me, I relate it here because it underscores, I think, two of the most attractive aspects of croquet. The first is the fact that *any* player can, with practice and patience, improve his or her game dramatically. Second, and more intriguing, is the fact that on any given day, it's possible for *any* player—even one ranked far below his or her opponent—to win, and win handily.

My victory over John Solomon is hardly the only proof of this phenomenon. Much more impressive is the fact that the 1982 USCA International Challenge Cup Team won fifteen of its thirty-two matches against Scotland (7-7) and South Africa (8-10), with five of those victories attained under unfamiliar English rules. Among these Americans were fifteen-year-old Kiley Jones, some players who took up the game just a

An historic 1985 meeting in Nottingham of the USCA and Great Britain teams. Left to right back row USA, Jack R. Osborn (captain), Kiley Jones, Jim Bast, John C. Osborn, Ted Prentis and Ray Bell. Seated Stephan Mulliner, Keith Aiton, Dr. Eric Solomon, David Openshaw (captain), Nigel Aspinall, and Keith Wylie.

few years earlier, and a number of malleteers who hail from places that their English, South African and Scottish opponents had never heard of. For American players to come from historically unimportant places and yet be able to compete on some of the world's most revered greenswards is reward enough; to hold our own against classically trained opponents is a welcome bonus. Clearly, our instructional efforts to upgrade the level of American play were starting to pay off.

If you turn to page 258 you will find the statistical data on how this trend has continued over the ensuing years with winning matches against Bermuda & Canada in 1983, respectable loses to Australia (1984), Ireland (1985) and Great Britain (1987) and two wins over International Champion teams in 1986 and 1988. Along with the introduction of the USCA's own International Rules National Championships in 1987, further progress in our quest for parity is exemplified by the establishment of a series of home and home international rules competitions between the USCA and British association for the appropriately named Solomon Trophy. Although we have lost the first two encounters (20 to 1 in 1988 at Cheltenham and 15 to 5 at Palm Beach Polo & CC in 1989), this Anglo-American "Ryder Cup" type series will continue to provide the incentive to our better players to improve their skills at both games.

All of this, and the USCA's role as a founder member nation of the newly formed World Croquet Federation, insures America's increasing stature on the international scene. In July of 1989, five Americans were among the eighty to qualify for the first ever World Croquet Championships in London, a feat that would have been impossible a mere decade earlier. Again, it would be great to report that they had joined Greg Lemond and Mark Calcavecchio in bringing home the croquet titles to go with the cycling and golf honors of Greg and Mark, but such is not the case . . . this year. Unseeded American Tremaine Arkley, 1984 USCA Rookie of the Year, made it to the final sixteen before losing to New Zealander Bob Jackson, one of the sport's all time greats. The real point is that we were there, and will be again next year.

1987
US/INTERNATIONAL
CROQUET
CHALLENGE CUP
APRIL 5, 10—12

U.S.A. vs GREAT BRITAIN

And The 8th United States Croquet Association

NATIONAL CLUB
TEAM CHAMPIONSHIPS
APRIL 6—10

Both At:
PGA NATIONAL
Palm Beach Gardens, Florida

4

THE OBJECT OF THE GAME
(With a Keynote on Vocabulary)

As we examine the basic points and objectives of the American 6-wicket game, let us stress the importance of learning and understanding the language of croquet. If you are to comprehend what follows, it will be impossible to do so without first distinguishing between such words as "roquet" and "croquet."

Soon enough, we're going to be throwing shorthand phrases around which will depress you no end if you don't understand them. You must, therefore, learn some basic croquet vocabulary even before you begin to play. Fortunately, croquet terminology is accurate and relatively brief.

In this chapter we will italicize key words. If they are not made sufficiently clear by the text, please turn to the back of this book, where there is a glossary of croquet terms. There, we define just about every croquet term you'll ever encounter. Here, we stick to the basics. They are:

roquet—A roquet is made when you hit your ball so that it strikes another ball.

croquet—The *croquet stroke* is the first stroke of the two you earn by roqueting another ball. To "take croquet," you place your ball against the roqueted ball and hit your ball so that both balls are moved.

rush—to rush a ball is to roquet it in a particular direction or to a particular spot.

deadness—every ball is said to be "alive" on all other balls at the start of the game. Thereafter, a ball acquires "deadness" by roqueting another ball. It cannot roquet that ball again until it itself has cleared its next wicket; until then, it's said to be "dead" on that other ball. If the ball roquets the "dead" ball again before the next wicket is cleared, the striker's turn ends and both balls are put back where they were.

The object of both the American 6-wicket and 9-wicket game is to beat your opponent(s) around a course of wickets and hit the finishing stake before he does (they do). The game can be played by either two people (singles) or four people (doubles).

In the 6-wicket singles game, each player plays two balls, either Blue and Black or Red and Yellow, and attempts to score 12 wicket points and one stake point for each of his balls for a winning total of 26 points before his adversary. In 9-wicket the total is 32.

In doubles, the game is played between two sides, each side consisting of two players. One team plays the blue and black balls and the other the red and yellow balls. Each player plays the same ball throughout the game. As in singles, the object is for one team to score the total of 26 or 32 points before their opponents.

In both games a ball scores a wicket point by passing through the wicket in the order and direction shown in the diagram on page 56. This is known as *running a wicket.* But a ball that has first hit another ball (roqueted) cannot thereafter in the same stroke bounce off and score a point for itself, except at the first wicket. A ball that has scored all its *wicket points* is known as a *rover.* The rover can score the stake by hitting it. When time has run out in time limit tournament games, and neither side has scored the total points needed for victory, wicket (and stake) points are added at the end of the time limit and the team with the most points is the winner.

Play is made by striking a ball with a mallet. The player who is doing this is called the *striker,* and the ball that he strikes, the striker's ball. The striker may never strike an adversary's ball with his mallet. But by striking his ball against any other, the striker may cause that ball to move and/or score a point.

The players play each turn in the sequence blue, red, black and yellow. A player is initially entitled to one stroke in a turn, after which his turn ends unless in that stroke his ball has scored a wicket point or hit another ball. When the wicket is scored, the striker is entitled to play one additional or *continuation stroke.* When another ball (whether opponent's or partner's) is hit, the striker is said to have made a roquet on that ball and is entitled to two extra strokes. He then becomes dead on that ball.

The first of these two strokes is known as the *croquet stroke,* and it is made after the striker moves his ball to, and places it in contact with, the roqueted ball.

If, in the croquet stroke, the croqueted ball is sent off the court, or the striker's ball is sent off the court without first having made another roquet, the turn ends. During the turn, a striker may roquet each ball he is *alive* on once. He may make a further roquet on each ball provided that his ball has scored a wicket point for itself and has thus *cleared* itself of its deadness. Thus, by a series of strokes that entitle him to continue, the striker may make one or more points during one turn. Such a series is known as making a *break*.

But *continuation strokes* are not cumulative—you cannot clear a wicket, hitting another ball in the process, and collect three strokes. If a player first clears a wicket and then, on the same stroke, hits another ball, he may either take one continuation stroke and not be dead on the ball he's hit, or he may choose to roquet that ball and take two strokes. If a player makes a roquet as a consequence of a croquet stroke—if his ball not only moves the ball he's taking croquet on but goes on to hit yet another ball—he immediately takes croquet on that ball and continues to play. But if, during a croquet stroke, a player scores a wicket for his ball, he is entitled to only one continuation stroke, which is his reward for clearing the wicket.

A ball is said to be *out-of-bounds* when its vertical axis rolls more than halfway over the boundary. It is then known as a *ball-in-hand*. This term is also used to describe a ball that has made a roquet, or any ball that must be picked up and moved.

After each stroke, all balls off the court are replaced one mallet head (or 9 inches) in from the point where they went out. This is also true of all balls within 9 inches of the boundary line after each stroke, except the striker's ball. These balls are replaced a mallet head in from the line.

With these introductory objectives in mind and before we explore any specific tactics or strategies, let's look at the court layout and direction of play along with the equipment you will be using for playing the game.

In Chapter 5 you will find a chart that delineates and correlates the different types of equipment available and its appropriate use by type of lawn, cost and level of play. Those who are planning to buy new equipment will find that this chart can keep them from wasting money on equipment better than they need—or from buying an inexpensive set in the belief that all official-looking equipment is more or less the same.

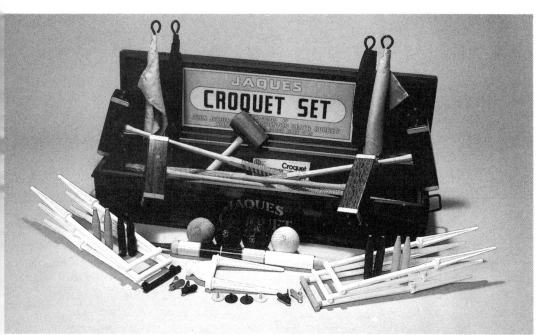

The Excalibur

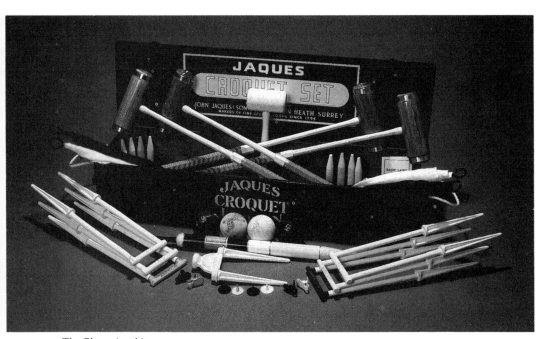

The Championship

5

THE COURT, EQUIPMENT, CLOTHING AND ACCESSORIES

THE COURT

Most of today's better American players don't play on their own croquet court and are quite content to perfect their game at United States Croquet Association clubs (see USCA Member Clubs, p. 264). Should you aspire to be a Class "A" tournament-level player and can't recreate the tournament lawn, you should, in any event, try to play on as close to a 105-by-84-foot tournament-sized court as possible. (Such courts can be divided into two courts for beginners and intermediate players and for practice sessions.)

Others make do with lawns that were never intended for use as croquet courts but have, with a bit of rolling and reseeding, proved perfectly adequate (see The Lust for Lawns, p. 189). Obviously, if your home is set on a lot smaller than one acre, there's almost no way you can create a quarter-acre rectangle for a tournament-sized court. Still, if you have a clear, level lawn that's 50 by 40 feet or larger, you have enough room for a proportionally correct, scaled-down court. Simply take care to maintain the 5-by-4 ratio or as close to it as possible.

Ideally, you will have four colored flags to mark the corners (blue in #1, red #2, black #3 and yellow #4), but whether you do or not, you should indicate the out-of-bounds line with one-sixteenth-inch string (#18) stretched at ground-level from corner to corner, affixed by a golf tee or metal pin at the corners. If you have a set of flags for the corners, they are *not* to be used in lieu of the golf tee or metal pin, as you may need to remove the flags for shots from the corners. Nor are lime or chalk recommended for boundary lines; even at their sharpest, they don't provide the definitive boundary line that USCA croquet requires. Corner

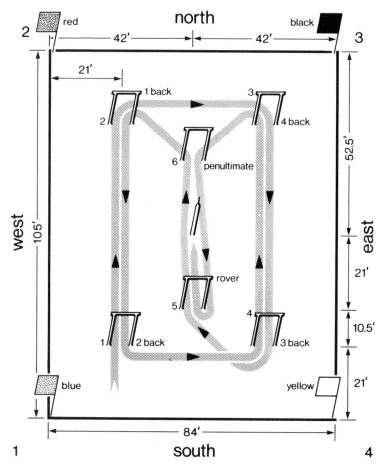

The layout and direction of play on the official United States Croquet Association 6-wicket court.

flags come with top of the line sets and boundary line sets are now also commercially made.

As diagram 1 indicates, each corner of the court is assigned a number. For purposes of description, the boundaries are designated North, South, East and West—regardless of the actual geographic layout of the court. The wickets are also numbered. With the exception of four wickets in the 9-wicket game, each wicket has two numbers, one referring to its order in the outward-bound direction, the other to its position in the homeward-bound direction.

If you have a 100-by-50-foot lawn and are playing 9-wicket croquet according to the official United States Croquet Association rules, you will set your two pegs 25 feet from each sideline and 6 feet from the North and

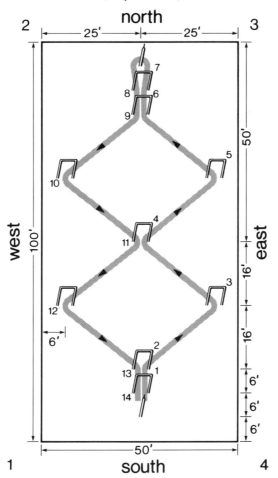

The layout and direction of play on the official United States Croquet Association 9-wicket court.

South boundaries. Wickets 1 and 2, as well as 6 and 7, are set 6 feet apart, with 1 and 7 set 6 feet from their respective pegs. The corner wickets (3, 5, 10 and 12) are set 34 feet from the North and South boundaries with their centers 6 feet from the sidelines. The 4th, or center, wicket is set 50 feet from the North and South boundaries and aligned with wickets 1, 2, 6 and 7. The 9-wicket court can also be scaled down, but not smaller than 30 by 60 feet.

The 6-wicket, 1-stake game is simpler to lay out. (Don't be fooled; this is the only way it's simpler than 9-wicket croquet.) The peg is set at midcourt—52$^1/_2$ feet from the North and South boundaries; 42 feet from the East and West sidelines. The four corner wickets are positioned 21 feet from their respective East or West sidelines. The two inner wickets are set

57

Corner flags and boundary lines: Boundary-line string should not be tied to corner flag since a flag may need to be removed during a match. Use a golf tee or metal pin pushed completely into the ground.

21 feet from the peg, with their centers 42 feet from the East and West sidelines. The inner wicket nearest the South boundary is known as the rover hoop. It is the last wicket to be made before completing the circuit, and, for that reason, is painted red across the top. The first wicket has a crown painted blue.

At the risk of repeating ourselves, we urge you yet again to spend a few minutes memorizing the order of play. Once you're out on the court, you won't be able to consult this book between shots, and you can be sure that your opponent will maintain perfect silence as you send your ball through a wicket that's not on the proper order of play. At that point—and only then—will he remark that your turn is over and that no additional shots are due you. If he is particularly disagreeable, he will cite not only the correct order of play but this paragraph as well. We would hate to see our text thus used, so—*memorize the order of wicket play!*

EQUIPMENT

The Mallet

"The croquet mallet," writes an English authority, with characteristic English understatement, "is a long-handled hammer." A $2^1/2$- to 4-pound hammer, to be precise, with a round, square or rectangular head that's most frequently made from a 9-inch-long, 3-inch-wide block of such exotic hardwoods as lignum vitae, teak, boxwood, rockwood or mahogany. The shaft is generally about 36 inches long and is made of ash, hickory or malacca cane. At the top of the shaft is the octagonal grip. Almost inevitably, some kind of string, leather or cork has been wrapped around this end for surer handling.

The mallet is the one piece of croquet equipment that can be personalized. As a result, once a fledgling croquet buff feels the onset of an addiction to croquet, he often can become obsessed with his mallet in much the same way as a runner can be preoccupied with a particular brand of running shoes. Does a square-headed mallet with brass fittings on the head perform better than a round-headed mallet? Does a player who holds his mallet in a way popularized by some great Irish players do better with a mallet whose shaft is 4 inches shorter than the standard English mallet? Does it make sense to buy any mallet not made by John Jaques & Son, Ltd., the English firm that has been manufacturing croquet equipment since 1850 and currently finds itself swamped with orders for mallets costing as much as $300?

Since a mallet is such a personal item which, like a golf club or tennis racquet, involves selecting one of appropriate weight for the individual in terms of the strength of wrists and arms, as well as the speed of the lawns upon which it will be used, here are a few general points to consider in selecting one for your use.

For play with one pound balls (Eclipse)

1) The stronger the player, the lighter the mallet required (except for very tall men or play on very heavy lawns). Recommended—3 pounds, plus or minus, 3 ounces.

2) The smoother and faster the lawn, the lighter the mallet. Recommended—2 pounds, 12 ounces to 3 pounds, 4 ounces.

3) The thicker or longer the grass, the more weight is advised since, in a proper pendulum-like swing, the heavier mallet head is expected to do more work than the arms. Recommended—3 pounds, 4 ounces to 3 pounds, 10 ounces.

4) Tall or lighter weight men or women may need heavier mallets on either fast or slow lawns.

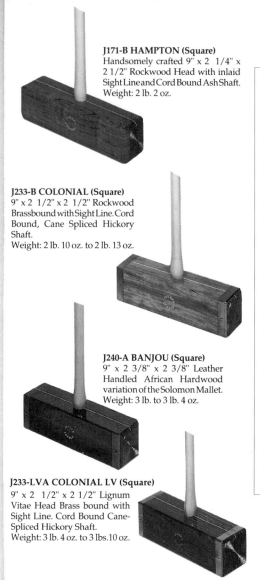

J171-B HAMPTON (Square)
Handsomely crafted 9" x 2 1/4" x 2 1/2" Rockwood Head with inlaid Sight Line and Cord Bound Ash Shaft. Weight: 2 lb. 2 oz.

J233-B COLONIAL (Square)
9" x 2 1/2" x 2 1/2" Rockwood Brassbound with Sight Line. Cord Bound, Cane Spliced Hickory Shaft.
Weight: 2 lb. 10 oz. to 2 lb. 13 oz.

J240-A BANJOU (Square)
9" x 2 3/8" x 2 3/8" Leather Handled African Hardwood variation of the Solomon Mallet. Weight: 3 lb. to 3 lb. 4 oz.

J233-LVA COLONIAL LV (Square)
9" x 2 1/2" x 2 1/2" Lignum Vitae Head Brass bound with Sight Line. Cord Bound Cane-Spliced Hickory Shaft.
Weight: 3 lb. 4 oz. to 3 lbs.10 oz.

SQUARE MALLETS

The increasing popularity of square-headed croquet mallets can be attributed to their use by more and more top level international players led by John Solomon and most of America's leading tournament winners. Some explain that they are better able to hit with the center or "sweet spot" of their mallet face when striking a ball lying on the other side of a wicket. Others like the fact that a square-headed mallet can stand up by itself when lining up or between shots.

J242-A SOLOMON (Square) (below)
The John Solomon autographed mallet has been played by more top International players worldwide than any other croquet mallet made in the history of the sport. The 2 1/4 inch square Lignum Vitae head with inlaid Sight Line is fitted with a fine leather grip handle on a solid Hickory shaft.

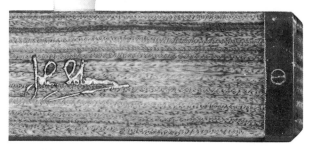

(Courtesy of Croquet International Ltd.)

J165-C HARDWOOD (Round)
9" x 3" natural Ash head with
Ash Shaft.
Weight: 2 lb.

J166-C HENLEY (Round)
9" x 3" stained Ash head with
color keyed solid polished Ash
Handle and Shaft.
Weight: 2 lb.

ROUND MALLETS

Still the classic shape
and most widely owned,
the round-headed mal-
let is a staple of many
clubs for general mem-
bership use. Often less
expensive than the
square style, they come
in a variety of woods
and weights.

J175-B ASSOCIATION (Round)
9" x 3" Rockwood Head, Brass-
Ringed with Sight Line. Cord
Bound and Cane-Spliced Hick-
ory Shaft.
Weight: 2 lb. 10 oz. to 3 lb.

J183-A CHAMPIONSHIP (Round)
Equivalent timber to Lignum Vitae with
9" x 3" Head Brass-Ringed with Sight Line,
cord bound Cane-Spliced Hickory Shaft.
Weight: 3 lb. 5 oz. to 3 lb. 10 oz.

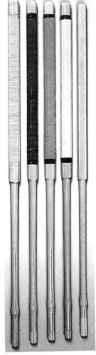

A B C D E F

**JAQUES OCTAGONAL HANDLE
AND SHAFT STYLES**
a) Cord bound cane spliced Hickory
b) & c) Porvair grip on cane spliced
hickory (dark/light)
d) Solomon Leather Grip solid Hickory
e) Polished Ash

For play with lighter (Class B and C, 12 to 14 ounce) balls

1) General rule: The lighter the ball, the lighter the mallet, regardless
of the strength of player or grass condition. A light ball may break when
struck by a heavier mallet, and vice versa. (Don't try to play with an
Eclipse ball with a mallet under 2 pounds, 6 ounces, or the mallet will
suffer.)

2) Play a Class B ball with a Class B mallet and a C ball with a C
mallet. (B mallets range from 2 pounds, 4 ounces to 3 pounds, 2 ounces
and C mallets range from 2 pounds to 3 pounds.)

3) On heavier lawns (grass 1 inch to $1^1/2$ inches), lighter balls will
travel further when struck by a heavier mallet of the same class.

Further generalizations in selecting your mallet include: Always start with a full length shaft (36 inches—plus or minus, 1 inch), regardless of your height. The length is needed for many shots (particularly the roll shots), and ordering a shorter one before you've played a while would be a mistake. Plain or string handles can be modified to leather or other fabric coverings, to one's taste as desired, by your local tennis or golf pro or croquet supplier.

Your mallet should be a pleasure to hold, swing and look at, to fully enjoy the sport.

It is not unusual for croquet addicts to own several mallets (for different playing surfaces and conditions), just as the tennis player or golfer has more than one racquet or putter.

Wood or Plastic Mallet Heads?

In recent years a number of space age plastics, resin impregnated laminates and synthetic wood mallets have been introduced on croquet courts around the world. Several of these have enjoyed a degree of popularity and have sparked conversational interest as to the relative merits of durability vis-à-vis playing characteristics.

Still unanswered, however, is the question as to whether they fully conform to the 1970 internationally accepted standard that the end faces of the mallet head be "made of wood or any other non-metallic material provided that no playing advantage is gained over wood." This regulation was initiated in 1901 to prevent the use of rubber on one face and metal on the other as was popular with what became known as "roque" mallets. The rubber end was used for dramatic roll shots, while the metal end made stop shots easier. Wood was considered to be the best balance between the two materials and since a player was only allowed to play with one mallet throughout a game after 1911, and during a turn since 1947 (unless damaged or taken out of play), it placed shot-making success on the man and not on the mallet.

What has now become clear, particularly with the simultaneous arrival of solid plastic composition balls, is that high impact plastic upon equally hard plastic makes many crucial shots such as rolls and split rolls very difficult to control. This is in sharp contrast with the playing characteristics of a compressible wood mallet face on a compressible cork centered (Eclipse) ball which provides the player with greater control of *all* the shots he must make in a match. Setting aside the strange sound of plastic on plastic, there also seems to be less traction or interactive "feel" created by smooth plastic faced mallets and solid plastic balls, with or without milling. All of this suggests that the plastic headed mallet is, in fact, "legal" since it clearly does not provide an "advantage" over wood.

Isn't it refreshing to realize that in some areas it is difficult to improve on "mother nature" and that hard wood mallets will continue to be favored by better players everywhere?

Whatever mallet you choose, there are a few simple rules that, if diligently followed, will enable you to make a mallet a once-in-a-lifetime purchase.

1) When it is not in use, never leave a mallet leaning against a wall; this will warp the shaft. Instead, hang it upside down between two pegs in a cool, dry place.

2) After a match on wet grass—towel your mallet dry. If you're unusually fastidious, you might, from time to time, waterproof your mallet head with a thin coat of shellac.

3) *Never* throw your mallet in anger at another player or, even worse for the mallet, at a tree or building. As tradition dictates, the only direction the mallet is *ever* to be thrown is skyward.

And that's it. For all its apparent delicacy, the mallet is a sturdy tool, and there's no reason to go overboard protecting it. In the 1930s, Harpo Marx air-conditioned a room specifically to keep his Jaques mallets properly cool, but no one who played against him ever remarked that his chilled mallets improved his game. Nor will you find it necessary to commission Louis Vuitton to protect your instrument on its travels between court and home.

USCA emblemed padded mallet cases, however, can now be seen on airplanes with greater frequency. If you anticipate that you'll be toting your mallet around the country with you, you'd do well to obtain one of these cases. Although an occasional airport security guard will decide that a croquet mallet could be used as a hijack weapon and insist that it be banished to the hold, you can sometimes convince the officials to let it be stored in the captain's cabin.

Even if you never play croquet and simply buy a class "A" mallet for its looks, you have, at the very least, become the proud owner of a conversation piece that has charms that, say, a baseball bat can never hope to equal. Some croquet addicts, upon reading this, may think of applying their mallets to our heads just for acknowledging that anyone might flirt with croquet for overtly social reasons. But our view is that it doesn't make any difference how or why people come to croquet, so long as they actually get to the greensward. In our experience, the gent who buys a mallet simply to impress his business associates or friends will inevitably find himself taking mallet in hand, improvising a wicket, or acquiring an indoor practice range in order to shoot a few impromptu hoops—and, not long afterward, will be heading off to the nearest lawn to try his luck at the thing itself.

The Wicket

For those whose memories of croquet are all about rubber-tipped mallets and thin wire wickets, no encounter with regulation croquet equipment is more disquieting than the first heft of a half-dozen Association croquet wickets. Not only do these wickets look heavy, they are heavy: each one is $4^{1}/_{2}$ pounds. That's because Association croquet wickets are made of cast iron that's $^{5}/_{8}$ inch in diameter, because they're 12 inches from crown to ground, and because they have star-shaped spikes that thrust 8 inches deep into the turf so there's no possibility that a firmly-stroked ball will unsettle them.

Wickets are also known as hoops, but that word, with its implication of vast diameters, is misleading. Hoops suggest vaulted arches that give balls plenty of room to bounce around before they get through, but Association wickets aren't like that at all. These wickets are $3^{3}/_{4}$ to 4 inches wide—a scant $^{1}/_{8}$ to $^{1}/_{4}$ inch wider than Association balls. There are three exceptions to this hoop width. The first is known as the "President's hoop," which narrows the opening to $3^{11}/_{16}$ inches for international championship play. Another is the "winter wicket." Jaques ($1^{1}/_{2}$ pounds) and Forster (14 ounces), called a "Challenge hoop," is made of thinner, $^{7}/_{16}$-inch or $^{5}/_{16}$-inch (Forster) diameter bent steel, giving the shooter slightly more margin for error on courts where the grass may be irregular and the ground may be frozen. Jaques has also introduced a heavier bent steel wicket called the Roehampton with $^{5}/_{8}$-inch upright which at $2^{1}/_{2}$ pounds provides some of the advantages of both.

Considering the weight and thickness of these wickets, new owners of Association equipment may be inclined to drive them into the lawn with

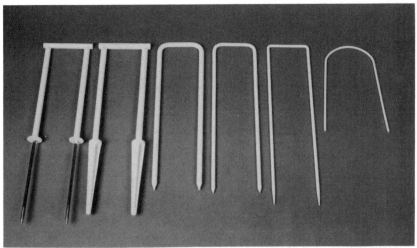

An array of wickets from left, the "Foxy" (for bowling greens or tennis courts), the Association (cast iron), the Roehampton (heavy bent iron), Jaques Challenge (winter wicket), Forster "C" class Challenge and "D" class Stratford.

the help of a hammer. Don't! At the very least, a hammer will chip the paint; at the worst, fracture the cast iron crown or upright, or, in the case of the winter wicket, distend the uprights. If you must use a hammer to set your wickets into the ground, put a block of wood across the crown first. If you are an equipment fetishist, there is a wooden hammer called a "smasher" that comes with most sets or can be purchased for just this chore. Also, now available from Jaques, is a "wicket drill" for the cast iron hoop which provides accurate and easier insertion of that style wicket.

Players who devote any time at all to the game or whose lawns are frequently used by others will soon discover that croquet balls will, inevitably, create grooves in the grass through the center of the wicket. These grooves give an equal disadvantage to every shooter and may well cause the ball to roll back into the jaws after it has passed through a wicket. This can prove to be costly if the match is a close one, so if grooves form in front of your wickets, you should, between games, rotate them—the important thing is to make sure that the outside wickets retain the correct alignment. To achieve this, simply rotate the wicket so that one of its present holes is used. Be sure to turn your wickets in the same direction so there is a clear, straight shot from one outside wicket to the next.

The Ball

The key ingredient in evaluating a croquet set is the ball. Compared to the lightweight plastic balls used in most backyard croquet, class "A" Association balls seem like the giant steel ball-bearings used by shot-putters. Designed in proportion to Association wickets, these balls weigh a pound, give or take $1/4$ ounce, and are $3^5/8$ inches (plus or minus $1/32$ inch) in diameter. They're made either of compressed cork covered with high-impact plastic or of a recently developed solid plastic composite. Whatever their center, their surface must be cross milled with grooves that conform to precise standards of depth and width.

Aside from the weight and diameter requirements set forth in both USCA and British Association standards, the ball played in all major tournaments throughout the world must meet another criterion involving its elasticity.

To meet this critical requirement, a ball must have a rebound coefficient of *between* 30 and 37 inches when freely dropped from 60 inches onto a 2-inch steel plate embedded in concrete. Any bounce greater would be considered too lively; any lesser bounce would be insufficient. USCA class "B," "C," "D" and "E" balls usually fall into either the low- or high-bounce category, and also vary in weight from 16 down to 9 ounces. These livelier balls are often found useful on heavy lawn as they require less strength to propel long distances. One problem that some solid plastic-composite balls have yet to overcome is a tendency to change rebound characteristics by as much as 10 inches after several hours play in hot sunlight.

Croquet balls: from (lower left) Class "C" Surrey, Class "B" Hampton (top) and Class "A" Eclipse (lower right).

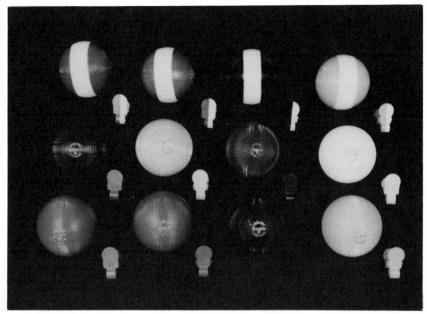

The Jaques Eclipse ball, long the world's standard by which all other balls are measured, is now available in First Colors (Blue, Red, Black & Yellow (bottom), Second Colors (Green, Pink, Brown & White) (middle) and new white striped First Colors (top) even with matching colored clips.

Since 1938, Jaques has enjoyed a leadership position in the production of its class "A" level, cork centered Eclipse ball. The World Championships and all major USCA and International Championships are played with the Eclipse ball.

An "A" class croquet set comes with four of these balls, solidly colored blue, red, black and yellow. In singles, one player will play red and yellow, the other blue and black. In doubles, each side plays either the red/yellow or blue/black pair.

There is another set of balls especially colored or marked so that two matches may be played on the same court at one time: in England this is called "double banking." To avoid the confusion that similarly colored balls would inevitably create, these "second color" balls are green (for blue), pink (for red), brown (for black) and white (for yellow). With "double banking" being increasingly employed in major tournament play where available courts would otherwise limit the number of entries, a white stripe around "first color" balls is proving a popular alternative. The white stripes on most American backyard sets of balls undoubtedly evolved from this need for multiple play in the 1800s.

The Finishing Stake (or Winning Peg)

Those who are planning to play 2-stake, 9-wicket croquet with English made equipment better order an extra "peg," because a basic Association set includes only one. It stands 18 inches tall, and is $1^1/_2$ inches in diameter; it is made of wood and, like the wickets, has a sharpened point to keep it firmly in place. It also has a narrow black wood or plastic spire on its top. This removable extension serves to hold the clips of the players who are shooting for the peg. (The designer was a believer in close contests: the spire is large enough to hold four clips.)

Although painted white, the peg has four bands of color on it, with blue at the top, then red, black, and yellow. These colors are hardly decorative; rather, they indicate the order of play. Aside from the "deadness board," the peg is the only spot on the court that gives this information, and even experts will find themselves consulting it when there is no strategic reason to, simply to keep themselves from one of croquet's most egregious and common errors: playing out of turn.

Jack Osborn has also decorated all his tournament mallet shafts with tape bands in this color sequence as a personal reminder to avoid this painful and embarrassing fault.

Stake (or peg): Center stake (or winning peg) has black extension for clips on top with colored stripes in sequence from blue, red, black and yellow downward to white base.

Colored clips indicate which wicket each ball is to play next.

Clips

In a game where a scoreboard is the exception rather than the rule, blue, black, red and yellow clips are attached to the next wickets that players must clear. A clip thus reminds a player—who may well be executing a series of shots that seem to have nothing to do with clearing wickets— which wicket his ball is for. And for knowing spectators, a survey of the clips indicates where the players are relative to the peg, thus providing what passes in croquet for the score for each ball and side.

On the outward course—the first six wickets—clips are placed on the crown of the wicket you're shooting for. On the homeward route—those same six wickets, cleared in the opposite direction—clips are placed near the top of the wicket's upright. When you're shooting for the peg, clips are placed on the peg's spire.

The only time a clip isn't on a wicket or peg is when you've cleared a wicket and are continuing your turn. Then it's attached to your shirt, belt or trousers' pocket. When your turn ends, it's promptly set on the next wicket your ball is for.

Because Association croquet is often characterized by defensive tactics

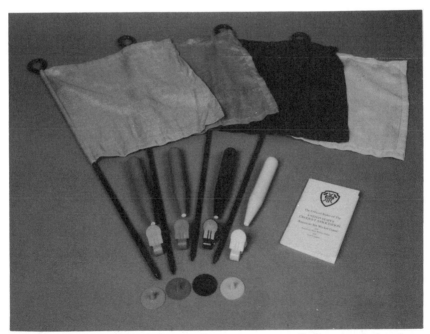

Croquet court accessories include corner flags, corner pegs and ball markers in the primary (or first) colors, Blue, Red, Black & Yellow, and of course the pocket size USCA rule book.

so seemingly perverse that players appear to be avoiding wickets, clips are absolutely essential. Most players *think* they're aware of where they're bound; with the clipped hoops, however, they *know*. In Association croquet matches, the only time a referee may offer advice without its being requested by a player is when he admonishes the shooter to set his clip correctly. Many is the croquet player who has avoided a humiliating error by this advice, or simply by noticing on his own, where he's ultimately going.

The Deadness Board

Even deluxe English croquet sets don't come with deadness boards, which means you're going to have to find yourself, at some early point in your croquet career, buying or building one of your own. For one truth we know: it is very difficult to do without a deadness board.

The function of the deadness board is to serve as a kind of interim guide, telling you and the spectators what balls you must not hit upon penalty of committing a foul and ending your turn. Let's say you're shooting with the black ball, and having cleared the second wicket, you roquet the yellow ball. A referee, another player, an appointed board-keeper, or, if necessary, a spectator, should promptly reveal the yellow square that's on the same line as the master black. This indicates to other players—and to your forgetful self—that you are "dead" on yellow unless you've cleared yourself by running the next wicket.

Let us say that by dint of clever shooting, you go on to roquet red. Now your red square is exposed and you're two-ball dead. Finally, you roquet blue. The blue square is opened, and you're three-ball dead. Woe to you if you end your turn without running your next wicket and "clearing" the deadness board, for you will then be in a terrible jam: balls that are not dead on you can dart fearlessly into courtspace you formerly controlled and use your ball as a steppingstone without fear of retribution. Darryl Zanuck's description of this state, though harsh, is exact: "When you're three-ball dead, you're just a worthless bum."

While variations of these boards have been homemade by innovative addicts using materials such as colored sink stoppers hung on nails and metal painted coffee tin tops on magnets, the most widely used in tournament play are the USCA approved boards of wood or weatherproof plastic with aluminum or clear plastic tracks with white sliding squares that either cover or reveal the color squares as play dictates.

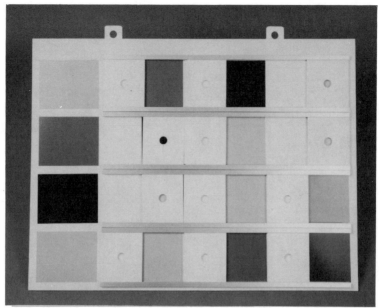

The Deadness board is helpful to both spectators and players since it advises them which balls may not be roqueted until the next wicket has been cleared. In this example, Blue (top left) is dead on Red and Black, Red is dead on Yellow, Black is dead on Red and Yellow (bottom left) is dead on the three other balls. (Courtesy Croquet International Ltd.)

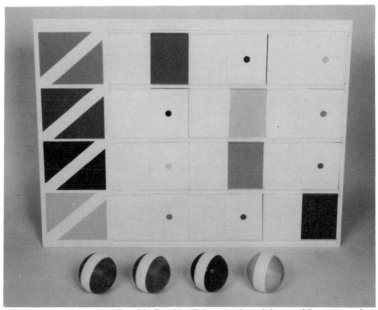

The recent increase in "Double Banking" has produced the need for a second set of balls, clips and a deadness board to match. Stripes added to "first color" balls and deadness board is one solution. (Courtesy of Croquet International Ltd.)

71

Three classes of basic equipment: Proportionate in weight, quality of materials and craftsmanship, components of class "A"–"C" and "E" types of sets are, from left to right: (1) "A"-class 3-lb. Lignum Vitae brass-bound mallet, 4¹/2-lb. cast-iron Association wicket and 1-lb. composition Eclipse ball; (2) "C"-class 2¹/4-lb. hardwood mallet, 2-lb. bent steel Challenge wicket and 14-oz. wooden ball; (3) "E"-class 18-oz. rubber-headed mallet, 1¹/2-oz. plastic-coated bent-wire wicket and 9-oz. wooden ball.

BALL TESTING
This involves random testing of different types of croquet balls by the repeated dropping of each ball in a set from a 60 inch height onto a thick steel plate imbedded in concrete. The height the ball rebounds is measured and compared with a standard to determine the elasticity and compression factors which influence the "liveliness" of each ball. "Liveliness" is one of the keys to the performance of a ball on court. The USCA videotapes these drop tests to provide an ongoing record as new ball models are introduced.

THE EQUIPMENT CHART

The most enjoyable croquet is played by those who use equipment that is appropriate to their lawns, abilities and aspirations. With the variety of croquet sets now on the market, it may be difficult to figure out which set is best suited for your type of lawn and your level of play. The accompanying chart should help you determine the set that's best for your needs.

The descriptions, weights and estimated costs of the sets and their components that we describe in the first four classes in this chart are largely based on the standards set by England's leading maker, John Jaques & Son, Ltd. American manufacturers such as Forster Mfg. and Harvard Sports (Spaulding), are beginning to develop better-quality sets to meet these standards. Abercrombie & Fitch, long a purveyor of quality croquet equipment, carries a selection of USCA approved sets including the top of the Jaques line. To find out where these sets are available in your area, contact the United States Croquet Association, Croquet International Ltd., or the firms listed in the back of this book.

For the purpose of this chart, all basic sets for USCA and British 6-wicket croquet will consist of the following:

4 mallets
4 balls (blue, red, black and yellow)
6 wickets
1 finishing stake (peg)
1 USCA Rule Book (includes rules for 6-wicket and 9-wicket croquet and golf-croquet)

Those who intend to play 9-wicket, 2-stake backyard croquet should be aware that unless otherwise indicated by an asterisk (*) on the chart, they will need to buy three additional wickets and one additional stake.

The following accessories are available and, in many instances, are included in the sets:

Clips (blue, red, black and yellow)
Corner flags (same four colors)
Ball markers (same four colors), used to indicate positions on the court when, because of darkness or weather, a game is not completed
Smasher (for driving wickets into the ground)

USCA Classification and Price Range	Basic Set Designations	Set Components	Weights
AAA AA A $1,000 TO $2,500	Custom (special order mallets) Excaliber Championship Association A & F International	MALLETS: Round/square, Brassbound, heads, grips. Cane spliced, sight line.	2¼–4 lbs.
		BALLS: Eclipse (or equivalent).	1 lb.
		WICKETS: (Association) Cast iron.	4½–6 lbs. each
		1 stake (peg), USCA rules, flags, clips and markers in a wood storage box.	75–77 lbs. per set
BBB BB B $500 to $1,000	Colonial Square Tournament Hampton Square A & F Cheltenham	MALLETS: Round/square, Brassbound, grips, sight line.	2 lbs. 4oz. to 3 lbs. 2 oz.
		BALLS: Eclipse (or composition).	13–16 oz.
		WICKETS: (Challenge) Winter/wrought iron/ bent steel.	1½–3 lbs.
		1 stake (peg), USCA rules, clips, in wooden box.	45–50 lbs. per set
CCC CC C $150 to $500	Henley *Challenge Collegiate *A & F American	MALLETS: Round, Bound or unbound heads, Plain or cord grips.	2–3 lbs.
		BALLS: Composition.	12–14 oz.
		WICKETS: (Challenge) Winter/wrought iron.	12 oz.–2 lbs.
		1 stake (peg), USCA rules, clips in a box or canvas bag.	30–45 lbs. per set
DDD DD D $100 to $300	Family *Stratford Garden (*9 Wicket/ 2 stake set)	MALLETS: Round head, Plain wood.	1½-2 lbs.
		BALLS: Composition.	9–14 oz.
		WICKETS: Light weight Wrought iron or wire.	2 oz.–12 oz.
		2 stake (peg), USCA rules in a box or canvas bag.	20–30 lbs. per set
EE E $60 to $150	Junior	MALLETS: Round head, Plain wood.	under 2 lbs.
		BALLS: Composition or Hardwood.	9 oz. (minimum)
		WICKETS: Bent wire.	2 oz. up
		2 stake (peg), boxed.	15–25 lbs. per set

Sizes (Dimension)	Court Sizes and Grass Level	USCA Approved/Recommended and/or Suitable for Use By:
36" shafts 9" x 3" heads	105 x 84 feet or scaled down to not less than $^1/_2$ size	Authorized for international championships by Croquet Associations worldwide and all USCA national, regional, sectional tournaments. Interclub, intercollegiate, invitationals, country, golf, tennis clubs, sports clubs and private club play.
$3^5/_8$" diameter		
$^5/_8$" diameter uprights $3^3/_4$"–4" span $3^{11}/_{16}$" for International play	Putting green (smooth and level) Flat to $^1/_4$" high	
33"–36" shafts	105 x 84 feet or scaled down to not less than $^1/_2$ size minimum	Country, golf, tennis and sports clubs (Challenge, winter or foxy wickets are often used on existing putting greens or lawn tennis court surfaces). Collegiate, private club and family play.
$3^5/_8$" diameter		
$^7/_{16}$" diameter uprights 4" span	Fringe (of golf green) $^1/_4$"–$^3/_4$" high	
33"–36" shafts	105 x 84 feet or scaled down proportionately to a minimum of 50 x 40 feet	Intercollegiate, interschool (intermediate), informal club and family play.
$3^5/_8$" diameter		
$^5/_{16}$"–$^7/_{16}$" diameter uprights 4" span	Golf fairway $^1/_2$" to 1" high	
30"-36" shafts	Scaled down from full size to fit available area	School, family and beginner play.
$3^5/_{16}$" diameter		
up to $^5/_{16}$" diameter uprights 4"–5" span	Fairway to low rough 1"–1$^1/_2$" high	
28"–33" shafts	50 x 40 feet, or to fit available yard area	Juniors, children, informal play.
3"-3$^1/_4$" diameter		
4"–6" span	Low rough, 1"–2" high	

CLOTHING AND ACCESSORIES

As the saying "You've come a long way baby" goes, so has the evolution of croquet attire, from the constrictive ankle length dresses and the starched shirt and tie and high top shoes of the turn of the century to the comfort and convenience of shorts, slacks and carefree, wash and wear cotton and blended shirts and tennis shoes dominating the courts of today.

As you've noted by now, there are many parallels between the evolution of tennis and croquet and nowhere is that more evident than on the courts of both today . . . with one exception. In croquet you can "color yourself" anything as long as its "WHITE."

Sharkskin blazer and pants from Jean Pearman's "Great White" collection of croquet attire. Jean, wife of US Croquet Hall of Fame's Dick Pearman, lives and designs in Bermuda.

USCA logoed wearing apparel is designed for on and off court comfort and playability.

For although anything from bathing suits to bluejeans may go, in the privacy of one's own backyard, the USCA dress code for all major tournament play is "white." However it has evolved, be it the Wimbledon connection or the simple truth that white does not absorb the sun's heat as colors do, croquet, as played at the top, remains sports' last bastion of sartorial conservatism and comfort.

77

This, no small tip of the hat to tradition, has not cramped fashion's hand in inspiring innovation in styles or fabric selection. Sea Island cotton, new absorbent polyester/cotton fibers and even "sharkskin" are artfully mixed with rain resistant manmade and "breathable" outer wear to cover the inevitable downpours which often occur in tournaments. Here the only act of nature that slows down the action is the presence of an inch or two of standing water and lightning.

It also cannot be denied that deeply tanned, or even sunscreen shaded players decked out in all whites lend more than a touch of class to any verdant court they play on.

In fashion   *Out of fashion*

In spite of the fact that some croquet fanatics are superstitious to the point of not changing all (or any) of the clothing worn in winning early round tournament matches for fear of changing their luck, gone are the days when one of our living Hall of Fame players insisted on wearing red socks and purple sneakers to appease his personal god of croquet.

Speaking of sneakers leads to the functional importance of comfort in playing croquet. Along with preserving the desirable smoothness of a good court, flat soled shoes, be they women's wedge heeled espadrilles or walking or tennis shoes that provide a solid comfortable base, are a must.

As for accessories, many USCA logoed niceties are now available, including blazer badges, ties, tie tacks, lapel pins, cuff links, clothing patches, glasses, mugs, key chains, belts, suspenders, visors, golf and tennis type caps and hats, mallet covers and that most indispensable item of all, the umbrella.

Having noted that croquet tournaments are one of the few sporting events played rain or shine, one of the sure ways you can spot a rookie to the sport is the absence of an umbrella. There is no rule that requires players to lend their umbrellas to their opponents. In fact, as in golf, it could be considered penalizable to receive outside assistance while taking a shot. The next time out a drenched rookie will undoubtedly be carrying his own umbrella and privately may remark on how quickly he is learning the game. And he is, he is.

Princess Diana may eventually enjoy a firm hold on the English throne, but as a child she opted for a left-handed Solomon grip.

6

GRIPS AND STANCES

THE GRIP

One of the more widely circulated pictures of Diana, Princess of Wales, is a shot of her as a spunky nine-year-old with a croquet mallet in her hand. Judging from the headlines and captions that have accompanied this photograph, the point seems to be that the Princess, in playing at a tender age a game thought to be the exclusive province of titled nobility, was "born to be Queen." As a budding croquet player, however, you will see that the *real* point of the photograph is that Diana is about to use the Solomon grip.

This is a significant piece of information because now that equipment has become more or less standardized, the grip is one of the few parts of the game in which personal preference can be expressed. And while it may seem a cruel irony that, if you are just being introduced to the game, you are confronted with a multitude of ways to hold the mallet, confront them you must. For everything you do later in croquet—from the simplest, 6-inch positioning shot to the most dazzling 80-foot cross-court roquet—flows directly from your ability to swing the mallet naturally and easily.

Every croquet player develops, in time, his favorite grip. That personalized grip is not, then, merely the ratification of an initial choice, but the gradual realization that one grip really produces more successful results than any other. We recommend that you read this chapter with a mallet in hand and, after each description of a grip, hit a few balls using that grip. Later, play a few games with the one that feels best. There will probably be some stiffness in your hands at first, but keep at it, periodically reviewing your grip to make sure you haven't, through fatigue or carelessness, let your hands slip into some other position.

How will you know when you've found the grip that's right for you? It's not necessarily when you make a shot that's previously eluded you, or win a game, or elicit questions from even greener players. Rather, it's a process of elimination; one day, having tried Lord knows how many grips, you'll just *know*. There you'll be, standing over a mallet *without* thinking about your grip—and in the perfection of that moment, you'll have found the one that best suits you. In that instant, your mallet will become what you most want it to be: a 3-foot extension of your arms.

Although some of the grips we're about to describe may seem somewhat tortuous, these are the grips that have been most widely accepted by players who have been at the game for decades. It may be scant consolation to you as you're twisting your thumbs around a mallet, but these grips are intended to be comfortable. For comfort is the ultimate concept in croquet; if you're standing over your mallet in pain, the studied consciousness that results can only be reflected in your shot.

However personalized the subject of grips may be, there's no reason to go it completely alone. If you're having difficulty and an "A"-level player—or, better yet, one of the game's greats—happens to walk onto your greensward, ask him to watch you hit a few. As in golf, a subtle adjustment in the grip may produce a dramatic improvement in your game.

Finally, whatever grip you choose, there's only one way to hold the mallet—as if it were a soft-boiled egg. Firmness is the key—you don't want to drop your mallet or watch it go sailing out toward the next wicket—but so is a certain tenderness. As Lord Tollemache says, "Remember that you are not holding a sledgehammer, but an instrument of touch." In a game where the best players often look as if they're having trouble staying awake, the hypertense, over-stressed, constricted malleteer doesn't have a chance.

The Standard (American) Grip

Many Americans will find that the most comfortable and effective grip depends on the widest possible separation of the hands. American courts have as much to do with this as anything else. Compared with English greenswards, which are rolled and manicured so frequently that an extraterrestrial, hovering over them, might think he had happened upon a nation of lawn worshippers, the bulk of our backyard lawns are bumpy and coarse. Consequently, a shot that would, in England, require a mere love tap will, on most American courts, necessitate a stronger stroke.

To try the American grip, the first step, if you are right-handed, is to grip the top of the mallet with your left hand. (The reverse would be true for a lefty.) The easiest way to think of the left hand position is to remember those schoolyard baseball games when the team captains would choose sides. One captain would toss the bat to the other, and, after it was caught, the captains would, by turns, grab the bat, with the winner being the captain who could grip the bat closest to the top of its neck. Skipping the interim steps, that is essentially what you do with your left hand: get it comfortably gripped at the top of the mallet without any part of your hand wrapped over the top and with your knuckles facing forward toward your target.

The standard American grip: With this grip, the knuckles of the upper hand face squarely forward. Side view: Notice that the knuckles of the upper hand face forward. Front view: The palm of the lower hand faces forward. Right: The American grip, with "pencil grip" variation.

The right hand goes, according to your preference, six to twelve inches below the left. The palm rests against the back side of the octagonal grip, and your index finger should be pointed down along the side or at the back of the mallet. As in other grips, the point is to keep the index finger and the pinky of the right hand from influencing your stroke. The second and third fingers of the right hand are the crucial ones, and if you've correctly positioned your hand, all they do is hold the mallet. If they affect your aim at all, you're doing something wrong.

Another variation of this basic American grip has the lower hand grasping the shaft as if it were a large pencil cupping the handle between the thumb and forefinger with the middle finger down the side and fourth finger against the back. We know of two world-class players who favor this "pencil" grip.

The British standard grip: The hands are held together near the top of the shaft.

The Standard British Grip

This grip is the same as the American grip but with one difference: here the hands touch at the top of the shaft. As your shooting skills improve or as you find better and faster courts to play on, you might consider bringing your hands closer together until you become comfortable with the British style. There is one advantage to this grip, and it is considerable: the closer your hands are to each other, the less either hand can dominate and, in the resulting imbalance, throw off the intended aim or strength of your shot.

Most frequently used with the center stance (for stances, see page 90), this grip is often also used in conjunction with the side-style stance with the bottom hand near the upper or slightly below it on the shaft.

The Irish Grip

This grip was introduced by a half-dozen brilliant players from Ireland who dominated the sport in the Edwardian era. It is particularly useful for those players who have trouble with their stroke because one hand exerts more influence than the other and consequently sends every ball off course. With the Irish grip, that error is almost automatically corrected. The hands practically cup the mallet. Both palms face away from the body, and both thumbs rest on the front of the shaft.

The Irish grip: Similar to gripping a golf club—hands cup the mallet with palms behind the shaft.

When used with a shorter mallet or with the hands set lower on the shaft, the Irish grip seems to increase accuracy—particularly in shots for the wicket at close range. A number of top American players and Champion Nigel Aspinall favor this grip for that reason. After a disappointing season some years ago, however, Aspinall switched to the standard (American) grip for many of his shots and quickly resumed his winning ways. Today he alternates these two grips for various shots, which suggests some latitude is permissible (or desirable) in this area.

The Solomon grip: A two-fisted grip with knuckles of both hands facing forward at the top of the handle.

The Solomon Grip

John Solomon recalls that he "invented" this grip as a child because it was simply the only way he could handle a mallet, which was almost as tall as he was. Later, he tried to switch to a more standard grip, but he soon discovered that for roquet shots and shots at the wicket he much preferred his own grip style. With more than fifty English and International titles to his credit, Solomon now includes several top-ranked American players among his devotees. His grip is unusual in that both sets of knuckles face away from the body. But John, like Nigel, also changed his grip for certain two-ball shots. Some players feel that separating the hands by an inch or two provides more control, power and steadier wrists.

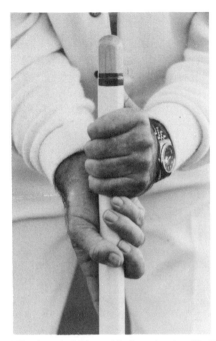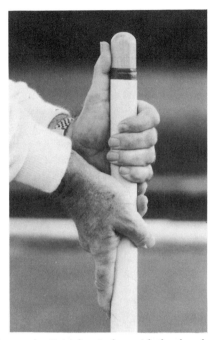

The South African (Osborn) grip: Similar to the British grip but with the thumb of the upper hand extending upward along the back of the octagonal handle.

The South African (Osborn) Grip

After years of experimentation, Jack Osborn has found a grip that enables him to hold his mallet exactly the same way every time he takes a single-ball stroke and during many of his two-ball strokes. The secret is the upturned thumb: with the pad of the thumb being fixed squarely against the back panel of the octagonal handle, the upper hand can't shift around the shaft. It also guarantees that the left elbow will remain tucked in during the stroke.

The Osborn grip is a modification of the grip used with obvious effectiveness by South African champions Tom Barlow and Reggie Bamford. Barlow uses a pencil grip with his right hand, which is lower on the shaft. Osborn (and Bamford) keeps his right hand next to his left in the standard palm-out grip at the top of the shaft.

He believes that this seemingly minor adjustment from the standard British grip he had settled on in recent years has, since his visit to South Africa in 1981, materially sharpened his long roquet and single-ball shots.

The Golf Grip

This may be the most natural grip for those who come to croquet from that other lawn sport, but it doesn't work as well on the greensward as it does on the fairway. For croquet is a game that ultimately rests on skills that are demonstrated at relatively short distances, and the golf grip tends to encourage fantasies of teeing off. Why do we include it at all? Because those whose arms are not strong may want to switch to the golf grip—and the golf stance and swing—for long shots. As in the Irish grip, both palms are cupped around the shaft facing each other and both thumbs rest on the top of the shaft. Here, however, the left thumb is almost covered by the right palm.

Golf Grip (and Stance): As in golf—palms face each other and fingers overlap or interlock.

STANCES
The Golf Stance

Those who have graduated to Association croquet from backyard competition almost invariably have mastered the golf stance. And with good reason: backyards are often bumpy, and it takes a hefty backswing to advance a ball even a few feet on such a lawn.

On the greensward, however, the golf stance is usually a liability. For one thing, it breaks the flow of the stalk, that apparently seamless series of gestures which enables a player to line up his shot and execute it without breaking stride. For another, it forces you to turn your head to check your aim. In short, it forces you to think at exactly the time when you ought to be finished with thinking.

Despite its drawbacks, the golf stance (see stance in figure on page 88) is well suited for long-distance shots on uneven or heavy lawns. To use it in a single-ball shot, stand at a right angle to the direction you want the ball to travel, taking care that the ball is just inside the left toe. For a long drive or double-ball shot, stand slightly in front of the ball. But no matter what kind of shot, a slow backswing is suggested, and, as you are often told in golf, let the mallet head do the work as you reach the point of impact and on into the follow-through.

In 1872 the cue stroke was outlawed, ending the use of the shot in which the narrow tip of the shaft was held like a billiards cue by a player who was, as often as not, lying on the ground.

In 1899 it was decreed that mallet heads had to be uniform, a crushing blow to those players who carried tiny mallets in their vest pockets for occasions when a regular mallet couldn't advance the fortunes of a hoop-bound ball.

As a result of these two edicts, croquet changed from a game well suited for contortionists to a more civilized and sportsmanlike contest played exclusively by erect bipeds—with the exception of backyard and roque, in which short (10-inch to 18-inch) handles still force the players to assume an inelegant squat or stoop to hit the ball. These edicts are a great boon for the fledgling croquet player, for, in choosing a stance, he must consider basically only three ways to approach a solitary ball that he wishes to hit.

The first, which we've shown you here, is the Golf stance. Although presented first, it is in fact the last we would recommend for playing on a level and smooth croquet court or for any shot requiring precision such as running a wicket. The other two are the Center and Side stances which are the most widely employed by serious players.

The Center Stance

For most players, this will be the only stance worth considering. The player stands directly behind the ball. He points his feet in the direction he wishes the ball to go. Neither foot exerts more influence than the other. And in swinging the mallet like a pendulum between his legs, the player has the greatest possibility of sending the ball in the direction he wants it to travel. One indication of its effectiveness is that the center stance and swing have been prohibited in golf forcing Sam Snead to change to a side stance.

The greatest advantage of the center style, however, is that it allows you to align your feet and shoulders with the target and thus to focus all your thoughts and energy into a fluid pendulum swing.

Start with your feet shoulder width apart, with your left foot from six inches to eighteen inches in front of your right (if you are right-handed, otherwise the reverse) and aligned parallel with the line to the target. The weight should be evenly distributed and your knees slightly flexed in an effort to create a solid, immovable base for the stroke. Again, comfort is the objective, so you should experiment with the distance your right foot should go back until you feel an even balance. The farther your right foot goes back, the more your weight should shift to the left foot.

Women tend to place their right foot farther back than men, since this stance provides somewhat more leverage during the swing than a more evenly squared, aligned stance. The latter is another variation of the center stance, which, in fact, is favored by some top International players who keep both feet closer together and at the same level.

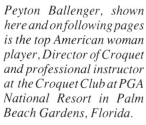

Peyton Ballenger, shown here and on following pages is the top American woman player, Director of Croquet and professional instructor at the Croquet Club at PGA National Resort in Palm Beach Gardens, Florida.

Left: Center Stance

Right: Center Stance with extended back leg.

The Side Stance

For those who are taking up croquet after years, or even decades, of physical inactivity, the side stance might prove sensible. Evolving from the era when long dresses prohibited swinging a mallet between the feet by the ladies, the side stance is seldom seen in tournament play today. It offers some of the power of the golf stance and yet delivers most of the control of the center stance. For all that, it is no instant solution to the challenge of standing over the ball without throwing off your aim—in this stance, it's more difficult not to twist the body slightly as you shoot.

To assume the side stance, face the ball and hold the mallet to the side of the foot. Your knees should be slightly bent. If desired, one foot can be moved forward to reduce even further any strain in the back and legs.

Side stance is often the choice of players with back problems since it allows for a more upright body position

Australian Win Dickinson prefers the side stance. An outstanding shotmaker, Win plays in a dress which according to Australian Croquet Council rulings may not have its hem higher than 17 inches from the ground.

English star Keith Aiton assumes a center stance with feet level and close together.

Once you have determined which stance seems to suit you best, and before getting further into the proper way to swing the mallet, let us literally take a few steps backward and introduce you to *the stalk*.

Richard Pearman stalks prior to taking a croquet stroke in an US International Challenge Cup Match.

7

THE STALK AND SWING

by John C. Osborn

STALKING—
The First Step

Perhaps the most common shot-making flaw the novice must overcome is his own enthusiasm. Just as it is true that one cannot run before learning to walk, it is equally impossible to hit the perfect shot without having aimed it properly. Even the best of players, with adrenalin flowing in the midst of a close game, occasionally approach the ball without the proper concentration, without remembering croquet's most basic law—always approach your ball properly (from behind).

It is difficult to convince neophytes that the most important moment in successful shot-making takes place *before* you swing your mallet. As John Solomon points out, "You can swing brilliantly, you can hit the ball with the precise degree of force you intend—but if the stance you've taken sends the ball off in the wrong direction, what does all that matter?"

Jack Nicklaus approaches a golf ball from behind, never from the side. So should you. On the green, Nicklaus looks at the hole, then at the imaginary line from his ball to the hole, and finally at a point on this line about three feet ahead of the ball. You should too. And, like Nicklaus, you should do all this before you are hunched over the ball—during what is known in croquet as *"the stalk."*

Welcome then to the "stalk." To begin with, depending upon the distance of your shot, stand from about six to twelve feet directly behind your ball. From there, draw an imaginary straight line from your target, through your ball, and make sure you are standing upon that line. The same way in which it is sometimes impossible to find an object right before your eyes, you will never be able to position your body and aim properly at your target by approaching your ball from the side. Now it is time to walk that line, and only if you are certain that your feet and mallet

The stalk: (1) Stand 6 to 12 feet behind your ball and draw an imaginary line between it and its target. Then (2) walk to your ball, keeping your eye on the shooting line. Finally (3), take a firm but comfortable stance.

are aimed properly, is it time to swing your mallet.

One of the most important things to realize here is that if there is even the slightest doubt in your mind of your aim, it is your swing itself which will reflect this. If you find yourself moving your feet or mallet once you have reached the ball, you are exhibiting such doubt. Start again, and having finally found confidence in your aim, only now can you freely concentrate on the swing itself.

Lord Tollemache said he could always tell when a player was going to miss his shot because, instead of shooting at once, he waited two extra heartbeats before taking his swing. In other words, the player was re-checking his angle, readjusting his mallet or feet when nothing should be on his mind but a smooth, slow backswing and an effortless stroke.

While we have inferred that the aim of your mallet is important to produce a successful shot, we will now go one step further to say that the detailed placement of your feet is crucial to guarantee a properly aimed shot. "Why," you ask, "should a beginner develop a foot fetish? We don't kick the ball, so what's the big deal?"

Let's pick up a mallet and stand about four feet in front of a mirror. Take aim directly toward yourself, and make sure that both of your feet and your mallet are aimed properly. Take a soft swing. Hopefully the swing will feel comfortable and you are secure that were you to actually hit a ball, it would travel toward its intended direction. Still, let's take one moment for an experiment.

Let the mallet rest in front of you and without altering your aim, stand upright. Now, while looking into the mirror and keeping your left foot still, redirect the toes of your right foot two inches toward the right. If you think your body is aiming as it was a moment ago, you are probably cheating. Relax your body and still standing upright, notice the new direction your shoulders have taken. Are your eyes still looking directly into their reflection? Now move your toes two inches more to the right, and it should be completely obvious that your body has taken on a new pose. As we exaggerate even further, moving your right foot more and more, you will realize that it will be almost impossible for your body to comfortably swing the mallet to the right. There is a good chance you have missed your target to that side. If you notice that both feet are pointed that way, you have failed to concentrate on the first step to the single-ball shot.

Finally, once you have finished your stalk, you are free to take a practice swing. Since your feet are properly set, you need no longer worry if your mallet falls into the same spot. Concentration on your stalk should now lead you to confidence in your feet, lead you to the time to concentrate on our second step: the swing.

THE SWING–
From Feet to Shoulders

Some of the best players in the history of golf have individual, unique swings. Likewise, baseball greats such as Babe Ruth and Mickey Mantle differed drastically in hitting styles. As in other sports, the swing of a croquet mallet can take on a very personalized appearance. We are, after all, different people. We are built differently, have different temperaments and have acquired grips and stances which may be unsuitable for another player. To find two players who handle and swing the croquet mallet in the identical fashion would prove a difficult task.

John Solomon has confessed that "it is almost impossible to describe how to swing a mallet." And yet, as in the art of swinging a golf club or a baseball bat, there are certain principles which should be followed.

As with the stalk, the position of the shoulders is vital in the croquet swing. It is the shoulders which should control the swing. Why? Simply because they are the truest part of the body. They are hard to twist, seldom move position and never fall to nerves the way other parts of the body might. They aim the shot and carry the arms which actually propel the mallet. So what can go wrong?

The worst culprits in a bad swing are the wrists. Very often you will hear a player yell out, "Oh, I twisted my wrists!" There are several reasons for this. The first reason, unfortunately, we cannot help, and that is the simple fact that in the course of a game, people get nervous. The wrists, in the midst of a swing, should remain firm, and as in golf and baseball, should be released, if ever, after contact with the ball. Often in the middle of a close game, a player will anxiously let the wrists do the work for him. Instead of pulling the arms back and through the ball, a player will seemingly forget that he has arms at all. Wrists take control of the entire swing, and it is almost impossible to keep the mallet in a straight line. Even the slightest twist of the wrists can lead to a very poorly hit shot.

There are two other reasons why the wrists can destroy a successful shot. It is the arms, controlled by the shoulders, which dictate the swing. Let's do another experiment. Assume a normal stance and place your mallet next to a ball and take a very small step or two closer to your mallet and try to swing. Now take a step or two closer. As you try to swing you will find it is almost impossible to swing the mallet without your wrists taking over. For some reason, even the best players tend to inch up on the ball when either nervous or attempting a long shot, and such movement can only alter a shot. The result is known as "hitting down" which will cause the ball to jump, detracting from both power and direction.

USCA National Champion Reid Fleming's head remains in one place throughout the down swing, contact and follow-through on this rush shot.

Now let's try it the other way. This time stand a step or two back and once again swing. Here problems arise as well, for as you realize that you will not make solid contact, the wrists will try to propel the mallet beyond the normal swing. This is known as "hitting up." What is important to understand is that your stance should remain the same in almost all single-ball shots. If you have either too little or too much room to undertake your swing, the wrists are almost forced to fix the imbalance. In the course of your stalk, make sure you are standing a consistent distance from your ball so that, unless another shot is called for, you will hit it square.

While your wrists might well be the most important physical monster you must master within the swing, the arms themselves can cause problems. Once again the stance is important. In the normal swing, the mallet should travel as a pendulum—it should make a smooth curve throughout the backswing and follow-through. And what if you are standing too far from your ball? Even if you resist the urge to guide with your wrists, it is your arms which will extend, pushing the ball instead of swinging cleanly through it. Your elbows should remain unmoved throughout the swing. However, if you are standing too far from the ball, this extension of the arms will shove the mallet instead of swinging it clearly. While your aim may survive this artificial swing, it is almost certain that the distance you wish to send your ball will be affected.

It is important to realize that the arms, in the course of a swing, should be a unit. In the midst of a tense game or, while making a long shot, a worse kind of "push" can occur. For whatever your grip, the bottom hand will probably be the dominant one. It will pull the mallet at the beginning of the backswing and propel it through the follow-through. The arms are a unit, and if the lower hand takes on an over-exaggerated force, you will be pushing the ball with only one side of your body. In other words, if you keep your right hand below and force the mallet with it, you will most certainly miss toward the left. Try it. While swinging with both hands will control the strength of your shot, pushing with one arm will probably distort the aim. If you find this happening, tighten up the upper or loosen the lower hand. Concentration is the key, and if you pay attention to your stance, control your wrists and swing through equally with both arms, the concentration should pay off with good results.

Finally, it is back to the shoulders. We stated earlier that, being the truest part of the body, the shoulders should never change position. This was, perhaps, an exaggeration, but the "do's and don'ts" are really quite simple in this respect. The fluid swing is essential in shot-making, and if your shoulders fluctuate in the course of this swing, you will most certainly jerk the mallet.

Hitting Down

Hitting Square

Hitting Up

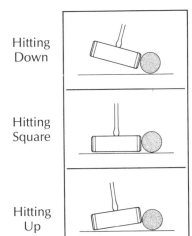

Hitting Down

Hitting Square

Hitting Up

As you watch other players and listen, if their screams after a miss hit are not, "Oh, I twisted my wrists," they will almost certainly be, "Oh, I lifted my head." In the excitement of seeing the results of a shot, even the best players occasionally look up to see the future, and, if this happens, even a spectator can foresee the results. Often it is not just lifting the head, but the shoulders dragged up by the head which will lead to a jerky swing. The stance and shoulders, the foundation of a good swing, must remain solid through the swing.

If you have not raised your head, another problem might well be that you are not pushing your arms, but the shoulders themselves. Players will often do this while hitting long shots or because of sheer nerves, and such an action can only hinder a swing. Lastly, do not let your knees bounce while swinging. The shoulders must remain stable throughout the swing, and bouncing about will only alter your balance, your shoulders, and finally the fluidity of your entire swing.

If it sounds as though there are a variety of disasters which can take place in the course of a swing, don't be too worried. As you practice and play more and more, you will become comfortable with your swing. As a beginner, it is important that you are aware of all potential problems. The ability to pinpoint a specific fault within the swing will help you improve by teaching yourself. While you might feel rigid and tense at the start, as time passes you will begin to relax. The swing of a croquet mallet should actually be a very relaxed experience. When a golf professional changes your golf swing, you will initially feel quite awkward. Soon, as in golf, the techniques you must master in croquet will become as comfortable as breathing.

Let us take a complete look at the single-ball shot. To begin with, take a moment to make sure you have stalked the ball properly. Two important aspects come into play here. 1) Be careful that you are standing the correct distance from your ball and 2), make sure that your body is well-balanced so that you lean neither forward nor backward during the swing. Now, sure of your aim, take a deep breath and concentrate on your swing.

The croquet swing should be a fluid motion, bringing the mallet back from the shoulders in a slow, controlled fashion. How far your backswing will go should be determined by the distance you are about to hit the ball. Practice will tell you this. As you bring the mallet down, be sure that you hit the ball squarely, a given result if you are standing properly. Do not jerk the mallet down, rather swing through the ball and follow-through completely. This follow-through is important to control the aim throughout the entire swing, and many players will pick a spot three feet in front of them to swing over. Make sure your shoulders remain in place, your wrists and arms remain constant and that you keep your head down even after the ball has been struck. If you have a target ball, don't worry—no one is going to move it while your head is down. And there you have it: the perfect swing.

For one last thought on this matter, John Solomon offers some wise words, "Any analytical approach to the swing means that you are not relaxed, and relaxation is the key to being a successful croquet player. It is rather like listening to music—there are two ways of doing it. You can listen to every note and establish its position within the framework of the whole piece or you can detach yourself from it, letting the music put you in an emotional frame of mind outside yourself. A croquet swing should be like that: a movement of the arms that is unconsciously performed and results in the perfect swing."

J. Archie Peck shooting the tie breaking shot to win the 1980 USCA National Singles Championship in New York. Record holding four times singles and two times doubles champ, Archie's shot-making streak from 1977 through 1982 earned him a place in the US Croquet Hall of Fame.

E.A. (Teddy) Prentis, IV, holder of eight USCA National titles including the 1983 Singles Championship, is regarded as one of the finest shotmakers in the sport. As the first "professional" instructor in the world, Teddy's pupils are in legion. He was inducted into the US Croquet Hall of Fame in 1989.

8

SHOT-MAKING

SINGLE-BALL SHOTS

Before undertaking a study of the game's tactics and strategies, one must understand that croquet virtuosity depends on your ability to perform the most basic skill of all—shooting your own ball. Lord Tollemache italicizes this notion: "the most difficult thing to do really well," he says, "is *to hit your own ball perfectly*." Tollemache's logic is impeccable on this point. The first shot of every turn is, after all, a one-ball shot. With few exceptions, running wickets entails a successful one-ball shot. The final shot of the game, the peg-out, is a single-ball shot.

Obviously, capitalizing on the opportunities presented by successful single-ball shot-making is essential, for you don't get those second shots if you don't take your first shot effectively.

To this end we encourage you to learn the following single-ball and two-ball shots, practice them well, and you'll better understand what we hold as croquet gospel: all winning strategy, from beginner to expert levels, is based on both your shot-making abilities and how accurately you are able to assess your opponent's skills.

With this in mind, pay close attention to the following sections. You will never be able to move onto the more complicated and rewarding two-ball shots without the ability to successfully hit your own ball well. Likewise, remember that your strategy will depend greatly upon how good a shot you will become; your game play is only as strong as the ammunition you possess. Of course, no one will ever hit all of his shots perfectly, but never should you cease in your quest for this state of perfection.

The basic single-ball shots are:

> the roquet
> the rush
> the cut rush
> the wicket shot
> the jump shot

The Roquet

To progress faster and more successfully than your opponent, the ability to hit another ball (or object ball), will often prove to be your first task. This key single-ball shot is called a ROQUET. Successfully completed, a roquet allows you to earn additional shots, begin "a break" (see page 148), and begin to use the other balls as steppingstones as you make your way about the court. While this shot appears quite vital, you will be happy to know it requires no further study than that which we have previously covered.

Building on the foundation of the fundamentals of the grip, stalk, stance and swing in the previous chapter, you should now concentrate on the aiming of your ball.

At the start of your stalk, draw a mental line straight through the center of both balls and approach your stance directly along the extension of that imaginary line from your ball to you. After reaching your ball, place the mallet behind it while you recheck the aim by matching the sight line or the top of the mallet with the line running through the balls. Then lower your mallet and your eyes to your ball for the stroke. Take a slow backswing, hit through the ball squarely at the bottom of the swing, looking up only after the ball is well on its way to the target ball. If, after all this, you find yourself missing short roquets, check that you are not looking up too quickly or that your stance is not improperly aligned. These are the most common causes for missing this essential shot.

Once you have made a roquet, you are now in the position of being "ball-in-hand." Explained simply, you are now both required and privileged to pick up your ball and place it next to (actually in contact with) the ball you have just hit. And yet, what if you had just hit that ball a bit harder? If you were intending to take your two additional shots to make your next wicket, the position that your object ball comes to rest, in relation to that wicket, will certainly dictate your odds on completing this task. Once again, the position of the balls on the lawn becomes important and leads us to a key form of the roquet—THE RUSH.

The Rush

If your ball is within two to three feet of another ball, you should not be content with simply hitting it. Instead, you must ask yourself where that ball would be of most use to you. Often this will involve driving, or "rushing" the object ball to a very specific location, and there are two basic problems which seem to arise.

The question of how hard you should hit your own ball is something which you must learn through practice. Obviously, rushing an object ball to a specific spot will take more power than it would simply hitting your own ball there, and this proves to be the cause of these problems. As we discussed in our look at the swing, when many players try to hit their own ball hard, they inevitably stand either too close or too far from that ball. While this may hinder aim in simply roqueting another ball, it can cause drastic results with a rush. The technique is actually the same with this single-ball shot, but now the importance of hitting your own ball squarely is magnified. By standing too close to your ball, your mallet will undoubtedly hit down on your ball and make it jump. If you are standing too far back, your mallet will then swing in such a way that it will hit up on your ball, your ball will skip or dribble on its way to the target ball instead of traveling smoothly upon the lawn.

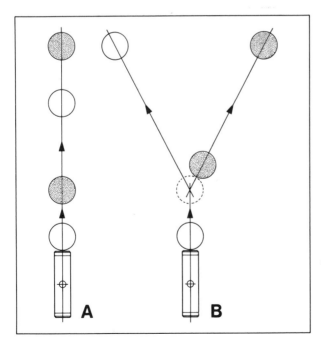

Straight rush and cut rush: Figure A: A straight rush sends both balls directly forward. Figure B: A cut rush allows the striker to send the roqueted ball at an angle to a pre-determined position.

107

While both authors agree that it is best to hit your ball squarely and smoothly with just enough power added to the swing to drive the roqueted ball the distance you want, the senior Osborn encourages those who tend to have their ball repeatedly hit the object ball near the top and discouragingly bounce or crawl over it without successfully moving it far enough, to step back three or four inches in their stance and hit up slightly as if attempting a "stop shot" (see page 128). His theory suggests that more energy is transferred by your ball if it strikes the object ball with minimal spin having been imparted to it, as would happen with a ball hit with a downward or slightly off square stroke.

Both of us also agree, however, that one should never rush a rush shot and that practicing this frustrating shot is well worth the effort if one is to avoid the embarrassment of seeing your ball jump clearly over the object ball during an important match. We know the feeling.

The Cut Rush

You will not always be lucky enough to have a "straight rush." More often than not, you will have to aim at one side or the other of the object ball to rush it to the proper location. If you have ever played pool or billiards, this should cause you no major problems, yet other people do seem to have a difficult time aiming the "cut rush" properly.

A good visual conception of the shot must be acquired. Instead of stalking your ball with an instinctive idea of where to aim, begin by stalking the line on which your object ball must travel. Stand behind the object ball and, once having drawn that line, imagine a ball on that line in contact behind the object ball. Your target should be at the center of that imaginary ball, and although it will take a moment or two extra to do this, only now do you have a true vision of where you should aim. Keep one eye on where your ball must make contact with the target, while returning to your ball, and only then are you comfortably ready to align your mallet. Just as a pool player will first put his stick to the ball he is shooting at, this brief little exercise should raise your confidence and allow you to swing in a relaxed fashion.

Once again, the power you will need for cut rushes is something you must learn from practice. As a rule of thumb, the more the angle of the cut, the stronger the stroke needed to move the object ball to its desired position. Even a slightly errant shot here will alter the results drastically, the most common of which is missing the object ball altogether. Our helpful hint here is to avoid trying too thin a cut shot . . . it increases the margin for error.

What you must remember is that all single-ball shots are hit in a similar fashion. Certainly it is true that each of these shots is vital to successful play, but keeping in mind the basics of shot-making should lead to both fast improvement and better results.

Shooting the Wicket

You have now made the perfect rush, gained position no more than two feet from your wicket, and are ready for what should be a direct, simple shot. You take a deep breath. You stalk, look down at your ball, confirm your aim and finally take what feels like a normal, easy swing. And what happens? The ball goes THONK into an upright and dies there, leaving you not only with a wicket unmade but with an impossible shot on your next turn.

This scenario is every croquet player's worst nightmare, for the invisible "troll" of the wickets will make you pay dearly. One poorly played shot at the golden arches has tarnished many a brilliant game. Perhaps the most exacting and vital part of a successful game, it is no surprise that shooting wickets has sabotaged the nerves of even the most determined

veteran player. And yet, is this shot so different from those already mentioned? Of course not! Like in every other single-ball shot in a croquet game, there are only one or two aspects one must keep foremost in mind.

The stalk again is important. Even if you are only a foot or two straight in front of the wicket, realize that your margin of error is much less than if you were shooting at another ball. A proper stalk not only emphasizes your aim, but will give you the time to concentrate on the shot itself.

Once you are set up correctly, the only major obstacle which remains is controlling your nerves. As we suggested earlier, watch out for the wrists and shoulders, for quite often a player will attempt to "push" or "pop" the ball through the wicket rather than swing cleanly. In a desire to get the shot over with, the urgency to swing with the wrists or nudge the shoulders forward overcomes the knowledge that a smooth, controlled swing is the key.

Another reason wickets are missed, stems from the use of unnecessary strength. A player will look at the wicket, notice how narrow it seems and suddenly believe that if he just hits it a little harder than normal, the ball will skid through the wicket before the wicket knows what's happening. Well, the troll is watching. What does happen is that the player hits without control, substitutes power for accuracy and spends the next few minutes watching his opponent take advantage of his over-enthusiasm.

While there are obviously several things a player must not do within the nerve-wrenching wicket shot, there is certainly one thing he must do— *follow-through*. It is rare that you will make a wicket without brushing at least one upright. What a proper follow-through will do is add extra forward spin to your ball, and even if the shot is poorly hit, this extra spin can carry the ball off an upright and through the wicket. Likewise, as in a well executed rush shot, hitting the ball squarely is vital.

This concern over the follow-through can help in two other ways. While we have mentioned that powering a ball through a wicket is dangerous, occasionally a player just a foot before his wicket will try to baby or tap his ball through. Concentration on the follow-through should help you to avoid this problem. Furthermore, now that you are relatively close to your "target," you can more realistically use the follow-through to help steady and aim your shot. Imagine that the mallet itself is making the wicket, and if you follow-through on that line, the swing itself should be truer.

Of course, croquet is never so simple that we are always a foot or two directly in front of a wicket. What do we do then if we are at an angle?

Shooting the wicket: Aim at the center of the wicket (1). Take a smooth swing (2), and, after making contact, carry through (3) as if you're trying to swing your mallet head through the wicket.

There are basically two techniques for hitting an angled shot successfully. In both cases the aim and swing are most important simply because the shot itself is more difficult. Aim with your site line so that your ball will just miss the inside edge of the near upright. Make a smooth even shot and make sure of a good follow-through and the natural roll of the ball should carry it on through. Sadly, if you hit the near upright, you will miss the

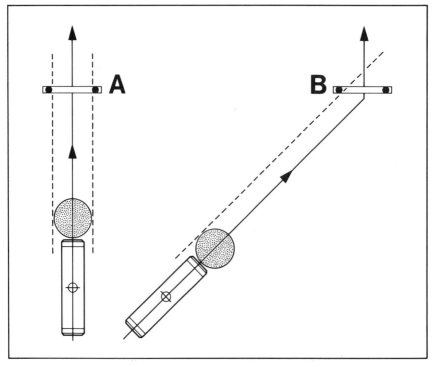

Shooting a wicket: A: From directly in front aim at space in center between uprights; B: from an angle aim to clear the inside of the nearer upright.

shot. While the temptation is to smash the ball through the wicket, the key here is to avoid a flat, sharply hit or "pop" shot which prevents the ball from starting its spinning roll before contacting the upright. A hard squarely hit shot causes the ball to skid rather than roll so that it dies upon hitting the upright.

For acute angles, the odds of making a wicket become more severe. There are times that you might be unsure that the wicket can be made with even your best shot. How will you know if a wicket is able to be made? There is no specific way to tell. Some people will say that if you stand behind the wicket, look through the uprights and can see a half or more of your ball, the shot is possible. There is no specific data about this, and depending upon your skill and the wickets themselves, shooting a wicket is a decision you must make, given the situation in the game. Most players have made desperation shots they felt were impossible, but if in doubt, you are probably best to adopt a different tactic unless you have no choice.

Another technique, if you are faced with a severe angle shot which you must make, is one of the few times you might indeed wish to hit down on the ball. As in the "jump shot," which we will discuss next, this technique will hopefully lift your ball up into the air, past the near upright and hit the far post. Here its spin should cause it to actually climb the upright, and even if it hits the ground it should sneak its way through the wicket. The margin of error is so slight in this difficult shot, that given the option, it is probably safer to adopt a different strategy rather than possibly giving your opponent the advantage of having your ball on the court.

The best way to avoid this kind of error—plus any others we're capable of inventing on our own—is to practice shooting wickets at every opportunity until wickets lose their capacity to intimidate you. It's like practicing foul-shooting in basketball or putting in golf: do the right thing often enough in practice conditions and you improve the odds you'll do the right thing in competition.

Don't think about just clearing the wicket; consider where you want your ball to stop on the other side and practice until you can put it within a foot of that spot. To make your practice more realistic, put another ball a few feet beyond the wicket and try to clear the wicket and stop a few inches shy of the other ball.

As a general rule, wicket-shooting need not be traumatic if you adopt a custom that some veterans use before any difficult shot at the wicket: go around to the other side and look back toward the ball. *If you can't see one half or more of it, you can't make it.* In that case, if the game situation permits it, play for position, not for a never-before-seen miracle.

The Jump Shot
(Or You Can't Get There from Here)

As we mentioned earlier, it is impossible to hit a perfect shot every time. Furthermore, since everyone will face a desperate situation sooner or later, holding a trick shot in your bag never hurts. When you are stymied by another ball or wicket, or have a difficult angled shot at a wicket, you may have to attempt what many consider the most dramatic shot in croquet. The Jump Shot. It is the favorite shot of the news paparazzi who can earn combat pay for lying down on the far side of a wicket as your ball soars straight into their Leica lenses at 60 miles per hour.

It can be achieved with surprisingly little practice by moving your stance forward with the ball parallel to your instep. Grip low on the handle, carefully aim at the top third of your ball and hit down hard—as if to take off the top of a soft-boiled egg—with one stroke of your mallet.

The ball should literally jump as the force of the mallet squeezes it into the ground on impact. Properly struck, your mallet should not hit the ground—but since it might while you're mastering it, it is best to practice on the sidelines rather than on the court, thus avoiding possibly unpleasant divots.

Be cautious. It is possible for a ball to jump not only through, but over a wicket and occasionally even over the finishing stake. If you have learned from the preceding chapters, we hope the need for such shots never occurs.

The jump shot: With the hands held midway down the grip (1), aim for the top third of the ball (2). The mallet makes contact at an angle (3). As the mallet head brushes the lawn (4), the ball jumps over the obstruction.

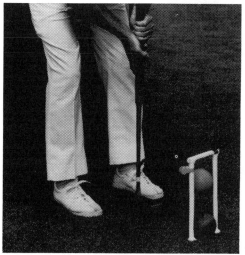

115

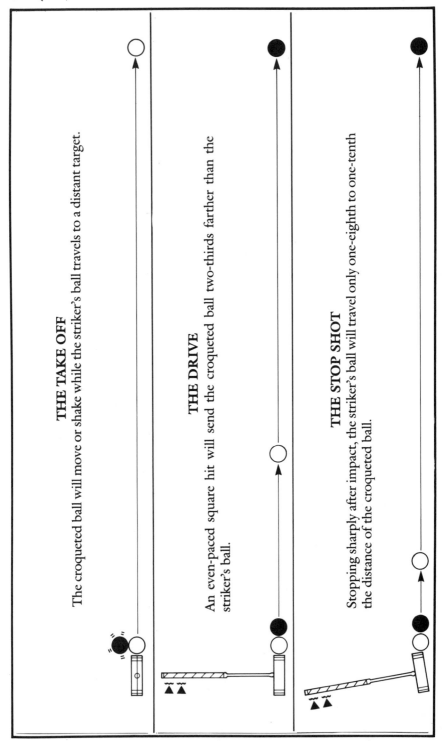

THE TAKE OFF

The croqueted ball will move or shake while the striker's ball travels to a distant target.

THE DRIVE

An even-paced square hit will send the croqueted ball two-thirds farther than the striker's ball.

THE STOP SHOT

Stopping sharply after impact, the striker's ball will travel only one-eighth to one-tenth the distance of the croqueted ball.

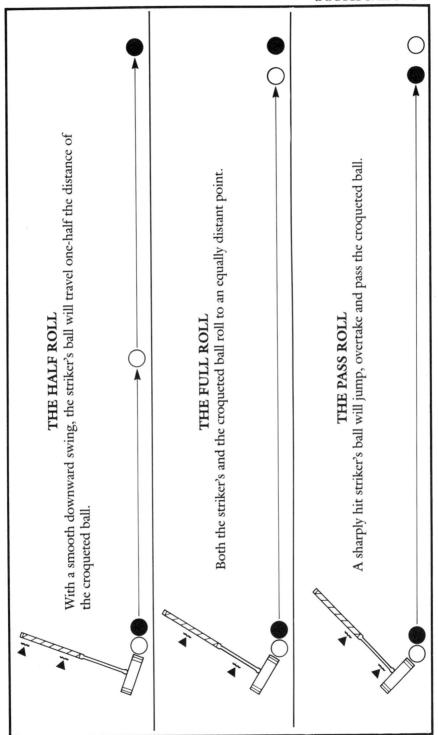

THE HALF ROLL

With a smooth downward swing, the striker's ball will travel one-half the distance of the croqueted ball.

THE FULL ROLL

Both the striker's and the croqueted ball roll to an equally distant point.

THE PASS ROLL

A sharply hit striker's ball will jump, overtake and pass the croqueted ball.

DOUBLE-BALL STROKES
The Croquet Strokes

One of the best-loved moments in childhood croquet begins when your ball strikes your opponent's with a satisfying thonk that elates you and depresses him. Seconds later he's begging for mercy, but you have none. Taking your ball in hand, you place it directly against his. Then, as if your ball were a bug to be squashed, you plant your foot on it. Having made sure your ball won't budge when you hit it, you smash it so hard that if you miss, your mallet will fracture your foot. But you don't, of course, and your opponent's ball rolls for a hundred feet, ending up perhaps in a bush or on a distant driveway, from which (because you, like your rules, are sadistic), he will be forced to take his next shot. Not that he will have another turn, for you make an incredible 15-foot shot through the wicket and go on to complete the course.

If that scenario seems too crude for you, you may remember a different version of croquet's most delicious moment. Disdaining violence after the initial contact, you take your ball in hand and place it a mallet head away from your opponent's ball. You're not going to smash him anywhere; instead, you take your two shots, one to position yourself in front of the wicket, the second to clear it as you move relentlessly, wicket by wicket, on toward victory. "Faster, faster!" you cry—as you race your way to the winning stake.

In Association croquet, we banish all that.

Violence isn't sanctioned.

Track spikes aren't necessary.

For in Association croquet, as in few other sports, strength and speed do not matter. Brains do. So does cunning. An appreciation of mathematics doesn't hurt. An instinctive understanding of Stoicism is an absolute necessity.

As we keep reminding you, winning croquet rests on your ability not to make single wickets, but breaks. You roquet another ball, advance it on the croquet stroke to a useful position, and then clear the wicket. Then you start the same process again.

In Association croquet, smashing your opponent's ball into the next county is a useless exercise in machismo. And putting your ball a mallet's head away from the roqueted ball and leaving that potentially useful ball behind is both illegal and makes absolutely no sense. Croquet is a game of position and a player's ability to maneuver the other three balls around the lawn is the cornerstone of successful croquet. But if you don't master the croquet stroke, you can't make a single break.

It is vital to acquaint yourself with the croquet shots covered in the next few pages. The name of the game is "croquet," and it is indeed your skill level in these croquet shots, those taken immediately after each roquet, that will determine how prosperous you will be as a player.

The basic "croquet," "double-ball" or "two-ball" strokes are: the take-off, the split shot, the drive, the stop shot, the half roll, the full roll, the pass roll, plus the peel and common shots.

Preparing to take croquet: Press your thumb under the lip of the roqueted ball (1) and place your ball into the imprint (2).

119

The Take-Off Shot

While we have said that positioning is the key to a controlled game, there is one exception, for it will not always be necessary to move the croqueted ball a long distance. If your partner's ball is in position in front of his wicket, leaving it there, while you go off on other quests, is often a good idea. Here, unfortunately, we have a problem. The laws of Association croquet dictate that once you have made a roquet, you must place your ball IN CONTACT with that roqueted ball and, on the croquet shot, must MOVE that ball. How far you must move it is completely up to you.

If, on your croquet shot, the croqueted ball simply shakes, or moves even a millimeter, you have performed a legal stroke. But what if you fail to meet this requirement? Under the rules, you have now created a fault—the balls must be replaced and the turn considered over.

One important and wonderful aspect of croquet is that it is a game for honor-bound gentlemen. In croquet, the striker is a referee, and as painful as it might be, should he realize that the croqueted ball has failed to "move," he is required to call this fault upon himself. With this in mind, it is now obvious that, as an exception, you must focus your attention not only on your own ball, but on the one from which you are taking-off.

The take-off: Make sure the balls are touching (1).

Then check to be sure that the "V" created by the tangent of the two balls points in the direction you want your ball to travel by laying your mallet flush against both balls (2) so that the shaft points to your target. To be certain the roqueted ball will move or shake, aim your mallet head (3) on a line pointing slightly toward and through the roqueted ball to point X.

Swing directly along that line (4) at point X.

4

If this revelation strikes fear within you, it shouldn't. The take-off shot is one of the most useful, if not the easiest, if approached properly. To begin with, it is vital that the balls be touching. If you learn anything from this book, learn how to be sure the balls are touching and stay together when you're making ANY double-ball shot. Before you set your ball next to the roqueted ball, place your thumb under the near lip of the roqueted ball, then lean your ball against it as you put your ball in that imprint. Your ball will sit in that imprint, and unless gravity reverses itself, the balls will not separate. If you take your stroke correctly, the roqueted ball will move very little, perhaps, but it will at least shake, and you have avoided committing a disastrous shot. On rough lawns, this might be problematical, but have patience, it pays.

As you will see in the accompanying photos, aiming will prove to be one of the easiest and most important aspects of the take-off. It is also one occasion in which your mallet will become a great aid. Place your mallet in front of the roqueted ball with the shaft aimed in the exact direction desired. Now take your ball and place it so that it is in contact with the roqueted ball and both balls are either in contact or an even distance from the mallet head. Take your time, and once you are secure that the aim of your shaft is correct, your preparation is complete.

What is hard for beginners to believe is that this aiming phase is vital. After a while you might feel comfortable without the use of the mallet, but if you find the roqueted ball isn't moving every time, it will pay you to recheck by using it again.

5

. . . as if the roqueted ball didn't exist (5), with enough force to reach your target.

Having set up the take-off properly, all that is left is to aim slightly into the imaginary line your shaft had once occupied. By aiming into that imaginary line, or "into" the roqueted ball, your ball now MUST and, believe it or not, WILL travel in the direction your shaft had been aimed. The ball you are taking-off from, in a sense, acts like a wall; as long as the balls are touching and your aim is correct, it is virtually impossible to miss hit the take-off. While you may have to hit a tad harder, the difference in strength of the shot is basically the same as if you were taking a single-ball stroke.

After practicing the take-off for a while, you will soon see that it is really very easy. You will also discover that, depending upon how much you hit into that imaginary line, you will be able to move that croqueted ball specific distances—be it an inch, a foot, or several feet.

When taking-off from a ball that is nine inches in from the boundary line, it is unwise to place your ball any place other than on the side between the ball and the string for the slightest miss hit could send the croqueted ball off the court and end your turn.

Finally, practice taking-off from both sides of the roqueted ball. Even experts will admit that they prefer to take-off from one side as opposed to the other. Try both sides, for although apparently relatively easy at first sight, the take-off is an underestimated and quite powerful tool in your shot-making kit.

The Split Shot

While the take-off is a necessary weapon in your arsenal, more often than not you will wish to move the roqueted ball to a spot more advantageous to your future plans. Let's look at an example.

Having just roqueted a ball close to your wicket, it would now be simple enough to take-off, make position and then score your designated wicket. But what then? Suddenly you realize that, although you are entitled to another shot, you have left a usable ball behind. If, however, instead of leaving that ball, on the croquet shot you were able to move the croqueted ball ahead of the wicket while taking position yourself, you would then have a usable ball waiting for you once you run the wicket. This is where the SPLIT SHOT comes in.

The split shot is not difficult if properly and patiently organized. Find

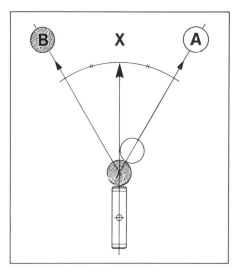

Split-shot: X is the aiming point for your mallet when you want your ball to go to "A" and the croqueted ball to go to "B."

1

Place your ball behind the roqueted ball (1) in such a way that a line drawn through both balls would extend to the spot where you want the roqueted ball to end up (point A). In this case, point A is on the far side of the wicket and slightly to one side. Then envision the direction of a line to the spot (2) where you want your ball to end up (point B). These two imaginary lines create a "V." Aim your mallet (3) at the midpoint of that V (point X).

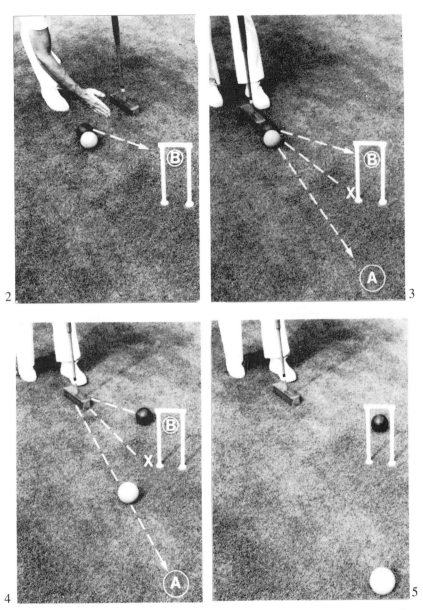

In this case point X is just to the right of the nearest upright of the wicket. Consciously avoid "steering" the stroke as you swing smoothly along the imaginary line to point X. In this case, the forward ball is to travel three times farther than the shooter's ball, and a drive shot was used. But no matter the desired distance, each ball should travel (4) along its respective imaginary line. Your ball ends up at point B—in this case, right in front of the wicket (5), which makes it a simple matter to clear the wicket on the continuation stroke.

the exact spot you wish to send the ball you've roqueted, and having done so, place your ball next to that ball so that an imaginary line can be drawn through and between the center of both balls and to that exact spot. (See accompanying photos.) At this time, having checked that the balls are touching, walk back and make sure your aim is true, for if you have aimed the balls poorly, the split shot will lead to quite unexpected results.

Now find the exact spot you would like your ball to land. With both spots in view, all that remains is for you to find the mid-point of the two locations. This will be where you will want to aim your mallet. While some players cut the angle in half, we have found that it is perhaps best to create another imaginary line between the two location spots and divide that in half. Once secure with that exact point, stalk your shot with an eye on it and aim carefully. All that is left is for you to discover how much power you will need to make your stroke, and though it will take some practice, soon you will become adept with the split shots. You may find on long splits that the two balls tend to "draw" or "pull" in toward one another. This is normal, but with some practice, you can compensate for it, by aiming the forward ball a bit wider than you would normally.

Beginners and experts alike have problems with split shots, not because they lack ability, but because they lack patience. It is vital to pick exact spots that you wish the balls to move to, not just vague locations. It is equally important to double check that you have lined up the two balls properly and that your aim is to a precise spot. Stalk the shot, for should you miscalculate any aspect of the split, the results could be dreadful.

The Drive Shot

You have mastered the take-off. Simple, wasn't it? And those split shots? You've figured out the angles without even breaking a sweat, but, hmm . . . yes, you have probably encountered one minor problem: the balls really aren't going the distances you wish they would. In this section and the few that follow, we can fix all of that and fill your cup of croquet shot-making.

Let's discuss the DRIVE SHOT, a shot considered the most basic of all croquet shots because it's the only double-ball shot where you assume a normal upright stance. Place two balls in contact, and for the purpose of these demonstrations, imagine we will be hitting them along a straight line in the same direction. Now, taking your normal stance, hit your ball squarely at the bottom of the pendulum swing and follow-through as you would in any single-ball shot.

What is important to realize here is that, if hit properly, your ball will travel a distance about one-third that of the croqueted ball. With that as your basic yardstick, all other croquet shots to follow will produce either more or less distance between the two balls. So let's take a look.

The drive shot: Assume an upright position for your mallet (1) and take a slow backswing (2). Take a clean swing (3) along the line of aim, hitting squarely at the bottom of the swing (4) and carry through.

The Stop Shot

If you're playing well, you'll have organized the court so that the balls are all ahead of the one you're shooting. In this constellation, you should be able to keep them in front of you—and to keep them there as you move your way around the court, clearing wicket after wicket with your ball in the process. The shot that better players find most useful, if not crucial to this feat, is the STOP SHOT.

The point of the stop shot is to move your ball as little as possible while sending your target ball far downfield. Experts can make the croqueted ball travel 7 to 10 times farther than theirs. You can, too.

There are several aspects of the stop shot which are different from the drive. To begin with, keeping your grip at the top of the mallet will produce the best shots. By keeping your hands high, you are actually allowing the entire shaft of the mallet to absorb the shock your ball would normally experience. Most importantly, though, is to have as little follow-through as possible.

While beginners have problems taking a shot with no follow-through, it is often because they forget the most valuable difference between the stop and drive shots. After approaching the balls and assuming a normal stance, take a small step about three inches backwards letting the hands bring the top of the shaft with you, which will raise the toe of the mallet while leaving the heel on the ground. What should occur now is that when you swing, you will be hitting up on the ball and you will find yourself pressing the heel of the mallet against the ground as you shoot. This is fine, since the lawn has now helped you to come to a halt in your stroke. Do not damage the lawn, of course, and do not actually TRY to drive the mallet into the ground. By standing back, your natural swing will do this on its own, and trying to dig the mallet into the turf will often result in missing your ball altogether.

Finally, for shorter stop shots, loosening your grip will aid the outcome. For longer shots, where you will obviously need a bigger backswing, grip your mallet with the strength you normally would, for you will certainly need an amount of control.

Practice, once again, is the key. The stop shot is probably the most physically abnormal and difficult to be at ease with, and the best way to practice is to place two balls in contact with one right next to a string. While shooting from the other side of the string, take note of how much your follow-through carries beyond it; the results should speak for themselves. You will, as a footnote, have more problems with the stop shots the heavier your mallet is. On the other hand, a heavier mallet will help you in our next two-ball adventure—the roll shots.

1

2

3

The stop shot: Having taken a step back from your usual stance, take a short backswing (1). As you swing, loosen your grip slightly (2), making sure that you jam the heel of your mallet into the ground as it makes contact with the ball (3). There is no follow-through (4) in this shot, so all the force of your swing will go into the forward ball.

4

The Half Roll

We have learned that the drive shot, taken from a normal stance, will carry your ball one-third the distance of that croqueted ball. The stop shot will send your ball anywhere from one-fifth to one-tenth that of the forward ball, depending upon your follow-through. Thus, we might ascertain that there are an infinite number of ball relationships we can achieve by changing one's stance, grip, follow-through and angle of mallet head and shaft. Let us take a look at the HALF ROLL.

Our objective is to send our ball one-half the distance of the croqueted ball. Like the drive and all roll shots, following-through is a critical factor. Except for the stop shot, every other stroke in croquet should consist of a fluid follow-through. It is, then, grip, stance and mallet angle we will concentrate upon in each roll shot.

Try to consider your mallet as a musical instrument; for every two balls shot, your hands should change position and grip another note on that instrument. For the half roll, your bottom hand should be placed, simply enough, about half way down the shaft, your upper hand placed higher near the top where it feels most comfortable. Next we need to focus on the angle in which you should strike the ball.

While in the stop shot we were hitting "up" on the ball, now we will actually hit "down" on it. To do this, effectively, you must alter your stance, moving about a step closer to the balls. Flex your knees so that you are comfortable, and you will see now that the mallet is approaching the balls at an angle of about thirty-three degrees. By doing this, you will be assured of striking down and through your ball (with the center of the "face" of your mallet), about midway between the center and the top of that ball. Now you are taking the direct force of the swing off the forward ball and placing more emphasis upon your own. Be sure to keep your body still, for the urge to play the shot with the body will lead to hitting your ball with the edge of the mallet's face and alter both the power and distance relationships. Before you begin your stroke, lift the mallet a bit off the ground and center the mallet's face with the desired contact spot on your ball.

Remember that each mallet is different and each player is unique. Try some shots. Should you be having problems, experiment with either hand placement or the mallet angle until the results prove consistent.

The half roll: Shift your weight and the angle of your mallet shaft forward (1) and, with your weight still forward, take a slow, smooth backswing (2). Hit down, striking the top third of the ball (3) with a smooth forward stroke and carry the mallet through (4).

The Full Roll

Let us say that tactics call for you to send both balls the same distance. Now let's think for a moment about our musical instrument. What would happen if we lowered our bottom hand further and increased our mallet angle just a bit? What you will find is that even should you fail to move your stance closer to your ball (which you should), to align your angle of impact, the sheer change in your hand placement will increase the impact on your own ball. Try it!

By moving your lower hand close to the bottom of the shaft, you will be taking the whip of the shaft out of the shot. The placement of the top hand should also be lower on the handle. Keep your body still and follow-through, experimenting until you find the hand placement and mallet angle which creates the best and consistent results. The chart on page 117 will serve as a good guide.

While the physics of all roll shots are the same, you do have one option, to either play the swing from a center stance through the legs or on the side. The side style is fine, but we do suggest the center style be attempted in that it provides both better body stability and aim. If you do feel attracted to the side style, keep your body still, play with the arms and make sure you swing with a straight stroke, not one which "wraps" around your body. Try both ways, always with the basics in mind.

What you should have learned by now is that hand placement is the key to controlling distance relationships between two balls. In fact, within the half roll and the full roll, there are an infinite number of variable distances achievable, countless notes for you to play. For instance, place your lower hand exactly between where it would be for a half and full roll. Try it and you'll have discovered the nuance known as the THREE-QUARTER ROLL.

1

2

The full roll from center stance: With lower hand nearing the head and upper hand midway down the shaft (1), the angle of the mallet increasingly forward along with the feet, with weight mostly on the forward foot (2) after a relatively short backswing, hit down (3) with sharp but smooth stroke and (4) follow through.

3

4

The Pass Roll

The trickiest roll played, known as the pass roll, is seldom used, even by experts, because of its difficulty. Here, the lower hand is placed at the very bottom of the shaft (it is illegal to touch the head of the mallet), and the shot is played at a sharply downward angle with a full follow-through. You will basically have to stand right over the balls and play them with a slight split, but if successful your ball should travel farther than the

The pass roll from a side stance: with her right hand almost touching the mallet head (1) Peyton stands with left foot level with balls, right foot extended and with weight and mallet shaft above the ball, takes a short backswing (2).

croqueted ball. Given the degree of difficulty of the shot, we encourage a great deal of practice before you include it in your repertoire.

Should you have a back problem and are unable to crouch low for some of these roll shots, try concentrating on increasing the mallet angle from an upright side stance.

3

Keeping her weight forward Peyton strokes down (3) hitting top third of ball and sees the back ball start to pass the forward one as she carries her mallet through (4).

4

Other Notes to Play

Let us now tie everything together by going back to the split shot. Hopefully, the problem you might have encountered of sending the balls the distances you wished, has now been solved. After lining up the split shot carefully, the unanswered question may now be answered. If the target ball must go twice the distance of your own, you must, after stalking, assume the half roll position. You will find that the larger the split angle, the farther your ball will travel. Without the croqueted ball impeding it there is not so much resistance. In these cases, instead of a half roll, you might try the drive stroke. If this sounds confusing, don't worry, it is, even to the experts. As a basic rule of thumb, however, the larger the angle, the less roll you will need. Unfortunately, only practice will take the guesswork out of this shot.

Finally, remember that before every two-ball shot, save the take-off. You must pay attention to the distances each ball must travel. Practice all of these shots, starting by hitting them softly and slowly build up to full court attempts. Soon you will be ready for controlled break play.

SITUATIONAL SHOTS
The Peel

Named after Walter Peel, the object of this stroke is to drive the croqueted ball, and occasionally both balls, through a wicket.

This is particularly helpful when the ball being peeled is your partner's ball, which has accumulated some deadness.

The peel: Make sure the balls are touching (1) . . .   1

If by luck or skill you manage to roquet the object ball into position in front of the wicket, take your ball and carefully place it so that you can visualize parallel lines running along each side of both balls as they pass between the uprights of the wicket. You'll do well to look at this alignment from both sides of the wicket before shooting.

Then, assuming you are not closer than a few inches from the mouth, stop shot the forward ball through the wicket and then run the wicket with your own ball on your second or continuation stroke. If both balls are within a few inches of the wicket, you may prefer to roll shot both through on your croquet stroke, taking care not to have your ball, mallet and the wicket upright in contact at the same instance, as this would constitute a "crush shot" fault.

2

4

... and then imagine parallel lines on both sides of the balls (2) which lead directly through the wicket. Stop shot your ball (3) so that the roqueted ball clears the wicket. Your ball should end up (4) in position so you can send it through the wicket on the continuation stroke.

137

There are occasions when your next wicket is not the same wicket as that of the ball you are peeling. In these instances, you will find it useful to attempt a split or roll stroke as you peel the forward ball while sending your ball to another spot on the court before taking your continuation stroke.

In this event, care must be taken to account for an inward pull exerted when splitting two balls. Align the balls with a slightly wider angle to compensate for this pull in a split shot or attempt more of a roll stroke, which provides somewhat more follow-through for the croqueted ball. Here, again, practice makes perfect.

The Cannon Shot

There are basically two kinds of cannon shots. One involves making a roquet in the same stroke as a croquet stroke and is more frequently used in the British than in the American game. British laws allow two or more balls to be placed in contact along the boundary line or in the corners. The object is to send the ball you are about to take croquet on and the ball your ball is about to roquet to different spots on the lawn in one stroke. In the USCA game this situation rarely occurs on or near the boundary lines because rules call for a separation between balls. It does occur occasionally out on the court.

The other type of cannon is useful when you wish to move a ball upon which your ball is dead (and thus cannot hit it directly with yours), by hitting (cannoning) another ball into it. Here, the object is to move the ball in the jaws of the wicket by cannoning it with the ball the striker has just roqueted or rushed to a spot nearby. If the two balls are carefully lined up so as to have the forward ball glance off the blocking ball in the croquet stroke, the striker's ball can be left in a position to clear that wicket on his second or continuation stroke. It is permissible that the ball being used to cannon away the target ball may itself be dead on that ball.

This form of cannon, which is often overlooked by even class "A" players, can be effectively used in a variety of other situations on the court, not just with a blocked wicket.

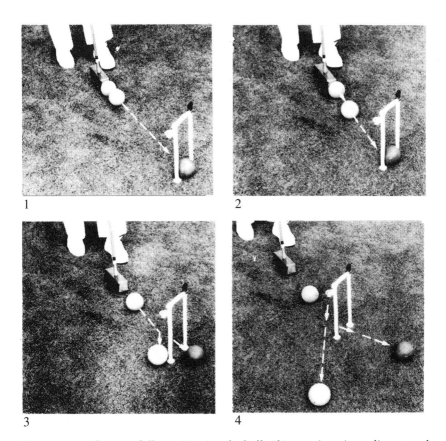

The cannon: After carefully positioning the balls (1) so an imaginary line extends through them to the targeted ball (the ball in the jaws of the hoop), take a stop shot. The roqueted ball rolls smartly (2) toward its target, hits the target ball (3) and knocks it through the wicket, enabling you to clear the wicket (4) on your continuation stroke.

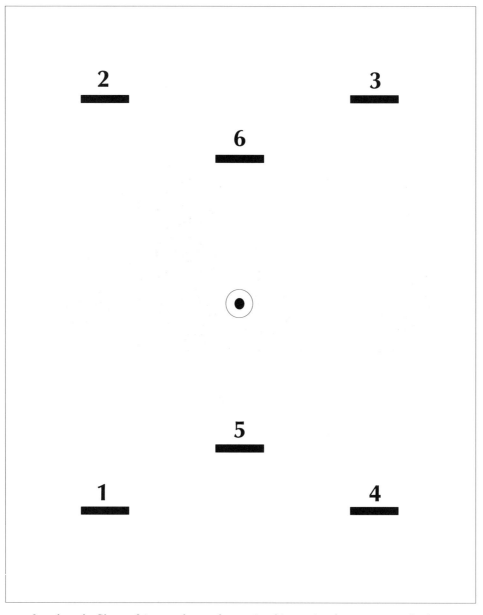

In order to let Chapter 9 (or your hopes of mastering this sport) make any sense, we implore you to memorize the order and positioning of the first six wickets on the court.

9

STRATEGY

When asked by the inquiring minds of the media, "Why the growing interest in the sport of croquet in America today?" the response inevitably focuses on the mental challenge presented by the tactics and strategic aspects required to play winning croquet.

Sure, shot-making skills are important but the most compelling appeal and reward of croquet is outthinking and outsmarting your opponent with your brain rather than brawn.

It is the unending quest for strategic mastery that keeps most great shot- making players on the courts for life.

For today's beginners, the good news is the tactics, which took the senior author 10 years to grasp three decades ago, are now theirs in a matter of months, thanks to books like this and instruction available through USCA schools, clinics and video tapes.

We have said that the key to successful strategic planning rests in your ability to assess accurately the level of your own shot-making and tactical skills as well as those of your opponents.

With this in mind, each shot you take should be weighed in terms of how much you will gain if the shot succeeds against how much you will be giving away if it fails. This principle of risk vis-à-vis reward is but the root of sound strategy and the one most overlooked by the neophyte.

If all this sounds like the description of a course in tactical warfare at West Point, you're on the right track . . . for croquet is, in fact, a warlike game.

Along with the basic objective of scoring the twenty-six points first, each team or player (in singles) should employ those offensive or defensive moves that will restrict the progress of opponents.

The primary offensive tactic is to utilize as many balls (both partner's and opponent's) as can be brought into setting up what is called a "break" in order to score as many wicket points in one turn as possible. By skillful use and placement of two or three other balls at wickets ahead of the striker's next wicket in proper sequence, the striker can make up to eleven wickets in one "all around break" during one turn. The ability to pick up and maintain a break is, as we shall learn in the following pages, the very heart of offensive strategy.

A key defensive tactic is separating the balls your opponent is playing in order to reduce their offensive potential. Another is taking your opponent out of position to make his next wicket, particularly when his ball is dead on his partner's ball. An opponent who is dead on two or three balls and can be kept that way has lost considerable offensive capabilities. Defensive strategy frequently aims toward placing your and your partner's balls on the boundary line far from the opponents to avoid providing them an opportunity to pick up a break for their side. This move often baffles spectators since it appears that no one is attempting to go for wicket points.

The more experienced player may choose more aggressive tactics, including enticing the less experienced opponent into taking shots that leave him on the field and vulnerable to being used to the advantage of the cagier player.

Remember, however, that it would be futile to master advanced strategy without the ability and confidence to make advanced shots. Again, the challenge of croquet is in mastering and balancing mental and physical skills.

OPENINGS

In American croquet all balls are dead on all other balls until that first wicket is cleared. As a result, there are two basic opening patterns to consider at this point. Assuming that all balls are being played by equally talented players (either singles or doubles), we'll start with the blue ball from one yard in front of the #1 wicket.

In diagram 1, blue clears the first wicket, then goes to the corner behind the #2 wicket.

Red clears the first wicket, in diagram 2, then goes parallel to or slightly behind the #1 wicket, but off the court on the West boundary.

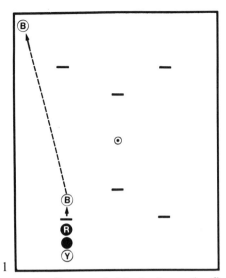 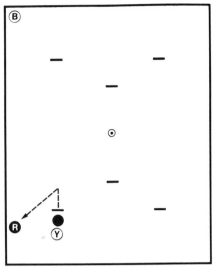

In diagram 3, black clears the first wicket, then gives blue a rush by shooting to a point between blue's corner position and the #2 wicket.

Yellow clears the first wicket (diagram 4). Now yellow has two choices, the most ambitious of which occurs if black has left himself more than a few feet out in the court. Yellow might do well to shoot at red. After yellow safely roquets red, it would then take off to black in the second corner in order to send it back to red and then stymie itself from being hit by the blue ball by going behind the #2 wicket (not shown). More commonly, however, and as we have illustrated here, yellow will go out of bounds a foot North of red, so that red will have a good rush upcourt on its next turn.

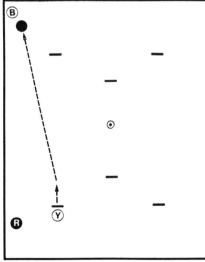 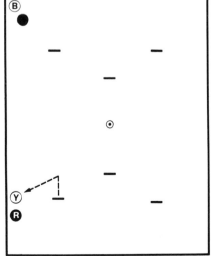

At the end of their first turn, it's fairly common for the balls to be in the positions shown in diagram 4. It's then usual for the following tactics to be used in the second turn:

Blue roquets (rushes) black to the front of wicket #2 (diagram 5). Then, with a split shot, blue sends black to the right of the wicket (diagram 6), blue clears the wicket (diagram 7), then rushes black to behind the #3 wicket (diagram 8).

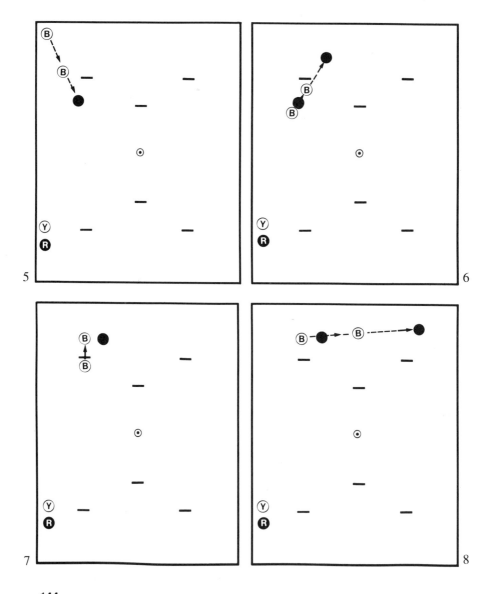

In effect, blue has begun a "two-ball break" and is in a position to make two or more wickets in this turn as we shall see in the next section on Breaks.

But let's assume, as sometimes happens, that blue fails to split black far enough behind the #2 wicket to get a good rush to #3. What then?

As common sense demands, blue clears the wicket, but instead of shooting at black, it could go off the court in the third corner (diagram 9) to avoid leaving two balls on the court for the red ball, which plays next, to shoot at. Or, as we illustrate here (diagram 10), blue can tap black, leaving it at the #2 wicket, and take off to yellow and red on the West boundary (diagram 11).

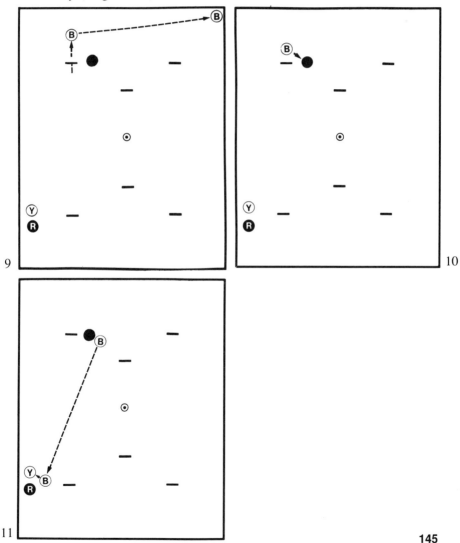

9

10

11

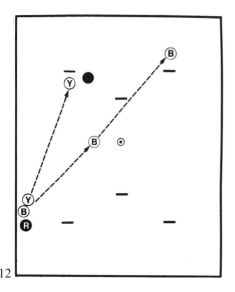

Blue could then tap yellow and on its croquet stroke send yellow to black at #2 wicket and go itself to a position behind #3 wicket on its continuation stroke (diagram 12). In this somewhat risky play, blue has achieved two desirable objectives: 1) he has effectively separated the opponents, leaving red, who plays next, a difficult long shot upfield at black and yellow (with luck, blue would have not left them too close together, giving red a double target); and 2) by going to #3 wicket, he sets up an opportunity for black to begin a "three-ball" break after making its #2 wicket off yellow. The risk, of course, is that if red hits in on either black or yellow the advantage and opportunity for a "break" shifts dramatically to the red/yellow side, since the hit will have been made at red's next wicket and blue is two-ball dead at #3.

There are other alternatives open to blue in this opening including attempting to get a rush on yellow to #3 wicket instead of sending it to black, but that requires yet another higher level of risk and shot-making skill than the last example.

146

Another opening (not shown here) used by top flight players who respect their opponents shooting too much to gather blue and black in the second corner is to join up in the first corner (behind wicket #1) with a line rush to the fourth corner where red and yellow will normally gather in order to distance themselves from the second wicket.

From here, it's too difficult to imagine, much less describe, the opening alternatives available to each player. The strategic permutations are one factor. But beyond that intellectual challenge is the other, more crucial determinant. That is, as we've said before, the shot-making ability of each player. Clearly, you would be more cautious against a good shooting opponent and not leave him any long, let alone short, shots.

From the spectator's point of view, the way to determine how much respect the players have for one another is to watch where they leave their balls at the end of their turn. When a player brings his balls together at a distant baseline time after time, you know he fears his opponent. On the other hand, when a strong shooter is doing battle with a less-than-stellar opponent, he may well decide to end his turn by leaving his ball at enticingly close range, or even at his wicket, the better to lure his opponent onto center court.

That moment—the equivalent of the moment when a matador bends to one knee before a snorting bull—is often the decisive one in a croquet game. For, if the weaker player misses, leaving his ball exposed, the stronger player can convert that steppingstone into making four or five wickets on his next turn. When that occurs, the virtual equality of field position created by these traditional American openings disappears and—just minutes after the opening shots—it would appear that our matador is certain to be awarded the tail and ears of the loser. But, as we will see, that is never a certainty until the last ball of the winning side is against the peg.

BREAKS

There is a breed of croquet player whose strategy is simplicity itself. Which is to say, a nonstrategy: the aim of this player is to clear the next wicket, and, having achieved that, to race to the baseline and hide. With apologies to feminists, this player, in croquet slang, is derisively known as "Aunt Emma."

It is certain that an Aunt Emma has, at some point in the history of croquet, won a game, but the annals do not record this victory. Nor should they. For Aunt Emma is exactly the kind of player the game doesn't need. Aunt Emma doesn't really want to win—*HE* wants the other players to lose.

Playing against an Aunt Emma can be tedium itself, for he lowers the game to a search-and-destroy exercise. But nothing is worse than two Aunt Emmas on a single court. Croquet is a game of confrontation, rewarding courage and faith. Two cowards attempting to have sport with one another is not croquet. And yet, unless your teachers and opponents force you to develop aggressive shot-making strategies, you will, for a time, become an Aunt Emma.

What fearful beginners and permanent Aunt Emmas don't want to confront is nothing more terrifying than the idea of making two, three or four wickets in a single turn with the help of the three other balls—in other words, making a break. This resistance to breaks is silly, for the seemingly effortless flow from wicket to wicket that a successful break makes possible is the very essence of winning croquet. Like the passing shot in tennis or the tee shot to the green in golf, a good break is a thing of beauty. Better yet, it is within your grasp.

One reason players shy away from attempting breaks is that the break which is easiest to describe and visualize—the two-ball break—happens to be the most difficult to execute.

The Two-Ball Break

Let's start with the two-ball break with the understanding that precision placement is crucial. Here it's essential that you keep the target ball ahead of you. Your ball should function as a kind of broom, sweeping the target ball ahead of you so you can use it to your advantage on subsequent shots. Picking up where we left blue and black at the #3 wicket (diagram 8 on page 144), black has been successfully rushed to a spot 3 feet in front of the wicket on the approach side and 1 foot off to the side from its center (diagram 1).

Having diligently practiced rushing, however, you won't find it an insurmountable challenge to advance the target ball to the designated spot near the wicket. On your next shot—the croquet stroke (diagram 2)—you are thus able to plan two shots ahead. First, you want your ball to end up in front of the wicket, giving you a clear shot through the uprights. Second, you want to move the croqueted ball to a point about 6 feet beyond #3 between it and #4 (diagram 3). How do you accomplish all this with a single shot? Very easily, as it happens. You simply make the shot which is the basic building block of successful break-making—the split shot.

MEMORIZE THE

2 **3**

6

5

1 **4**

NUMBERS OF FIRST SIX WICKETS

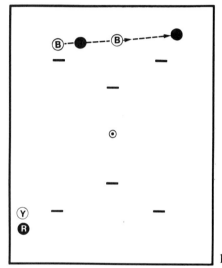

1

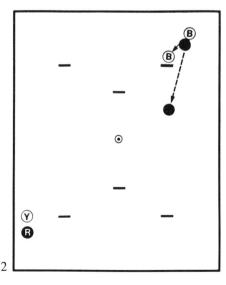

2

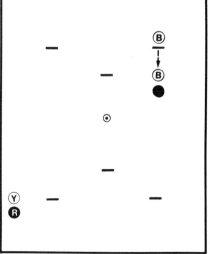

3

The success of this shot is important, for after you've cleared #3, you'll want to have a clear rush shot to advance the target ball to #4 wicket (diagram 4).

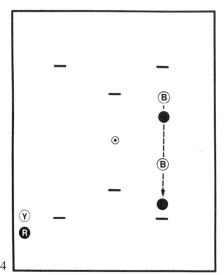

4

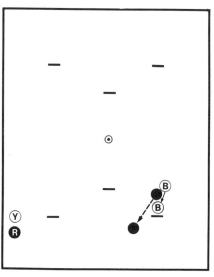

5

Blue now splits black 2 feet past and 1 foot to the right of #4 (diagram 5), runs the wicket with control so that blue has a rush on black to #5 wicket (diagram 6) and on its croquet stroke splits black 6 feet beyond the #5 and itself to position on the approach side of the wicket (diagram 7).

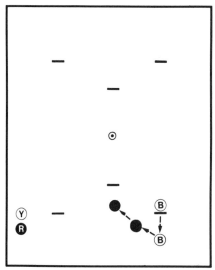

6

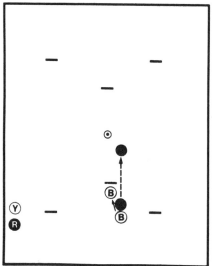

7

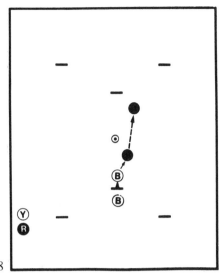

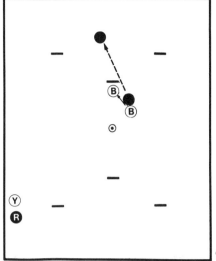

8   9

Then after running the #5 wicket, blue again rushes black up to the #6 wicket (diagram 8), splits black past and to the left of #6 (diagram 9), and after running #6 is in position to rush black to the 1-back wicket (diagram 10).

Blue has now successfully scored four wickets in this two-ball break (not counting the #2 wicket in the Openings section) and conceivably could continue all the way around the course of wickets. But as luck (and an errant shot) would have it, blue rushes black off the court, thus ending his turn (diagram 11).

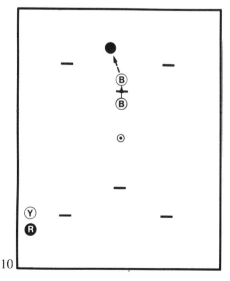

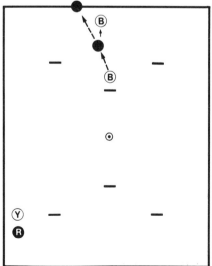

10   11

At this point, however, we want to address the question of strategic range. Assuming that you learn to make perfect split shots, should you split the balls, clear the wicket, rush the target ball to the next wicket, split the balls again, clear the next wicket, and so on, all the way around the court? Should you, in other words, perfect the two-ball break to the exclusion of all others?

No. You may take a two-ball break around the court. That would be an impressive achievement, a testimony to your inspired shooting and cool nerves. But for all its brilliance, the sustained two-ball break doesn't represent brilliant strategic thinking. The reason is simple: to sustain a two-ball break, you must ignore every other ball on the court. If you were playing solitary croquet that would be no problem, but unfortunately for the player addicted to the two-ball break, there is always an opponent waiting for his turn, knowing that the two-ball break can end with the slightest miscue. As we have just seen, such a situation occurred when blue accidentally rushed black off the court and thus ended its turn.

Wittgenstein said, "The limits of language are the limits of life." Ditto in croquet. If your strategic vocabulary is limited, you can't expect to see as much—or shoot as well—as better-endowed players. You must, therefore, be constantly vigilant to detect any weaknesses in your own game as well as to learn from other players.

If you are a true croquet player, this vigilance will be one of the attractions of the game. Croquet is, after all, not a terrifically physical sport. Strength scarcely matters. As long as you can stand, you have enough endurance. But a propensity for Machiavellian scheming, a willingness to prey on your opponent's weaknesses, and the fortitude to hang tough in a difficult situation and force it, by will and intellect, to bend your way—these are the hallmarks of every great croquet player's approach to the game.

Such a player understands very well that Association croquet is not just backyard croquet with different equipment. Croquet is not a version of miniature golf. And it is not, courtesy of the two-ball break, a form of leapfrog. For the skillful player, the entire court is his to dominate. For him, the idea of the game seems to be to shoot at everything *except* the next wicket. And yet, at endgame, it is, more often than not, this player who gobbles up a half-dozen wickets to take the victory.

By what method does such a player achieve all this?

By mastering the three-ball break.

What this player has come to understand is something you too will quickly discover: making a two-ball break all the way around the court is a very dicey proposition. At some point, you *must* pick up more balls. Only by using every ball on the greensward do you have any hope of fending off your opponent and—almost as an afterthought—achieving victory.

The Three-Ball Break

With blue and black on the North boundary as the result of blue's breakdown during his two-ball break, we begin the red/yellow side's turn with the balls in diagram 12. For his patience, red is now in a position to pick up a three-ball break with a bit of courageous shooting, starting with the rushing of yellow up the lawn toward #2 wicket (diagram 13).

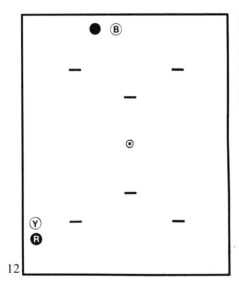

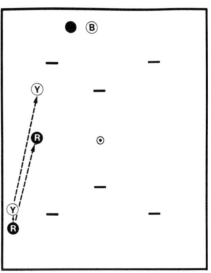

12

13

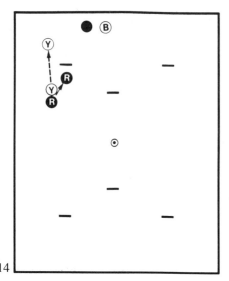

14

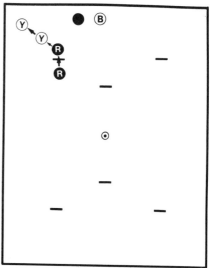

15

Instead of splitting yellow to the right of the #2 wicket (as blue had done earlier with black in starting his two-ball break), he splits it to the left (diagram 14), runs the wicket and then rushes yellow toward the second corner (diagram 15). At first glance, it appears he has forgotten that he is for #3 wicket across the court. Not so—for in order to establish the three-ball break he must get a ball across and down the court *near* #4, where it becomes known as the "pioneer" ball, while at the same time picking up the black or blue ball on the North boundary. This risky maneuver

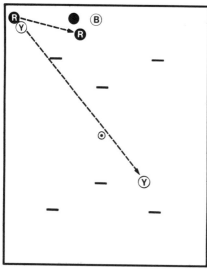

16

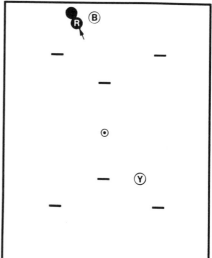

17

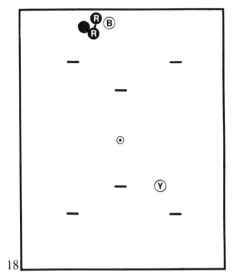

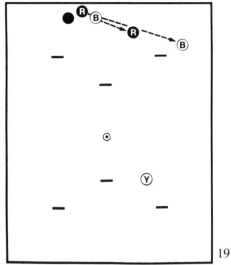

requires a split shot with a stop shot stroke that stops his ball near black and blue, while yellow is sent almost to #4 (diagram 16).

Red then softly roquets black (diagram 17), and on his short take-off croquet stroke gets behind blue (diagram 18) in order to rush it to #3 wicket, which red is now for (diagram 19). Being now ball-in-hand, red places his ball behind blue and after splitting blue to the far side of #3 (diagram 20) and running the wicket, he softly roquets blue a few feet (diagram 21) and takes croquet with blue aimed to go to the approach side

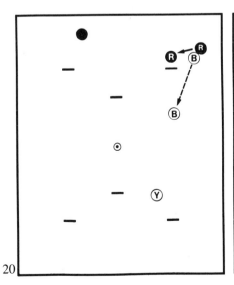

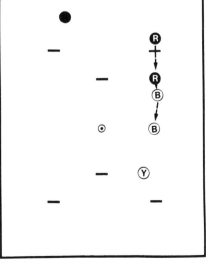

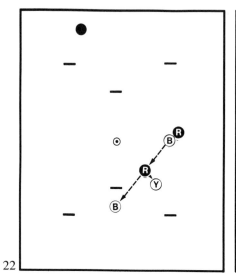
22

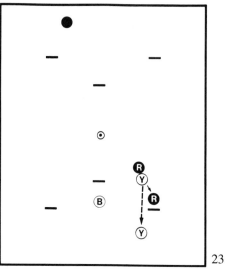
23

of #5 wicket (diagram 22) and in the stroke stops his ball so that it has a rush on yellow to #4 wicket (diagram 23). After hitting and then splitting yellow to the far side of #4, red runs the wicket so that he can roquet yellow again softly (diagram 24).

With blue as a "pioneer" ball already at #5, red now lines up yellow so that on his croquet stroke it will be sent as the "pioneer" ball up to #6 while his split shot brings him to the blue ball at #5 (diagram 25).

After roqueting blue, red splits it to the right of #5 wicket (diagram 26)

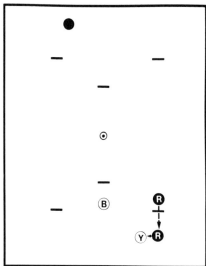
24

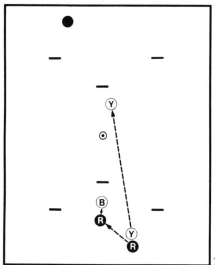
25

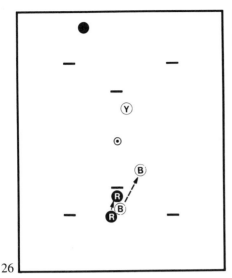
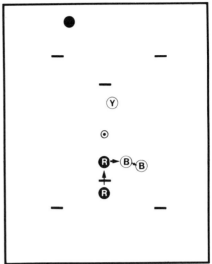

and runs the wicket with control in order to roquet blue again (diagram 27). He then aims the blue to a point between the #6 and 1-back wickets and plays a half roll shot, stopping his ball close enough to roquet yellow, which is waiting at #6 (diagram 28).

At this point, you can see that after using the three balls in making four wickets so far in this turn, red is now in a position to pick up the fourth ball (black) after running the sixth wicket (diagram 29).

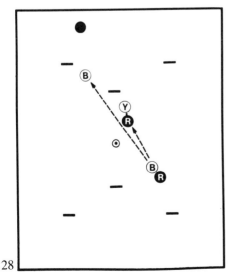
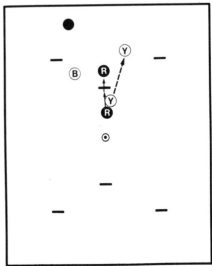

The success of the three-ball break rests in keeping the "pioneer" ball ahead of you and in front of the next wicket your ball will be for after it makes the one you are now for (or as the English say, the next wicket but one).

By adding the fourth ball to the task of making multiple hoops in one turn, break-making is made much easier.

There are moments in learning to play croquet when, suddenly, a light bulb flashes over your head or the muse lands on your shoulder and whispers in your ear and all the pieces magically fit together.

What has been mystifying becomes clear and through this newfound understanding your game takes a quantum stride forward.

Over the 30 years of attempting to help beginners learn how to play this challenging mind-bending game, there seems to be one point in the comprehension curve where this magical moment occurs most often. That is when someone grasps the full significance of the four-ball break.

In the book *Winning Croquet,* the four-ball break was presented as an exercise, and while I still believe it should be practiced at every opportunity, we have moved its description up here to follow the three-ball break in the hopes that you will better see why it is the most desirable status to try to achieve in your strategic planning.

In a game, establishing a four-ball break is your best way of coming out the winner. So try this rewarding approach to mastering this break.

The Four-Ball Break

If you have attempted to master the two- and three-ball breaks and have had some difficulty, breathe easier, for we have saved the best for last.

With the four-ball break we introduce an exercise that is not only instructive but also great fun.

To begin, place the black ball 3 feet in front of the #2 wicket and the blue ball 6 feet to the left of the center stake.

Now place the red ball a foot in front of yellow, which is one mallet head in from the boundary behind wicket #1 (diagram 1).

You are playing yellow. Start the break by rushing red to about 3 feet on the approach side of the first wicket, then split red to the right and about 5 feet in front of the wicket. Run the wicket on your continuation shot (diagram 2).

Now looking up the court we see the black "pioneer" ball waiting at #2 wicket and the blue at the pivotal spot by the peg—but no ball at #3, which

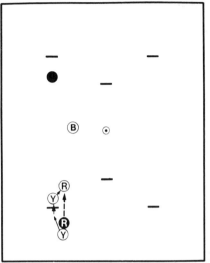

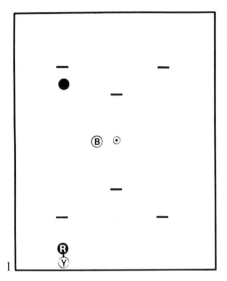

will be needed after making #2. After softly roqueting red, you line up the croquet shot so that it will go to #3. Instead of a long split shot to get yellow up to #2, you have the relatively easier option of making a straight-ahead half roll shot, stopping your ball near blue at the peg while red goes to the third wicket (diagram 3).

You now softly roquet blue and in the croquet stroke take off to black at the second. In the process you will split the blue somewhere between the peg and the sixth wicket (diagram 4).

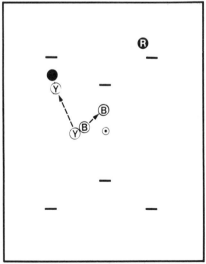

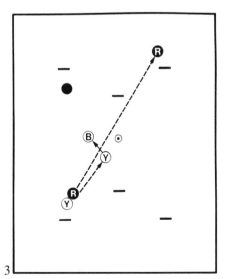

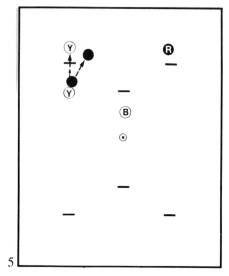

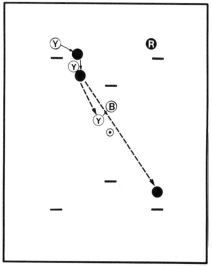

After roqueting and splitting black to the far right side of #2, you run the wicket (diagram 5) and gently roquet black again. With another hefty half roll, send black to #4 and you (yellow) to blue at the pivot in mid court (diagram 6).

By now you will realize that using the pivot ball in these straight-on half roll shots is far easier than the pinpoint rushing required in the two-ball break or the wide split shots needed in the three-ball break.

So again you softly roquet the blue ball and take off to red at the third, splitting the blue ball slightly to the east of the peg this time (diagram 7).

By moving the blue pivot ball around the peg to the side of the court where your next wicket is, your next roll shot will find it in more or less a straight line with where you will be sending the next "pioneer" ball.

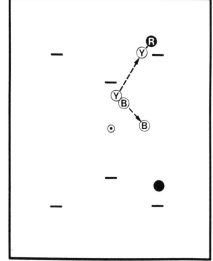

In this case, after making the third wicket off red (diagram 8), then roqueting it, you will be sending it to the far side of #5 wicket with your half roll bringing you once again back to blue (diagram 9).

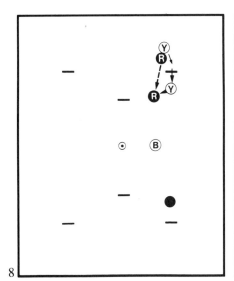 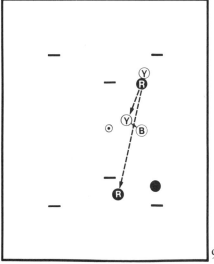

8   9

From here the whole concept of the four-ball break should become clear and you should be able to repeat the action of sending the "pioneer" ball to the next wicket but the one you are for and using the "pivot" ball to ease the way.

This of course looks easier on paper than on the lawn so in practice sessions take a bisque (or take-over shot) each time a shot fails. By counting the number of these bisques needed to make all twelve wickets, you can measure your improvement after each practice session.

Once you've mastered the four-ball break, why not practice a three-ball version by simply setting up the start the same way but eliminating the pivot ball at the peg. You'll soon appreciate the value of learning and practicing how to pick up and maneuver all the balls into your breaks.

LEAVES

Unlikely as it may seem as you're clearing your third wicket and bearing down on the fourth like an ace reliefer throwing fastballs with two out in a late inning, your turn will eventually end. At that point your opponent will step onto the court and attempt to rout you as you are, even now, trying to rout him. This is invariably an unhappy moment. It can, however, be made less unhappy if you've given him nothing much to shoot at.

Knowing when your turn is going to end is a little like knowing the hour of your death; you're sure to miscalculate. Where you end your turn is, in reality, the byproduct of more variables than anybody can generalize about, but one broad truth must be remembered.

Do not be tempted to leave either of your balls out on the court or at a wicket unless both balls of your opponent are dead on them and/or they are dead on each other. To do so will surely invite him to attack and remove that ball or send it back to his partner ball to set up a break for his side.

If you have managed to keep control of your break, you should plan to separate your opponent's balls, preferably by leaving or sending the one that shoots after your partner ball to that spot near your partner's next wicket. You then join up with your partner at some safe distance from the next opponent ball to shoot. This "divide and conquer" tactic combines the best of both defensive and offensive strategies in one play and can be employed frequently throughout a match.

One other sensible way to end your turn, paradoxically, is to do just as Aunt Emma would—shoot for the boundary at a point on the line a few feet from your partner ball.

The argument for what may seem to a novice to be a cowardly and boring shot is simply that you don't want to become a steppingstone for your opponent. If you go to the boundary and your opponent comes after you, the odds are good that he'll be attempting an approach shot of considerable distance. He may well miss. If he does, and you're not dead on his ball or your partner ball, you'll have a splendid opportunity to pick up a two-ball or three-ball break.

But even if your opponent does manage to make contact with your ball, he'll be taking croquet from the boundary. Unless you've left your balls too close together or one a few feet out on the court, he will not be able to get in a rush for his next wicket or another ball. Still, he may be foolish enough to try for a long boundary shot. And, because the odds are against him, he may end up with a bad leave for his pains.

If he's any kind of strategist, however, your opponent won't attempt any of the above. Instead, he'll do exactly as you've done; respecting your shot-making ability, he'll keep his distance and shoot for a distant boundary line. What may then ensue is not the kind of thing that dazzles spectators—you hit your next ball a few inches down the line, he taps his ball a few inches along his line in order to set up a good rush or tempt you to attack, until finally someone makes the mistake of giving the other player an opportunity by leaving a ball on the court.

If you find yourself resisting this style of play, you will probably benefit from a few games in which you don't shoot for the boundary. They will probably be very short. You will probably lose. And then perhaps you will understand why veterans try to keep their opponent's balls as widely separated as possible; try to keep their opponent's balls wired or stymied from all but a distant ball; and try to end their turns with their own balls together at a distant boundary in preparation for the break they intend to start on their next turn.

END OF THE GAME AND PEGGING OUT

The sweetest sound a croquet player can hear comes at the end of a hard-fought game. Having cleared the rover wicket with both balls and having shot one of them against the peg, the soon-to-be-victorious player sends the last ball against the peg with a resounding thud. It all seems so inevitable: it's late afternoon, the shadows are deepening, there's no breeze. This is a moment out of Fitzgerald, out of Waugh, and somehow you know that it will be followed by icy drinks, much laughter, a shockingly expensive dinner, perhaps even a spot of late-night wickedness.

Yes, it is a beautiful moment. There is, however, one small problem—it's not inevitable. All too often, a player on the verge of victory hears that final thud of his opponent's ball against the stake *before* he takes his final shot.

As we've pointed out, one of the greatest similarities between croquet and life is that it's possible to lose at any moment. In other sports, such constant vigilance isn't required. In basketball or football, for example, a team that's leading by 40 points in the last quarter is virtually guaranteed the victory. Even if their opponent hears the voice of God and becomes divinely inspired, the clock militates against a comeback.

But in croquet, a player can be seemingly out of the match when one careless shot by the opponent, usually the result of mounting nervous tension, can completely turn the tide as the opponent "snatches defeat from the jaws of victory."

163

The most common way for your side to finish after the second ball clears the rover wicket is by rushing the partner rover ball to the stake and on the croquet stroke knocking that ball against the peg, and then your own.

Preferably this will be done just after your second ball has run the rover hoop, but if you're widely separated from the partner ball you must join up with it on some boundary line to set up a rush for one or the other of your balls (depending on their respective deadness), back to the finishing peg on a subsequent turn.

Should you fail to get a good rush on your partner to the peg, another tactic would be to roquet your partner and take off to the opponent ball that follows your partner's ball in sequence. After roqueting the opponent's ball, you send it back to your partner ball on the croquet stroke and, on your continuation stroke, go to the peg.

All of this assumes your partner's ball is alive, both on the ball you have just sent him, and on yours. If you have been careful not to give the opponent's ball that now follows you too good a shot, and he misses, your partner then roquets the other opponent ball you've kindly delivered him, takes off to get a good rush on your ball near the peg, and after roqueting you closer, pegs out first your ball then his own for the win. If, however, your balls are dead on one another, you have fewer choices. You can shoot at a ball on which you are alive and use your croquet and continuation strokes to get to the peg, or you can shoot directly at the peg.

10

EXERCISES AND DRILLS

Since the early 1980s, the USCA has conducted an increasing number of croquet schools and clinics to help beginners develop their playing skills. Top teachers from around the croquet playing world, such as John Solomon, Bernard Neal, Nigel Aspinall and John McCullough from England; Ron Sloane and George Latham from Australia; Ian Gillespie, Reginald Bamford and Tom Barlow from South Africa and dozens of other internationals have joined ranking American pros like Teddy Prentis, multiple USCA title holder and the world's first professional instructor at Palm Beach Polo and Country Club, Johnny Osborn (NYCC), Bob Kroeger (Newport Casino), Peyton Ballenger (PGA National) and others as faculty members of these fine schools. Their students have all taken away a keen understanding of how valuable practice can be and have learned that practice can also be fun when it is properly organized.

Class of 1989 USCA National School in Palm Beach Gardens, Florida.

The object of the following set of drills is to enable you to reach the point where you can make the most of the shots used in croquet with comfort. There is no shortcut to achieving that end except practice, but if you think of each exercise as a game and compete against yourself or another player, you too may find these drills surprisingly pleasant . . . and productive.

SINGLE-BALL DRILLS

Touch Shots—Playing to a Specific Spot

One of the most difficult things to judge in croquet is just how hard to hit the ball to get it into position to make a wicket or to approach a ball on the other side of the court. This exercise is designed to improve your sense of touch in distance shooting.

Begin with four balls lined up next to each other on the north or south boundaries. Hit the first one a few inches in, the second a little further, and so on until all four balls have been struck to form a diagonal line into the court with the fourth ball at the end of the line farthest in toward the opposite boundary. Pick up the first three balls, and using the remaining fourth ball as your starting point, continue hitting the balls from the boundary further down the court. Each ball should stop just beyond the one before it. If you undershoot, retrieve that ball and shoot over it until it lands in the proper place. The object of this exercise is in taking the greater number of strokes in making it across the court. You should be able to do it in forty or fifty strokes. Fewer strokes would mean you are less accurate in your placements.

Rush Shots

The object of the exercise is to develop control in rushing. Using two balls, place one a foot in front of the other on the north or south boundary. Softly rush the forward ball a few feet (known as a "Dolly rush" in England) so that the ball you are hitting remains behind it in position to rush it again. The goal of the exercise is to rush the forward ball down the court without picking up your ball or moving the ball in front other than by the rush. In order to maintain control of where the balls land, you should not try to cover too much ground at one time. If you "cut" the rush (i.e., hit the forward ball on either the left or right side instead of squarely in the middle), you will find the forward ball moving to the right or left of your ball. You can regain control of the forward thrust by cutting your rush back the other way. Forty to fifty strokes to cover the length of a full-sized court should be about right.

G. Nigel Aspinall is featured in two video tapes "Croquet . . . a Primer" and "Fundamentals of Shot-making" which include recommended exercises and are available from the USCA.

DOUBLE-BALL DRILLS

Split Shots Around the Wicket

The goal of this exercise is to improve your sense of how much split and how much stop, drive or roll you need in order to control both balls in a croquet stroke at the wicket. Using eight balls, place them (two each) in a 180-degree arc 3 feet from the wicket. Aim them in such a way as to place your ball in position 18 inches in front of the wicket and located by a marker (you may use a coin for this) and the forward ball to a marker you have placed 5 feet on the far side of the wicket. Repeat the exercise on the other side of the wicket, still aiming for the same positions.

Stop and Roll Shots

These shots, from stop to full rolls—and the infinite variations in between—are the most common croquet shots in the game. The *stop shot* is frequently used to place the striker's ball in position in front of a wicket and the forward ball on the other side of the wicket in position to continue play once the striker clears the wicket. A stronger hit—often called a "beefy" stop shot—is the mainstay of three- or four-ball breaks as the forward ball is sent to a "pioneer" position at the next hoop but one, and the striker's ball is sent either to a pivot ball in the center of the court or a ball at the next wicket.

167

This exercise should train the shooter in the differences between the stop and roll shots. Beginning at the boundary line behind one of the corner wickets, stop shot a ball so that the forward ball lands near the wicket and your ball stays as close as possible to the boundary. Repeat the play with a drive shot, with the forward ball to the wicket and your ball one-third the distance. Repeat it again with a half roll, then a three-quarter and finally a full roll, bringing both balls to the wicket.

Practice making long shots by repeating the exercise from the north or south boundary, sending the forward ball to the nearest center wicket, and then the farthest center wicket. Repeat the shot two more times, and by increasing the roll each time, bring your back ball closer to the wicket without letting the forward ball move much beyond it.

For long half roll shot practice, begin at the center on the boundary line, aiming the forward ball to the nearest center wicket and the striker's ball to end level with the corner wicket. Next shoot the forward ball to the stake and the striker's ball level with the nearest center wicket. The third exercise should send the forward ball to the corner wicket diagonally across the court and the striker's ball level with the peg.

The Split Roll Shots

As with other split shots, the roll is used both for delicate wicket shots and long shots to set up or maintain a break. At the wicket, it is frequently used to place both the striker's and his partner's balls in position.

Beginning at the boundary line in a corner, roll both balls to position at the wicket as in the earlier split drill. Repeat the exercise from side boundary. Be careful in each of these shots to split the roll to assure a clear shot with the striker's ball through the wicket on the continuation.

For long split roll shots, begin again in the corner and roll your ball to position at the center wicket and the forward ball to the peg. From here, pick your own targets and increase the width of the splits and the distances to be covered.

Wickets and Boundary Shots

There are numerous other exercises, such as shooting a wicket from different distances and angles. One can never overpractice wicket-running. We suggest that you start from relatively close in, and, as you develop an ability to make the wicket consistently from that distance, gradually increase the length of your attempts.

Another good exercise is to place your ball at various distances from a boundary and shoot at balls a mallet head in from that boundary. The trick is to make sure that neither ball goes out of bounds. This "touch shot" can only be mastered by repeated practice.

Perhaps the most productive exercise we know of is the four-ball break. As described in the preceding chapter, this is the one exercise that brings all of the shots previously described into play in a drill you can truly enjoy as you learn—and which will improve your game with every attempt.

THE CROQUETATHON

In "Winning Croquet," the Croquetathon was called CROQUETATH-LON. The removal of the letter L, however, eliminates a syllable and makes it less of a tongue twister.

The British Association and the USCA have devised several croquet exercises that we have found to be extremely helpful to both beginning and veteran players alike and particularly useful to those clubs that wish to inspire more active and rewarding play for their members. One such exercise that adds in the interest-retaining element of competition is the croquetathon.

The croquetathon allows a large number of players to participate on limited court space and attempt shots which are essential to the game. The events are designed to offer a basic understanding of the various shots required in playing a real game while offering a fun, competitive exercise to novice and champion alike.

A player may compete in a croquetathon individually, as a member of a team, or both. Teams should consist of two or four players. Each team should have a balance of a more experienced player with a less experienced player or players. Two teams should be paired with each other to compete in the same events at the same time in order to keep each other's scores. Each team has a captain to keep the other team's score, and players of each team take alternate turns rather than each player taking three or five attempts at one event in a row. It's particularly important in the last event that a member of the opposing team keeps the stroke count of a competing player. To facilitate posting of scores, a tournament director should have a list of all players grouped by teams and a space to mark the individual event scores for each player.

The longer version of the croquetathon takes about three hours for eight four-man teams per court, with several events taking place on one court at a time. The shorter version takes about two hours. While court positions or sequence for events 1 through 4 can vary, the last event requires all of the court and must be played last.

USCA members clubs use it both for introducing new members to the various shots of the game and for allowing its membership to compete on a large scale in one two- to four-hour-long event.

Experience in conducting croquetathons over the past five years has suggested that the following format is a more productive version than that presented in "Winning Croquet." By using the short version, which requires less time, it can be combined with a Golf Croquet event with top finishers of the croquetathon paired against each other to produce overall winners for the event.

RULES OF THE CROQUETATHON
SHORT VERSION

Event 1
Three attempts at shooting a hoop from a distance of five feet directly in front of the hoop.

Points Awarded for:

	Points
Hitting the hoop	1
Hanging ball in jaws of hoop (touchable by straight edge down nonplaying side of hoop— use edge of mallet's head)	2
Clearly running hoop (not touchable from playing side of hoop)	3
Total possible event points	9

Event 2
Format and points are the same as event 1 but shots are now taken from 15 feet.

170

Event 3

Three attempts at shooting at a ball placed one mallet's length in front of a corner hoop from a mallet's head in from the nearest side line. After hitting it, you are to split the roqueted ball, and after making the corner hoop, roquet the other ball again. Then take your two earned shots and make the closest middle hoop.

Points Awarded for:

Making roquet and not hoop	1 point
Making roquet, split shot and corner hoop	2 points
Making roquet, split and both hoops	3 points
Total possible event points	9 points

Event 4

Five attempts shooting at the center stake from side boundary.

Points Awarded for:

Within one mallet's length from stake	1 point
Within one mallet's grip length of stake	2 points
Hitting stake	3 points
Total possible event points	9 points

Event 5

In as few strokes as possible, each player plays one ball through the 12-wicket, one-stake course from start to finish counting strokes. Par is 35; in the event that the player's score is over 35 the net result will be a minus number to be subtracted from the player's total score of the preceding events. In the case of a player scoring lower than 35 the net result will be added to the player's total score.

NOTE: While the last event is an excellent exercise in teaching the proper direction of playing the wickets on the court it can be eliminated if time constraints dictate. Simply total the scores of the first four events and should a tie occur, have a shoot out by repeating event number 1.

CROQUETATHON
LONG VERSION

Events 1, 2, 3 and 4

Are the same as the short version only five SHOT attempts are made instead of three. The scoring systems for each are also the same but with 15 points becoming the maximum for each event.

Event 5

Is the same as in the short version.

In both total all the scores to determine the winner. The individuals and/ or team with the most points wins the competition.

An example of early croquet variations
from the June 1, 1972 issue of

THE ILLUSTRATED LONDON NEWS

THE INDEX CROQUET MALLET.

This mallet is so contrived as to become a register, by which the player can tell the bridge his ball should next be passed through in the order of play. Two series of grooved rings (A B and B C, Fig. 1) are painted on the shank of the mallet. There are seven rings in each series, of seven diverse colours—the two series being counterparts of one another, inversely placed. A black belt is at each end, and a white one (at B) in the centre. An elastic ring (R) is drawn over the shank of the mallet, capable of being moved along the coloured rings, and rested in any of the grooves. Fig. 2 will show the object of this contrivance. The hoops, or bridges, are painted in colours to correspond to the rings upon the mallet, and set upon the croquet-ground in the same order of succession. The first seven bridges, between the starting and turning stakes, are respectively represented (in colour) by the first series of seven coloured rings on the mallet; while the seven bridges to be passed through in returning to the starting-stake have their representatives in the second series. The white belt in the centre stands for the turning-stake. The mode of registering will now be understood. At the commencement of the game the elastic ring is over the black band, contiguous to the head of the mallet. When the player ceases his turn of play he moves the elastic ring into the groove of colour representing the bridge he has last passed his ball through, and there leaves it, to point out the one he is next to play at on resuming his play. The elastic ring placed over the white belt in the centre tells that the stake has been tolled, and when resting on the last

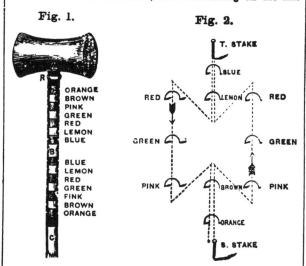

Fig. 1.

ORANGE
BROWN
PINK
GREEN
RED
LEMON
BLUE

BLUE
LEMON
RED
GREEN
PINK
BROWN
ORANGE

Fig. 2.

T. STAKE
BLUE
RED — LEMON — RED
GREEN — GREEN
PINK — BROWN — PINK
ORANGE
S. STAKE

THE INDEX CROQUET MALLET.

coloured ring it will indicate the "rover." The index mallet also points out the order of succession of the balls. These are painted to correspond with the seven coloured rings on the mallet, a black ball making the eighth. Thus upon the mallet's shank there is an index—a double one, indeed—to the order of their succession.

11

VARIATIONS

ROQUE

Over the past century countless variations of the game of croquet have evolved in America. The predominant spinoff is roque (pronounced as in "broke"). Roque was first played in 1899, when the British Croquet Association outlawed mallets with rubber tips on one end of the head and metal or an equally hard substance on the other end. Angered by this ruling, the Americans who headed the National Croquet Association dropped the "c" at the beginning and the "t" at the end, and "croquet" became "roque." It was this transformation of the game that, more than any other factor, guaranteed America's descent to the cellar in the world of international croquet.

Croquet was introduced at the Paris Olympiad in 1900 and its American hybrid cousin, roque, was played as an Olympic sport at the 1904 St. Louis Olympiad, where the gold medal was, inevitably, won by an American. But roque's first appearance as an international sport was also its last. It continued to prosper in America, particularly during the Depression, when the WPA installed hundreds of clay-and-sand courts bordered by concrete in the Midwest and South. Roque is still played today under the auspices of the American Roque League, last known to be headquartered in North Carolina.

Unfortunately for the cause of Association croquet, many Americans still confuse roque with croquet. In parts of Kentucky, for example, roque is played on clay courts with short (10- to 18-inch) rubber-and-metal headed mallets under the auspices and rules of the Kentucky Croquet Association.

Roque and the countless other variations of croquet—"Robber" and "Polo Croquet" being the most widely known—succeeded in muddying the American croquet scene and encouraged manufacturers and players alike to create their own interpretations of the game. While all this was going on, however, the rest of the English-speaking world was following the British Croquet Association laws, refining and consolidating its game and the quality standards of its equipment.

It is instructive to consider the roque-and-croquet career of Archie Burchfield of Stamping Ground, Kentucky. Frequent winners of the Kentucky championships, Archie and his son Mark modified their roque mallets to conform to international standards, learned the 6-wicket USCA rules, and, in their first attempt at a national title, won the 1982 USCA Doubles Championship in New York. Clearly, succeeding at Association croquet is possible for those who have started their croquet careers playing what the USCA considers a "variation" of the game.

Those who have learned their 6-wicket lessons well, however, are sometimes not immune to the charms of variety. Of the many variations, the USCA constitution recognizes its own 6- and 9-wicket rules, the international 6-wicket croquet as set forth in the laws of the Croquet Association, Hurlingham Club, London and the New World Croquet Federation, plus a traditional favorite played in both countries, golf croquet.

GOLF CROQUET

The one variation of the game that seems to have successfully crossed international boundaries and with only minor differences in starting position or court layout can, in fact, be played competitively by one and all throughout the world. This is golf croquet.

Until recently it was played in America, primarily on 9-wicket, 2-stake court settings, on lawns measuring as much as 200 by 70 feet. And mostly it was played in three places: Old Black Point in Connecticut and on 6-wicket, 1-peg courts in Hobe Sound in Florida and the Ocean Reef Club in Antigua. Pronounced "crow-key" by its practitioners, its popularity undoubtedly rests on the fact that it is relatively easy to learn and thus provides beginners with a game they can enjoy almost immediately.

The USCA has found golf croquet an effective introductory game or exercise for large groups of beginners; it encourages its clubs to teach and play this variation competitively in "C"-level tournaments until those new players can move up to the Association game.

Many Americans and British top players enjoy playing this variation when time precludes a full Association match.

In England the winners of their annual Golf Croquet Championships are most frequently those you will also find in the British Open and Presidents Cup finals.

So what is golf croquet?

First of all, golf croquet is *not* real croquet; it is a steppingstone towards croquet. It's about as different from Association croquet as checkers is from chess. Though many of the movements are similar and the same equipment is used, the tactics of the two games are far removed in both interest and complexity. Why then do we bother to explain it?

First, because it is a good introduction to a croquet court and it teaches the sequence of wickets, which is the same as in Association croquet.

Second, it gives excellent practice in some of the basic strokes of croquet, such as running the wicket, the roquet and rushing. It also teaches the neophyte how to play with control—that is, to play a ball to a chosen spot.

Here the similarity between croquet and golf croquet ends. For the croquet shot itself, which is the characteristic shot of Association croquet, is not used in golf croquet at all.

Golf croquet is a game in which the winner of a wicket is the side that makes that wicket first with one of its two balls. The similarity with golf is that everyone is going for the same wicket at the same time. The important difference is that the balls are allowed to interfere with each other. Imagine, if you can, the glee of being able to knock your golfing opponent's ball away from a "gimme" putt causing him to take his next shot from wherever it ends up. No wonder golf croquet is fun.

The balls are paired as in croquet—red with yellow and blue with black—and doubles or singles may be played. A point is scored when one side manages to run a wicket in order with either of its balls; the winning side in a timed game is that which has scored the more points at the end of a game. If a short game is being played, the number of points is 7 and these consist of six wickets as in croquet, followed by wicket number 3 if a decider is needed. For a middle-length game, 13 points are played; in this case the six wickets are played twice and wicket 3 is the decider should there be a tie after 12.

The balls are played strictly in sequence—blue, red, black, and yellow. Unlike croquet, there are no extra shots and turns. For example, if red makes a wicket all players then turn their attention to the next wicket and black has the first shot in approaching that wicket.

There are several rules that differ from those of croquet. First, it often happens that in trying to run a wicket the ball gets stuck in the "jaws"—that is, it starts to run the wicket but does not get completely through. In this case (in our advanced rules game), it must be hit back to the playing side of the wicket on its next turn before that wicket is again attempted. If, however, it was placed in that position by an opponent's stroke, the ball may then on its turn continue straight through to score the point. A ball may also score the point by being rushed through the wicket by either side.

Secondly, a player may not anticipate the running of a wicket by deliberately going on to the next hoop.

Thirdly, jump shots, where the ball leaves the ground, are not allowed. This rule is intended to protect the lawn from possible damage and also to make the stymie a useful tactic. The full rules for golf croquet may be found on page 249.

We cannot praise the usefulness of this variation highly enough nor encourage its use in connection with large groups of non-croquet players more strongly.

GROUP AND BENEFIT EVENTS

Since real croquet is far too complex to expect a large group of neophytes to be able to play at a first time outing, golf croquet is ideal.

Golf croquet is, in fact, the number one form of croquet the USCA suggests to charity or fund-raising groups to employ when it is asked for suggestions or help by the organizers of these events.

Photo courtesy of Robert Phillips

A combination of wicket shooting contests and golf croquet are employed at an annual pro/celebrity benefit event in New York.

ROLEX

in conjunction with

THE UNITED STATES CROQUET ASSOCIATION
and the
NEW YORK CROQUET CLUB
cordially invite you to attend the

1989
US CROQUET HALL OF FAME CLASSIC
PRO / CELEBRITY CROQUET TOURNAMENT
and the
CHAMPAGNE PICNIC LUNCHEON

*...uring stars of Broadway hits
...cluding "Me and My Girl"*

*Benefitting
...Central Park Conservancy
...u've Gotta Have Park! Day)
and the
...dation of America Educational Fund*

May 20, 1989
at the
...ork Croquet Club Courts in
...ark, New York City, New York

Per person (tax deductible)

*Croquet Casual Attire
...572-4345, Celia – Rain Date: May 21*

...ICKETS WILL BE HELD AT
...ROQUET COURTS

Rolex Watch, USA President Roland Puton shows his shot-making skills during benefit pro/celebrity tournament.

NY Croquet Club's own favorite soap opera star Christine Jones with actresses Carmen de Lavallade and super Ruth Warwick at the Rolex US Hall of Fame courtside picnic.

177

Another useful and fun form of croquet activity for large groups of neophytes is the Wicket Shooting Contest originally popularized at the Croquet Foundation of America's benefit black tie (white sneakers optional) Balls in New York and Palm Beach.

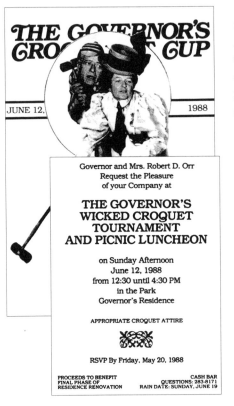

THE GOVERNOR'S CROQUET CUP

JUNE 12, 1988

Governor and Mrs. Robert D. Orr
Request the Pleasure
of your Company at

THE GOVERNOR'S WICKED CROQUET TOURNAMENT AND PICNIC LUNCHEON

on Sunday Afternoon
June 12, 1988
from 12:30 until 4:30 PM
in the Park
Governor's Residence

APPROPRIATE CROQUET ATTIRE

RSVP By Friday, May 20, 1988

PROCEEDS TO BENEFIT
FINAL PHASE OF
RESIDENCE RENOVATION

CASH BAR
QUESTIONS: 283-8171
RAIN DATE: SUNDAY, JUNE 19

This concept involves selling tickets for shots at a wicket from 5 to 15 feet away for prizes. Conducted outdoors or indoors (uses special welded wickets firmly set into carpeting), this event cannot only be used in fund-raising, but has proven to be great fun for shooters and spectators alike.

The Croquetathon, The Shooting Gallery and Golf Croquet can be mixed or combined to make major themes for groups of all sizes from meetings and conventions to benefit Balls or Picnics.

The Governor of Indiana's Mansion Restoration Committee recieved local USCA assistance for their benefit picnic.

Setting up the Wicket Shooting Gallery at the Beach Club for the Palm Beach International Croquet Ball.

CORPORATE AND CHARITY EVENTS FEATURE CROQUET FOR PUBLIC RELATIONS, PROMOTIONS AND FUND RAISING

The increasing popularity of the sport of croquet has not escaped the attention of Charity and Benefit Committees across America.

Wicket shooting at a US Croquet Hall of Fame Ball in New York (White sneakers optional).

As noted, the USCA is frequently asked to provide assistance in helping various organizations to organize or even provide management support for such events. Unfortunately the limited human resources of the Association prevent its direct involvement in these often worthwhile activities but are sometimes able to recommend sources who can provide their services for a fee. In these cases the USCA or the Croquet Foundation of America (which is the tax deductible [501(c)3] educational affiliate of the USCA) can provide a special "official" sanction for an event in exchange for a contribution from the affairs organizing body. For further information, see page 270.

USCA Tournaments such as the National Club Team Championships (top) and the National Open Singles & Doubles Championship (lower) are the pinnacle events of the USCA sanctioned schedule each year.

John C. Osborn, three time co-winner of the USCA National Club Team Championships, 1983 & 86 with his father Jack and in 1988 with Kiley Jones.

1988 USCA National Open Singles Champion, Reid Flemming (right) with Doubles Champs, Teddy Prentis and Bart Richardson (second and third from left) with runner-ups Carl Behnke and Lisle Guernsey.

12

TOURNAMENTS

HANDICAPS AND BISQUES

Tournament croquet is the very heartbeat of the current boom in the popularity of the sport in America. Be it at the family club or national championship level, tournaments are the focal points which combine the competitive challenge and the highly social aspects of croquet. This unique convergence has proven to make tournament events appealing to players, spectators and the press alike.

As I write this chapter, sitting courtside at the Round Island, Connecticut, estate of Pat and Fred Supper, a match is in progress between an Executive Vice President of a major toiletries company and his partner, the retired Director of NBC-TV's nightly network news and their opponents, the diminutive five foot, 100-pound secretary of the USCA and her partner, a retired US Air Force Captain.

They are playing in the Quarter Finals of the first Greenwich Croquet Club Invitational Tournament which is also being held at the new club's courts at the municipally owned Bruce Park Lawn Bowls and Croquet greens. This July event is the culmination of several years of diligent work by local USCA members in obtaining the joint use of the town's park facility. Their success has opened the doors for over 95 residents to launch what has become the third largest USCA club to date.

In the course of this four day event, the 36 invited players will attend three cocktail and dinner parties hosted by club members, enjoy courtside lunches and refreshments daily and partake of a champagne picnic during the Sunday finals in the park. Daily results, accounts and feature articles have appeared in the Greenwich newspapers and a segment on WABC-TV Eyewitness Newscast covering the event was shown on the New York stations Thursday evening program.

Participants in the historic first annual Greenwich Croquet Club Invitational.

Having lost three of my five doubles matches, thus being eliminated from final round play, allows me the opportunity to make the point that to lose in such pleasant and casual surroundings in the company of friendly people is clearly no loss at all. With a few exceptions, this view will be shared by my fellow competitors who also subscribe to the old adage, "It's not whether you win or lose, but how you play the game."

For me, the ultimate winner will be those of you who, because of the media coverage or through friends exposed to the tournament, have been attracted to the sport. If you now find your way onto a court and into a tournament you too will begin to enjoy the unique blending of competitive social activity that sets croquet apart from other sports.

Croquet tournaments range in scope from informal half day sociable shooting contests or golf croquet to week long, multi-flight major USCA championship events with upwards of 100 competitors competing on as many as ten or twelve courts.

The heaviest tournament action takes place within member clubs' internal competitions—some clubs have as many as five tournaments a year—and the popular invitationals, where host clubs invite members of other clubs to compete with and/or against their members.

While the USCA recognizes several tournament formats—single elimination, round robins, block play, etc.—the standard double elimination format seems to be favored for most club play.

DOUBLE ELIMINATION FORMAT

The double elimination tournament allows each player or team to play at least two matches. Thus, should a player lose one match, he or she is still capable of winning the tournament.

Example of a Double Elimination Tournament Ladder

1. For 8 sides (singles or doubles), A through H on ladder, if only one court is available for the tournament. Fourteen or 15 1½-hour matches can be played over a three day period.

2. If two courts are available, the tournament can be condensed into two days and the time limit for each match can be extended up to two hours. In this event matches 1 through 6, 8 and 9, would be played on Saturday. Matches 10 and 11 would be played at 9:00 A.M. Sunday, matches 7 and 12 at 11:30 and the semi-finals as shown.

    NOTE: Examples of ladders for odd numbers of entries including distribution of seeding and byes are available from the USCA office.

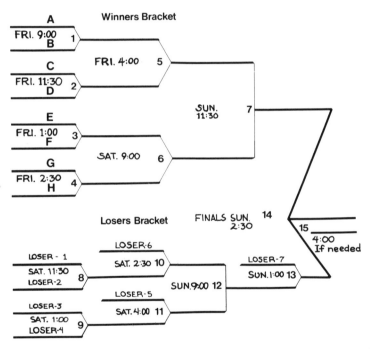

As in the case of a straight single elimination, the top four to eight players or teams are seeded. Note that losers of upper-bracket matches play other losers until a final winner of the lower bracket then plays the winner of the winners' bracket in the finals. Should the winner of the losers' bracket win that match, then both will have lost only one match and one more match must be played to decide the champion. Should the winner of the winners' bracket win the first game, the tournament is over.

When you set up a double elimination tournament, the winners' and losers' brackets for the given number of players should be drawn first. Schedule the finals first and work backward, starting with the losers' bracket before proceeding to those matches in the upper bracket which have not yet been scheduled. If you do this correctly, the first round matches will all be upper-bracket matches and the losers of the first matches will not play again until later in the tournament.

BLOCK & LADDER
TOURNAMENT FORMAT

Another tournament format which is growing in popularity, particularly in larger invitationals and USCA titled events where the participants who will have traveled some distances and would like to be assured of more than two matches of play before being eliminated, is the combination of "block and ladder" tournament.

Since the number of matches in this format is increased, provision for more courts or extending the length of the event is the key determinant.

In the example we will use to illustrate this format we will increase the numbers of entrants to 12 and organize them into two blocks of 6 with the top seeds evenly distributed between them. Each entry (singles or doubles) will then play each other within the block for a total of five matches. From these two blocks three top finishing entrants will advance to an elimination ladder of six with the winners of each block given a bye until the second round of ladder play.

The winner and runner-ups of the block play will have been determined by 1) number of wins; 2) by record of play against others in the block; and in the event of a tie, 3) by net points scored.

The ladders for the finalists may be played under either single or double elimination formats. In this single elimination example one loss would find an entry out after playing in six matches while all tournament participants would have played a minimum of five.

Example of Block & Ladder Format

Block 1

	SEED #1	SEED #3	SEED #5	SEED #7	SEED #9	SEED #11	GAMES Won/Lost
SEED #1	░						
SEED #3		░					
SEED #5			░				
SEED #7				░			
SEED #9					░		
SEED #11						░	

Block 2

	SEED #2	SEED #4	SEED #6	SEED #8	SEED #10	SEED #12	GAMES Won/Lost
SEED #2	░						
SEED #4		░					
SEED #6			░				
SEED #8				░			
SEED #10					░		
SEED #12						░	

Single Elimination Ladder

WINNER BLOCK ONE

③

SECOND BLOCK TWO

①

THIRD BLOCK ONE

FINAL

SECOND BLOCK ONE

②

THIRD BLOCK TWO

④

WINNER BLOCK TWO

Challenge Ladder

There are also season long "challenge ladders" which provides clubs with an opportunity to develop a ranking within their membership, which in turn serves as a basis for establishing a handicap range that can be meshed into the USCA National Handicapping System.

First, arrange your club's playing membership in order of their known (or assumed) skill with the best at the top of the list and the less experienced below them. Lower ranked players are then encouraged to challenge those up to two above them to a match. If the higher ranked player loses (or is unable to play within a reasonable time) his place is assumed by the challenger in the club ladder. The matches are usually played without handicaps but handicap ladders can also be used in this type of extended competition.

HANDICAPS AND BISQUES

The United States Croquet Association, like its British counterpart, uses a handicapping system of bisques to equalize match play between players or teams with different levels of skill. The USCA bisque rules allow a player to replay any given shot. The British Association bisque rule provides an additional continuation shot at the end of any stroke in the turn. The American bisque is mostly used to correct an error and continue play; and, in the USCA game it may be used to attempt a different and more rewarding shot.

Aside from its primary function of being a "great equalizer," the bisque is also a most valuable tool in learning how to play the game. Use it in practice sessions and you can measure your improvement as it takes fewer and fewer "take-overs" to achieve your practice goals.

In Part 5 of the USCA rules (see page 231) you will learn the basics of how bisques are used under game conditions. One thing the rules don't tell you, however, is to be sure to USE your bisques in matches. Don't, whatever you do, let foolish pride lead you into "going to bed" with a bisque with which you might have won a game.

BISQUES IN HANDICAP TOURNAMENT PLAY

A handicap tournament provides for players of different caliber to compete reasonably equally. Naturally the best players in the tournament will receive few if any bisques and players of less skill will be awarded more. Depending upon the difference between skill levels of players within a tournament or club, bisques may range from zero to twenty. Generally, the best player in a tournament should receive no bisques. The bisqueing of players should be based on singles play. However, until recently developed USCA guidelines, no proper comparisons between the best and worst players existed and players would be awarded bisques by the tournament committee, based upon their general level of play.

In 1986, the USCA launched an ambitious program of providing officers of USCA clubs, districts, sections and regions with handicapping authority and by 1989 a comprehensive list had evolved resulting in a national handicap system similar to that of golf. USCA clubs are now able to use guidelines to establish their members' handicaps so that they can play in handicap (and non-handicap) tournaments throughout the country.

When a handicap tournament is broken down into flights according to skill level, usually the bisque differential is not greater than four or five. Quite often the players may play "net" bisques by subtracting the number of the best player's bisques from the number of bisques the higher handicap players have. This results in fewer bisques for each player with the best player playing at "scratch." "Full" bisques refers to matches played where all players are entitled to all designated bisques rather than playing off the lowest handicap.

In doubles handicap tournaments, the partners' handicaps are combined and then averaged and the pair with the lower number of bisques is subtracted from the higher pairs average, who then are awarded the bisque difference with only the higher handicap player on the team receiving the bisque(s). See Part 5, Rule 30 a & b.

As the cornerstone of the five charter USCA member clubs, the New York Croquet Club's whimisical mallet and ball weilding Statue of Liberty illustration by Linda West symbolizes the sport's increasing quest for more croquet courts.

13

LUST FOR LAWNS

by Jack R. Osborn and Dr. Carlton H. Mabee

There can be little doubt that the better the lawn you have to play on, the faster your croquet skills will develop. It's unlikely, however, that most of the readers of this book have ever seen, let alone played on, a really good croquet lawn. Many more will have played on garden or backyard grass that was probably not flat and most certainly was uneven or bumpy. Simply put, the ideal lawn for first-class croquet will be as *flat, hard, smooth and fast* as possible because such a lawn reduces the element of chance and allows you to play a more advanced game with exacting shots and sophisticated tactics.

Unlike the British Isles, where climate and soil conditions are reasonably constant throughout, American conditions vary broadly. To attempt to provide a comprehensive treatise on the proper grass type or care and feeding of lawns from Alaska to Florida would fill several books.

Do not despair, however, for even those of you who think your lawns are beyond hope may find some helpful hints below. Existing backyard lawns with rolling or sloping areas dotted with trees can, with a little care, be great fun to play on.

Your most important concern should be the length of the grass. If it is too long, it will cause you to "force" your shots, with an inevitable toll of accuracy. Long grass will simply not allow you to attempt, let alone master, many of the roll or split shots. When you are forced to smash every ball, there is a tendency to hit down and cause the ball to jump as if it had hit a bump. Your first step in improving your lawn, then, is to determine what variety, blend, or mixture of grasses you have growing and cut it as low as it will tolerate. See the following chart for the minimum cutting tolerances of many varieties:

SUGGESTED MINIMUM CUTTING HEIGHTS
OF SELECTED TURFGRASS SPECIES

Relative Cutting Height	Cutting Height	Species
Very Close	0.2 inches	Creeping Bentgrass
	0.2	Velvet Bentgrass
Close	0.3	Colonial Bentgrass
	0.3	Annual Bluegrass
	0.3	Bermuda Grass
	0.4	Chewings Fescue
	0.5	Perennial Ryegrass
	0.5	Zoysia Grass
	0.5	Rough Bluegrass
	0.5	Buffalo Grass
Medium	0.75	Kentucky Bluegrass
	1.0	St. Augustine Grass
	1.0	Centipedegrass

Relative Cutting Height	Cutting Height	Species
Medium	1.0	Carpet Grass
High	1.5	Red Fescue
	1.5	Meadow Fescue
	1.5	Bahiagrass
	1.5	Tall Fescue
	1.5	Fairway Wheatgrass
Very High	3.0	Canada Bluegrass
	3.0	Smooth Brome

Cutting any species of grass below its minimum level will damage it severely. Reducing height of cut to its minimum level will increase the cultural intensity necessary to maintain it to a maximum. Raising the height will reduce the amount of care. Lower the blade of the mower slowly over a period of time so as to allow the plant to adapt to its new height. You may want to consider overseeding with another variety of grass which will tolerate a lower cut.

Your next concern should be the smoothness and texture of the lawn. Uniformity of texture in a greensward will help impart predictable rolls of a croquet ball. Lawns plagued with crabgrass, clover, daisies, plantains and other grassy and broad leafed weeds should be rectified in time by the selective use of pre- and post-emergent herbicides (be careful if you are planting grass) and weeding tools. Mowing at minimum height regularly enough so as never to cut off more than one third of the blade will help control weeds while providing a trimmer, faster surface.

As for leveling an existing irregular lawn, it may take you a few years to achieve an excellent lawn. Become adept at top-dressing with sifted soil and seed, filling and rolling back the turf, and removing some subsoil and relaying the turf. For smaller high spots, a hollow-tined fork will enable you to remove soil from beneath without disturbing the grass.

For more demanding leveling problems you may want to modify the landscape severely by bringing in the bulldozers. After killing the existing vegetation on the court area with Round-up, bulldoze the topsoil into a pile off the court, level the subsoil, perhaps install drainage if the subsoil is impervious, and return the soil to a flat plane. At this point, to prevent soil impacting, mix your existent soil 60-70% with sand (masonry sand is good), and have a tractor operated rototiller thoroughly mix it together. Sand can also be incorporated into the topsoil off site before returning it to the court. Let the top-mix settle completely before you plant. Probably the most common error we see in first attempts at court construction is the non-compacting or not allowing the soil to thoroughly settle before seeding. This can lead to large irregularities in surface smoothness and levelness after play begins. The ideal situation is to have no more irregularities than can be eradicated with top-dressing within the first year.

If you're contemplating the installation of a new court, we urge you to talk first with the golf course superintendent or greenskeeper of a local country club to determine the type of drainage and grass he uses for his putting greens. The chances are good that he'll recommend constructing a court similar to USGA specifications. Successful establishment and maintenance of greens quality turf varies tremendously from one region to another. In the northern climates creeping bentgrass is favored over most other varieties and offers an unsurpassed playing surface. But in the cool humid regions of the west and east coast, velvet bentgrass and chewings fescue (perhaps combined with colonial bentgrass), hold up extremely well. And in the south improved Bermuda grass cultivars and some of the new cultivars of zoysia grass are used, again with the possibility of winter overseeding. In the arid, non-irrigated parts of the country buffalo grass may deserve a try.

Until contractors familiar with the installation of croquet courts become available, you might also check with a tennis court builder to discuss appropriate methods of leveling the area to be used. Tennis courts of impervious material usually have a slight pitch to them and this principle can be applied to a croquet court at 1-3 inches per 100 feet if the court is not expected to drain well. However, a properly constructed first class greensward can and should be perfectly flat.

Of the two methods of putting in grass—seeding or sodding—seeding, although less expensive, takes longer to become playable. Sodding is often faster, but the cost is higher. In either case, other factors to be considered are the watering systems for proper irrigation and drainage.

Ideally, a peripheral sprinkler system should be put in to avoid sprinkler heads on the court itself. Reasonable drainage can be achieved by a layer of gravel a few inches thick 5 to 6 inches under the topsoil.

Two of the finest seeded croquet court installations we know are to be found at the PGA National Resort in Palm Beach Gardens, Florida, and the prestigious Meadow Club of Southampton, Long Island. The last, with 38 tennis courts, is now the largest lawn tennis club in the world. Eight of their newest tennis and their two croquet courts were installed with identical playing surfaces. Club grounds superintendent, Anthony Olender, who supervised the project, provides these suggestions:

After the ground is properly leveled, it should be raked, limed and fertilized. Once the ground is ready, seed with creeping bentgrass at a rate of 3-4 pounds per 1,000 square feet. Overseeding is recommended for the next two years. Creeping bentgrass provides an unsurpassed playing surface.

However, if the selected site has a good, desirable grass, such as blue or fescue, already established, it can be overseeded with bentgrass. This would permit playing the following year.

Follow-up care is essential, therefore you should consider the following:

1) Installing an irrigation system.

2) Purchasing a small lawnmower suitable for greens, such as a Jacobsen.

   a) set the cutting height at about $^5/_{16}$" or $^1/_4$".

   b) court should be mowed at least three times a week.

3) Program of regular fertilizing, top-dressing, aerating, dethatching, and controlling weeds, fungus and insects.

The Meadow Club of Southampton's two croquet courts adjoin lawn tennis courts installed at the same time. Decorative statuary shares the practice space between the courts.

In sharp contrast with the several year development program above, and as a good example of how difficult climates can affect the planning and time required to create good seeded courts was the six month installation of the USCA's five full-sized, international quality courts at their headquarters at PGA National Resort in Palm Beach Gardens, Florida.

With the goal of having fully playable courts ready for the US International Challenge Cup matches between the USCA and Great Britain'in early 1987, Luke Majorki, then General Manager and Superintendent of PGA National's four championship golf courses, began the installation in August of 1986.

After moving some trees, clearing and grading the acre and one fourth of court space, bulldozers were used to level the subsurfaces. Five hundred feet of drainage pipe were installed in a herringbone pattern on each of the five courts and covered with 4 inches of washed pea gravel. Ten inches of medium sized sand was then spread over the gravel and carefully leveled and rolled to a flat grade. A peripheral irrigation and electric control system were installed. After tilling peat moss into the top few inches of sand, the greens were again levelled and rolled to a flat grade. The base was then fumigated with methyl bromide and covered with plastic film for 48 hours.

The greens were then sprigged with Tifgreen #328 Bermuda and the borders sodded with Tifway #419. The courts were top-dressed and fertilized lightly twice a week. In December, the greens were overseeded with Derby perennial ryegrass for the winter months.

Because of the tight schedule to meet the tournament dates, Majorki employed a variety of chemicals to both speed the growth and protect the young grass. "It takes a year for a green to mature," said Majorki, "but we didn't have that luxury." But by opening date in January, six months after ground breaking, Luke and his crew were rewarded with praise such as, "I have died and come up in croquet heaven," by USCA officials and members alike.

August   1. Bulldozing to
level subsurfaces.

2. Herringbone tile
drainage laid.

3.

4.

September 3. Four inches of pea gravel covers drainage base.

4. Levels of sand, pea gravel and base.

5.

6.

October 5. Peripheral irrigation, electric installed.

6. Fumigating base with control system Methyl Bromide and cover for 48 hrs.

7.

8.

November 7. Court surface sprigged with #328 Bermuda and cut in.

8. Top dressing and fertilizing.

9.

10.

December 9. Overseeding with Derby Rye for the winter season.

January 10. Ready for Opening.

The five court complex at USCA's headquarters at the PGA National Resort in Palm Beach Gardens, Florida, receives substantial rainfall throughout the year. The sand based courts were installed with care to provide maximum drainage. The above photo taken in the middle of a three inch rainfall shows some accumulation both on the court and along the near side.

The right hand photo was taken five minutes after the rain had stopped with the court completely playable, while courtside puddles still remain.

There are many other examples of the geometrically increasing new court installations across the country, many of which are being blended into extraordinarily beautiful backyard landscapes. Courts such as those at Fred Supper's in Greenwich or Russ Aiken's in Newport, Rhode Island, are but two "home" courts that leap to mind.

Russell Barnett Aiken's Pegasus Court, with its perfect lawn and Greek temple.

Sodding, or the laying down of already growing turf on a preleveled court site, has also proved successful at several USCA member clubs. By calling in a talented neighboring golf course superintendent to supervise its installation, the Beach Club of Palm Beach had two tournament quality lawns in play within two months of putting down the sod. And at the Pinehurst Hotel and Country Club in North Carolina, in what must be considered the most ambitious croquet installations to date, three full-size courts were carved out of a sloping hillside in front of the golf clubhouse, sodded with putting green grass in June of 1982, and were ready for the Southern Regional USCA Championship play in late August. These three beautiful tiered greenswards at the country's leading golf complex, gave Pinehurst the distinction of being the first site in America with four international quality croquet courts. Of historical note is the fact that the first sport facility installed by James Tufts, who created Pinehurst in 1895, was a croquet court.

View of the Pinehurst Golf Club House from the middle level of three tiered croquet courts.

Whether starting a croquet court from scratch or improving an existing lawn, a program of continuing maintenance is a must. Cultural activities such as aeration, verticutting (dethatching, top-dressing, irrigating, fertilizing, and mowing while concurrently implementing a disease control program), will keep turf looking and functioning as close to perfect as possible. For *these reasons* golf, tennis and other clubs that have the equipment and staff to care for the courts properly are ideally suited as sites for croquet clubs.

Similarly, resorts, hotels, inns and retirement communities are able to establish and maintain excellent facilities. Colleges and schools often have lawn areas that can be utilized effectively, and, with encouragement from interested faculty and alumni, can even be improved to first-class level.

Another opportunity for establishing courts rests in the parks and recreational departments of towns and cities. If properly approached, these agencies can be convinced of the healthful, social and beautification benefits of croquet facilities.

In New York City, Denver, Greenwich, Beverly Hills and San Francisco, for example, local USCA clubs are playing on lawns originally set down as lawn bowling greens. The New York Croquet Club share lawns with the New York Lawn Bowling Club, an arrangement that has worked well since 1960. These lawns served as the site for the first nine USCA National Singles and Doubles Croquet Championships from 1977 through 1985.

As a result of the media coverage of the Nationals in New York City, a number of other USCA clubs, in approaching their local authorities, have suggested that with any new installation their parks department might consider one which could serve both croquet and lawn bowling *or perhaps lawn tennis* to maximize the use of the facility.

For the record, the area required by a Lawn Tennis Court is 60 feet wide and 120 feet deep. Two lawn tennis courts side by side equals the size of one regulation (120 x 120) lawn bowling green. While two modified (60 ft. x 90 ft.) croquet courts will fit on one bowling green, three tennis courts provide sufficient room for two full size (84 ft. x 105 ft.) championship croquet courts, and one and one-half bowling greens.

The principal concern of players of croquet and bowling is ensuring the smooth surface of the lawns; this can be achieved by properly plugging *or closing* of the holes created by the wickets when the bowlers *or tennis players* are to use the lawn. Special "Foxy" wickets (see page 65), which leave smaller holes are now available, while regular wicket holes can be sprinkled with grass clippings or topped with grass plugs. Otherwise use a fork-like tool inserted into the ground around the hole to tease the soil together, thus closing the hole. Sprinkle top-dressing over the area and smooth. Avoid filling the holes with soil, which will ultimately cause a mound to develop around the wicket.

While we're on the subject, ruts may be worn between the uprights with constant play and wickets should be rotated from time to time. To do this, simply remove the wicket and reset it with one upright in the existing hole and the other in a new one to the side. Make certain that all wickets are kept in line with one another by rotating them in the same direction. Then fill the remaining old holes with grass clippings or tease the soil together as above.

View of the New York Croquet Club and New York Lawn Bowling Club courts in Central Park.

USCA Los Angles District President, Cesare Danova, shows USCA Vice President, Libby Newell, the Roxbury Park courts, now the home of the Beverly Hills Croquet Club, after successful negotiations with the Beverly Hills Parks Department and the Lawn Bowling Club.

The interest in croquet continues to grow and with it the passion for fine lawns. The USCA greens committee is accumulating a great deal of information about court installation and care and Dr. Carleton H. Mabee, greens committee Chairman, has nearly completed a book on this very subject which will be available to the public in the near future.

US Croquet Association's Administrative Director, Anne Frost, keeps clubs and at-large membership happy and hopping with over one new club a week joining the USCA since 1986.

14

CLUBS

No one really knows how many croquet clubs exist in America today. But we do know those who have become affiliated with the USCA. The basic categories of membership in the United States Croquet Association are: At Large Members (Adult, Couples and Juniors), and Member Clubs. Most of the USCA member clubs fall into one of the seven general categories described on the following pages.

We also have learned over the years that the one common thread, starting with the family-type club, that marks the successful club is the presence of an individual (or core group) whose energy, enthusiasm and instinctive organizational abilities serve as the principal thrust in either starting a croquet playing group "from scratch" at home or working within an established sports club or facility to create a croquet presence. This essential ingredient, this "mover and shaker," if you will, can usually get support from others to get the croquet ball rolling.

Many of our new USCA Clubs have, in fact, been started by folks who initially joined the Association as individual At Large Members and later built up a core group of friends into a club in order to take advantage of the broader benefits available to clubs.

It is to this person (or group) we extend our encouragement and invitation to join the USCA, either as an At Large Member or as a Club. We hope you will join in the fun.

As noted earlier, well over 350 croquet clubs have been established in America during the 12 years since the USCA was founded, with 200 of these joining from 1986 through late 1989. It has been estimated that this growth rate has outstripped all other English speaking countries combined and that there is no letup in sight.

In fairness, there are undoubtedly more opportunities for new clubs to be launched in the United States than in the United Kingdom and Commonwealth countries where some of their formal clubs have been established for over a century. American croquet clubs, like Americans themselves, are a more diverse lot, ranging from family size to major real estate developments and resorts with no two exactly alike. On the following pages we will take a look at some of these and for a listing of active 1989 USCA clubs see page 264.

Family Clubs

Family clubs are private home-based groups with a one- or two-family core. Neighbors or other family members are added as their interest is raised. Play is primarily centered on one or two backyard courts that often are improved each year by the landowner as the playing level increases. Members of these clubs enjoy the sport for the opportunity to compete among themselves, where differences in age or sex are minimized and fun is the key ingredient.

Family and private clubs differ only in the number of non-family members sharing the courts. (1) The Round Island Mallet Club in Greenwich is the name of Pat and Fred Supper's family estate. (2) Casa Woodfin is Jerry and Gene Woodfin's beautiful home court in Indian Wells, California. (3) The Perrysburg Croquet Club in Ohio is John Donnell's growing groups' favorite greensward.

Private Croquet Clubs

Private croquet clubs represent an expanded, organized group, from 5 to over 100 members, for whom croquet makes up either a substantial part or the whole of the club's activities. These clubs are composed of adults who recognize the competitive challenge the game poses plus those who enjoy the social aspects. They often establish more formal croquet facilities, with one or perhaps several courts, and share the cost of proper equipment and maintenance. In some instances, they utilize a single member's or several members' home grounds or arrange to play on semipublic or public grounds.

(1) Harbor Point, Michigan, is the summer home of John J. Kilpatrick's Harbor Balls & Mallet Club. (2) Robert Clayton's home court is one of several that serve the Quantuck Bay Croquet Group on Long Island, NY. (3) Mrs. Carvel (Susie) Linden's seaside courts in Spring Lake, New Jersey, are home to the USCA's oldest charter member, Green Gables Croquet Club (1958).

203

Country, Tennis and Sports Clubs

Country, golf, tennis and sports clubs are primarily dominated by activities other than croquet, which is presented to their membership as an individual sports alternative. A Croquet Committee is usually established to coordinate the use of courts, equipment, tournaments and social activities for those of the club's members who are interested. If appropriate, separate assessments may be used to fund USCA annual dues, equipment needs or social functions related to the croquet group.

The Bon Vivant Country Club's courts in Bourbonnais, Illinois.

Croquet at Rhode Island's Newport Casino, home of the International Tennis Hall of Fame.

Bellerive Country Club, St. Louis.

204

It is not surprising that country clubs, tennis clubs, yacht clubs and other sports clubs, whose membership may not all participate in the club's primary sports activities, are finding that croquet has become a very attractive addition to their facility. Recent studies have shown that croquet players outspend tennis players in the food and beverage operations and make solid contributions to a club's bottom line.

But it is the club's members, who have been exposed to the charms of the sport at other clubs or resort facilities, who are pressing their management and boards into installing proper croquet courts and joining such prestigious USCA members as Grandfather Golf and Country Club in North Carolina; Royal Palm Yacht and Country Club, The Everglades, Card Sound, Indian Creek, Key Largo Anglers and The Beach Club in Florida; Vicmead, Merion Cricket, Newport Casino, Agawam Hunt, Meadow Club of Southampton, and Ballymeade along the Atlantic seaboard; Bellerive Country Club in St. Louis; The Morningside, Fairbanks Ranch and The Sherwood Country Clubs in California.

Royal Palm Yacht and Country Club in Boca Raton, Florida.

Resorts, Hotels and Inns

Resorts, hotels and inns are increasingly adding croquet to their selection of activities and this represents an exciting and positive trend for the sport. Facilities range in size from a single small court at a New England inn to full-size international level courts at major resort complexes and hotels.

These installations provide numerous aesthetic, social, recreational and promotional benefits, including an attractive and functional use of open space, plus an added sports and social activity for members, guests and local residents, who may also arrange to utilize the courts and amenities as the site for a local private USCA club. These hostelries also benefit from the ongoing publicity opportunities that surrounds croquet tournaments and events.

1

2

3

4

In 1987 a new program called the USCA Resort/Hotel/Inn Network was established to provide special services and attention to its member clubs in this category. Network participants who advertise in the US Croquet Gazette are provided with free omnibus listings in advertising placed by the USCA in croquet publications around the English speaking world.

In addition, if they have a sufficient number of adequate-sized, well-maintained courts (two to four), they may serve as sites for USCA teaching clinics/schools and qualify as a venue for a USCA sponsor supported tour event in the coming years. As a USCA member organization, the hotel/resort/inn can provide interested guests with individual USCA applications and enlist them as members of their non-resident "club." This attracts new upscale guests as well as encouraging frequent return visits.

USCA Resort/Hotel/Inn Network members include:

(1) The Breakers, Palm Beach, FL

(2) Blantyre, Lenox MA

(3) Gasparilla Inn,
    Boca Grande, FL

(4) Lantana Colony Club, Bermuda

(5) Meadowood Resort,
    St. Helena, CA

(6) Pointway Inn, Edgartown, MA
    and :

The Enchantment, Sedona, AZ; The Inn at Rancho Santa Fe, CA; Jekyll Island Club Hotel, GA; Madden's, Brainerd, MN; Meadow Lane Lodge, Warm Springs, VA; Palm Beach Polo & Country Club, West Palm Beach, FL; PGA Sheraton Resort, Palm Beach Gardens, FL and Pinehurst Resort & Country Club, NC.

5

6

207

Schools, Colleges and Universities

Schools, colleges and universities are adopting the sport. The USCA Collegiate activities were launched in November, 1980, with the Harvard and Yale Croquet Clubs' first competitive match. Since then USCA National Collegiate Championships have attracted teams from the Crimson and Blue, Brown, Princeton, Vassar, Columbia, Wellesley, University of Virginia, University of Florida, St. John's College, Washington & Lee, Catholic University, University of Miami, University of California (Berkeley) and the U.S. Naval Academy. As has been proven at Oxford and Cambridge in England, future USCA champions will come from intra-school tournaments (fraternities, sororities and campus clubs), plus inter-school, state, regional and national competitions.

The 1988 Yale Croquet team with coach Michael Charrier at right.

Retirement Groups and Communities

Retirement groups and communities represent another contingent that is expressing mounting interest. Croquet offers a great deal of enjoyment and satisfaction as a healthful competitive outlet for those unable to participate in more physically demanding outdoor sports.

Real Estate Developments

While many real estate community developers offer golf, racquet sports and aquatic amenities, relatively few, to date, have recognized the image building promotional advantages that croquet offers to their sales efforts. Urban developers who seek a unique consumer appeal, while conforming to local open or green space requirements, are finding croquet courts an ideal activity alternative.

Demographics

As the membership in the USCA mushroomed over the first decade it became clear that this phenomena was not a passing fad and that its roots were firmly set in some fairly well-to-do ground. This was not surprising, given the relatively high cost of installing good croquet courts. What was surprising, however, was the degree of affluence these early members and clubs had relative to such participants in sports as golf and tennis, whose formative expenses had to exceed those of croquet.

In 1987 the Croquet Foundation of America, in conjunction with the United States Croquet Association conducted the first demographic survey of the USCA membership.

Here are some of the highlights of this study:

WHO. . .
57% Male, 43% Female
Average age 43
58% 35 to 64 years old
Average Household Income: $150,000
25% Net Worth of $1,000,000 plus
88% Professional/Managerial

WHAT . . .
72% Married
94% Attended College
85% Own Home
Average Market Value $375,000
28% have additional properties
Average value $600,000

WHERE . . .
48 States (6 neighbor countries)
42% Florida, California and New York
75% Belong to Country Clubs
93% Travel (Average 13 trips)

Of the USCA clubs 68 percent were Family and Private, while Country, Tennis, Sports Clubs and Resorts, Hotels, Inns and Developments accounted for 26 percent and College, Historical and Retirement Communities, the other 6 percent.

The results of the full survey are available from the USCA.

THE CROQUET FOUNDATION OF AMERICA

The Croquet Foundation of America, Inc., is a non-profit [501 (C)(3)] organization dedicated to growth and development of the sport of croquet in the United States. Founded in 1979, its principal source of income is through the tax-deductible contribution of individuals, and the proceeds of the Annual Fall US Croquet Hall Of Fame Awards Dinner and special Croquet Balls, parties and events throughout the year by member-clubs and organizations.

By providing funds for the creation of educational materials, public information services and organizational assistance through the United States Croquet Association, the CF of A encourages the understanding and direct involvement of individuals and clubs ranging from school and college levels through Senior Citizens and Retirement organizations as to the social and recreational rewards of playing the sport of croquet.

US Croquet Hall of Fame members attending the 1988 awards dinner included (Back row, L to R) E.A. Prentis III, John Young, Nelga Young, Libby Newell, Jack R. Osborn, Barton Gubelmann, Herbert Bayard Swope, Jr. and Cathy Tankoos. Front row, 1988 Honorees, Fred Supper, (Mrs.) Ned Skinner (Kayla), and Cesare Danova.

15

U.S. CROQUET HALL OF FAME

(and Other Famous Folks and Media Friends of Croquet)

When something as old and familiar to most every American as croquet begins to enjoy, what appears to be, a sudden renewed popularity and vogue, the big question is always "Why?"

After all of the social, physcological and physiological attributes of the sport have been analyzed and sorted out the answer inevitably comes down to the people who have become involved, enveloped and then dedicated to sharing its challenge, fun and rewards with others.

Many of these good folks may have never been, nor ever will be "Great" players, but whose enthusiasm for, and support of, croquet has contributed immeasurably to the current re-emergence of the sport.

To attempt to recognize all of these boosters on these pages would be impossible, so instead we will identify some of those who have been chronicled in earlier literature on the sport including the inductees into the U.S. Croquet Hall of Fame, participants of "celebrity" and benefit croquet events as well as a few of the many friends from the fourth estate who have spread the good word over the years.

U.S. CROQUET HALL OF FAME

Each year the trustees of the Croquet Foundation of America consider individual nominees whose contributions to the growth and enjoyment of the sport of croquet in the United States would merit their induction into the U.S. Croquet Hall of Fame. Since 1979, its inaugural year through 1989, the following distinguished American croquet players have been elected.

MEMBERS OF THE U.S. CROQUET HALL OF FAME 1979-89

Pictures of many of these Hall of Fame inductees have appeared in prior pages of this book and identified in the captions.

Others are numbered and pictured here.

1. George Abbott*
2. Paul Butler*
   Cesare Danova
3. Margaret Emerson*
4. Raoul Fleischmann*
5 Andrew Fuller
   Samuel Goldwyn*
   John David Griffith*
6. Mrs. Walter Gubelmann
7. Mr. Walter Gubelmann*
8. William Harbach
   W. Averell Harriman*
9. Moss Hart*
   Howard Hawks*
10. William Hawks*
11. Milton "Doc" Holden*
    Louis Jourdan
12. George S. Kaufman*
13. John Lavalle*
    Mrs. Carvel Linden
    Tom Lufkin
15. Duncan McMartin*
16. Hilda McMartin*
17. Harpo Marx*
    Jean Negulesco
    Elizabeth B. Newell
    Jack R. Osborn
    Richard Pearman
    J. Archie Peck
18. Mrs. Ogden Phipps*
    Edmund A. Prentis, III
    E. A. (Teddy) Prentis IV
19. Richard Rodgers*
20. Mrs. Richard Rodgers
    Michael Romanoff*
21. George Sanders*
22. Fred Schock, Jr.*
23. David E. (Ned) Skinner*
    Frederick M. Supper
    Herbert Bayard Swope, Jr.
    Herbert Bayard Swope, Sr.*
    Catherine Tankoos
25. S. Joseph Tankoos*
26. Francis O. Tayloe*
27. S. Cortland Wood
28. Alexander Woolcott*
    Gig Young*
    John Young
    Nelga Young
    Darryl F. Zanuck*
 * Deceased

1.

2.

3.

5.

4.

8.

6.

7.

9.

10.

11.

12.

13.

15.

16.

17.

18.

19.

20.

21.

22.

23.

25.

26.

27.

28.

Other Famous Friends of Croquet

The first Hall of Fame Dinner in 1979 was held at The Tavern on The Green and was preceeded by a "Pro/Celebrity" event sponsored by Faberge at the New York Croquet Club Courts nearby. The winning "Celebrity" was Billy Talbert of Tennis fame.

Among those vying for the Faberge Cup held here by Georgette Mosbacher (then Mrs. George Barrie) were Margeaux Hemingway (left) and TV's Kristy Witker and Donna DeVarona.

Over the years many celebrated people from the worlds of music, movies, media, sports, theatre and television have picked up croquet mallets for charitable and promotional reasons or just plain love of the sport.

"60 Minutes" stars, Harry Reasoner and Morley Safer participated in the 1979 Hall of Fame Pro/Celebrity event. Morley later became a USCA Media Award winner for his croquet segment on the CBS show.

1. ABC TV's Peter Jennings,
2. Author, George Plimpton,
3. World boxing champ,
  Sugar Ray Leonard,
4. Canadian super songstress,
  Anne Murray
  (President of the
  Pugwash Mallet Club),
5. Jeopardy's Alex Trebek,
6. Bradway's Kevin McCarthy,
  John Callum and
  Jo Sullivan Loesser,
  and croquet buffs,
7. Larry Hagman,
8. and Chief Justice,
  William Rehnquist.

1

2

3

4

5

6

7

v

8

USCA AWARDS FOR OUTSTANDING CONTRIBUTIONS TO THE SPORT OF CROQUET BY THE MEDIA

"To what do you attribute the recent dramatic growth of the sport of croquet?" is the most frequently asked question by media representatives in interviews.

The answer, we honestly believe, is the mounting serious attention the ladies and gentlemen of the media themselves have given the sport via print and broadcast over the last several years.

What was barely a trickle a decade ago has become a flood of articles, stories and pictures from journalists across America and the rest of the English speaking world.

Since 1980, the USCA has endeavored to identify these individuals, and the media firms who employ their talents, in order to express its appreciation through the presentation of awards to those many contributors whose work has been deemed particularly outstanding.

Too many to list herein , we present a sampling on these two pages.

Palm Beach Daily News Sports Editor, Mike Strauss, shares anecdote while receiving his award from "60 Minutes" veteran Harry Reasoner.

Photographer of the Year Robert Phillips (two time winner for Travel & Leisure in 1982 and Town & Country, 1985) accepts award from CBS TV's Morley Safer.

Among other USCA media award winners are:

1. *Jane Pauley, NBC TV's "Today Show" whose Willard Scott also signaled fair weather for the USCA.*
2. *ABC TV's "Wide World of Sport" and Hughes Rudd,*
3. *Authoress, Town & Country and European Travel & Life contributing Editor, Nancy Holmes,*
4. *Sportscaster, Dick Schapp,*
5. *CBS TV's "On the Road," Charles Kuralt and,*
6. *Author, "Winning Croquet," writer (New York Times Magazine, New York Magazine & Vanity Fair) and bon vivant, Jesse Kornbluth.*

1.

2.

3.

4.

5.

6.

UNITED STATES CROQUET ASSOCIATION

The United States Croquet Association is the national not-for-profit organization for the development, coordination and promotion of the sport of croquet. Twenty years from conception to fruition, the USCA was formally launched in 1976 when its long time goal of codifying the rules of the American version of this centuries old sport was fulfilled. The USCA, with its growing list of Member Clubs, sponsors National, Regional and District Championships and sanctions Club Championships and other croquet events. The USCA is also responsible for the selection and sponsorship of the US National Team which competes with England, Scotland, Ireland, South Africa, Australia, Bermuda, Canada, New Zealand and other croquet playing nations.

16

UNITED STATES CROQUET ASSOCIATION RULES
(With a note on British and American Rules)

First published in "Croquet, the Complete Guide to History, Strategy, Rules & Records," by James Charlton and William Thompson (Scribner's, 1977) and subsequently in the book "Winning Croquet" by Jack Osborn and Jesse Kornbluth (Simon & Schuster, 1983), there have been six printings of the USCA Official Rulebook for American Six-Wicket, one-stake and Nine-Wicket, 2-stake Croquet.

Since their adoption in 1976, the rules of the American six-wicket game, as with the English Laws of Croquet over the past century, have been changed and modified as the game has grown in popularity. These rule changes are a natural evolution of the sport, the same as they have been for any other of our modern sports. They result not only from the desire but also the need to clarify the intent of the rules, simplify their interpretations, communicate the rules clearly by removing ambiguities and inconsistencies, encourage competition, and provide fairness and equity throughout the various levels of play. It is to this end that the USCA, through its Rules and Referees Committee, strives to incorporate these changes which will improve the sport while maintaining its character.

To those readers of this book who possess any of these earlier versions, we urge you to study the following newly revised rules with particular attention to the shift to the Standard Rules of those previously in the Advanced Rules section.

One should also note that the Advanced Rules section has been renamed Optional Rules.

Furthermore, a new section entitled Experimental Rules has been added. These rules are intended for use in occasional, non-tournament play in order to permit their testing by players over a trial period. It is hoped that the player input resulting from the use of these rules will give sufficient data to their impact on the game, resulting in either their rejection or adoption as USCA Official Rules. Experimental rules may not be used in any USCA sanctioned events unless prior notice of the intention to use one or more of these rules is provided the players.

To assist you in the enjoyment of the sport, the USCA publishes a pocket size (3¹/₂" x 6") version of the rules which is distributed to its members and is available to nonmembers by ordering through the USCA office.

Each of the convenient rule booklets consist of the following sections:

Section I—The Court and Setting, Equipment and Accessories
Section II—The Object of the Game
Section III—Customs and Etiquette
Section IV—Rules of the Standard American 6-Wicket Game and Advanced Game
Section V—Rules of the American 9-Wicket Game
Section VI—Rules of Golf Croquet and the Glossary

Since we have covered Sections I and II in Chapters 4 and 5 and will put the Glossary in the Appendices section, we will begin this printing of the Official Rules of the United States Croquet Association with the third section dealing with Customs and Etiquette.

Should you decide to take this book with you to the croquet courts we will further its usefulness with the following table of contents to help you locate the rules you will most certainly want to find fast in the course of a heated match.

Section III—Customs and Etiquette

Section IV—Six-Wicket Rules and Court Setting

Section V—Nine-Wicket Rules

Section VI—Golf Croquet Rules

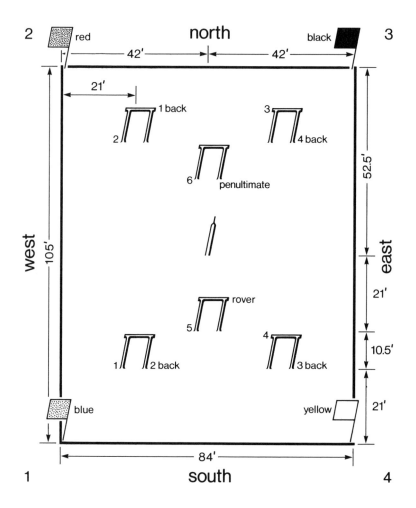

Official
United States Croquet Association
6-Wicket court layout

Smaller courts are frequently used based on available space

THE UNITED STATES
CROQUET ASSOCIATION
AMERICAN SIX-WICKET GAME

THE COURT AND SETTING,
EQUIPMENT AND COURT ACCESSORIES
Section III

CUSTOMS AND ETIQUETTE

The following, while not including specific rules or penalty related action, should be considered important and helpful to the conduct and enjoyment of the game.

Presence on Court

A player should not remain on the court in line of sight or area of distracting visibility while his opponent is playing, or move onto the court until play has finished.

Expedition of Play

A player should play as quickly as possible and in doubles should avoid wasting time in prolonged discussion with his partner (more than 45 seconds is considered excessive). In tournament play a 45 second time limit is usually enforced for each shot. While each player is entitled to the full amount of this time, near the end of time limit matches (usually 1 hour, 20-30 minutes) players should play expeditiously despite the desire to take as much time as possible to protect a lead in score.

Spectators

Spectators should abstain from audible comments on the game, from offering advice to players during a game, and from calling attention to any error committed or about to be committed by any player. A spectator may reply to a question by a player on a point of fact with the consent of his adversary. A player should not take advantage of any error or omission unnoticed by himself or his partner to which his attention has been drawn during the game by the comments or attitude of the spectators.

Advice and Aids

No player is entitled to advice from anyone other than his doubles partner. It must be a matter of conscience how a player acts after receiving unsolicited information or advice. Warning a player other than his partner that he is about to run a wrong wicket or play with the wrong ball constitutes advice, and in tournaments players and spectators should not so warn.

A mark should not be made, either inside or outside the court, for the purpose of guiding the striker in the direction or strength of a stroke. A partner may use his mallet to indicate a spot, but it should be removed before the stroke.

Calling Faults

As soon as a fault is observed by any player, it should be called. A fault must be called as soon as it is observed and a striker should call against himself any fault that he has committed.

Questionable Stroke

A player about to play a stroke, of which either the fairness or the effect (i.e., possible fault or when aiming at a ball in or near a wicket) may be doubtful, should himself suggest to his adversary that a referee be called to watch the stroke. The striker or opponent should signal for a referee or umpire by holding his mallet vertically above his head.

When the Players' Opinions Differ

If a ball has to be replaced because of the carelessness of a player, the offending party should ordinarily defer to the opinion of the other. When the question is whether a roquet has been made on a ball or whether the ball has moved, the positive opinion is generally to be preferred to the negative opinion. If there are any reliable witnesses, the players should agree to consult them in order to resolve the differences; but no player should consult a witness without the expressed permission of the other player.

Testing the Position of a Ball

The striker should not test whether a ball has run a wicket by placing his mallet against the wicket without first consulting his opponent. Any such test should be made by a referee if available or in conjunction with the opponent. The same principle applies when the question is whether a ball is out of bounds, or may be lifted, moved, or wiped, if the position of replacement is critical. Any such decisions made between strokes should be made jointly.

When Calling a Referee

In tournaments, a referee should always be called before a questionable stroke, and all disputes should be referred to a referee. If the opponent fails to call a referee before what he should have realized to be a questionable stroke, he should not appeal. He should confine himself to requesting the striker to take the initiative in calling for a referee if another such stroke is to be played. But it may be that the adversary is of the opinion that the striker is making faults such as "pushing" or "double tapping" in an unhampered stroke; if so, he should inform the striker with a view to a referee being called to watch a stroke.

Should any player feel that an opponent is making repeated faults (and the referee concurs), such as failing to move or shake the roqueted ball in his croquet stroke, he may request that a referee watch all such subsequent shots.

Standards of Conduct

Courtesy and good sportsmanship are required of all players, officials and spectators.

Players are under an obligation to avoid acts that may be considered detrimental to the game of croquet. It shall be so considered if during the course of a match a player swears at an official, spectator or opponent in a voice that can be heard by any person; uses profanity or insulting, abusive or obscene language in any way that may be heard by any person; uses obscene, insulting or abusive gestures; throws in any manner a mallet or deliberately throws or hits a ball in the direction of an official or the spectators.

Any spectator who, on behalf of a player before, during or after a match, abuses an official or player, will be warned and directed by the Tournament Director to desist. If the abuse continues, the person may be directed to leave the tournament area. In a case of flagrant abuse the directive to leave may be given without a warning. Any such instance should be reported to the Grievance Committee.

Umpires

An umpire is any person appointed at a tournament by a referee of that tournament to act with the following limited powers:

   a) As a referee to judge whether a ball hits another ball, moves or shakes the croqueted ball in the croquet stroke, or hits the stake in attempting to stake out.
   b) As a referee to judge whether a ball has completed the running of a wicket or is on or off the court.
   c) As a referee to judge any questionable stroke.

Section IV
THE RULES OF THE STANDARD AMERICAN SIX-WICKET GAME

PART 1. USE OF MALLET

1. A player must hit his ball with either striking face of his mallet. A bevelled edge adjacent to the striking face shall not be considered part of the face. A mallet head is usually nine inches in length (when it is not, a nine inch designation should be marked somewhere on the mallet for measurement purposes). He may hold any part of the mallet shaft but cannot touch the head of the mallet nor rest the shaft on the ground during the stroke. See Part 9, Penalties, Rule 55 a.

2. a) The striker may not push his ball. Note: A push means maintaining contact between mallet and ball for an appreciable period or any acceleration following a check of the mallet head after its initial contact with the ball. See Part 9, Penalties, Rule 55 a.

   b) The striker shall not strike his ball audibly or distinctly twice in the same stroke (double tap) or maintain contact between mallet and ball after his ball has hit another ball, except that no fault can be committed under this rule if the cause of the second hit is the result of a roquet. See Part 9, Penalties, Rule 55 a.

3. a) A stroke begins when the striker's mallet strikes the ball. A stroke ends when all balls set into motion as a result of the striker's stroke have stopped rolling or have crossed a boundary line.

   b) It shall be counted as a stroke if, with the intent of striking his ball, the player's mallet hits a wicket and not the ball, or if he drives his mallet into the ground without contacting the ball, or misses the ball entirely.

   c) A player may waive or pass his turn. He must audibly so declare by stating the color of the ball playing and the intention to waive the turn. Once the announcement has been made, the turn has finished and may not be replayed. A player who has waived out of turn is subject to Rule 47.

4. a) If a ball lies so that a player cannot strike it squarely, he may not place another mallet against the ball and hit that mallet with his own.

   b) The striker may not move or shake a ball at rest by hitting a wicket or stake with the mallet.

   c) The striker may not strike his ball so as to cause it to touch an upright or the stake while still in contact with the mallet (crush shot).

d) The striker may not strike his ball when lying in contact with an upright or the stake other than in the direction away from the upright or the stake (crush shot). For a, b, c and d above, see Part 9, Penalties, Rule 55 a.

5. In the course of the stroke the player may strike only his own ball without touching another ball with his mallet. See Part 9, Penalties, Rule 55 a.

PART 2. STARTING THE GAME AND WICKET #1

6. The toss of a coin determines the starting order of play. The side winning the toss has the choice of playing first and third with blue and black or second and fourth with red and yellow.

7. All balls must start from the starting area which is a space $12^5/8$ inches wide, three feet south of the first wicket parallel to the South Boundary so that a ball could be placed at either end of a mallet's head (nine inches) or anywhere within that area and be three feet from the wicket. Balls must start in order of colors shown descending on the center stake (Blue, Red, Black and Yellow) and they will play in that rotation until the end of the game or being put out of play by completing the course.

8. Any ball that has not made the #1 wicket cannot receive more than one stroke per turn.

9. A player who has not made wicket #1 may drive his ball and hit any other ball which has likewise not made that wicket, so as to put it into position, out of position, or through the wicket. This ends his turn unless his ball also makes a clear passage through the wicket, which entitles his ball to one continuation stroke. The other ball which has thus been put through the wicket shall be considered to have made the wicket but is not entitled to a continuation stroke.

10. A player who makes the #1 wicket is entitled to one continuation stroke (Exception:, Rule 21 a but is nevertheless dead on all balls that have not made #1 wicket. See Part 9, Penalties, Rule 55 a.

11. A player who drives through *any* wicket *in order* and in the same stroke hits a ball that has not made the #1 wicket is not penalized and is entitled to a continuation stroke (Exception:, Rule 21 a) with the other ball remaining where it lies.

12. Any ball that has made #1 wicket may not block or impede the stroke of any ball that has not made the #1 wicket. If it does, the offending ball is

marked and becomes ball in hand immediately preceding the turn of the ball not in the game and is replaced immediately after that shot. If the marked space becomes occupied by another ball, the lifted ball is then placed three feet directly north of the #1 wicket (which is also the #2 back wicket).

PART 3. MAKING A WICKET

13. To score a wicket point, a ball must make a complete passage through a wicket and in the proper direction. This shall be visually observed by seeing whether any part of the ball breaks the plane of the playing side of the wicket. This shall not be tested by placing a mallet against the approach side of the wicket.

14. A ball stopping in the wicket, or one which goes through but rolls back into it, has not made the wicket.

15.a)   If a ball is for a wicket but on the wrong side, it may be played through the wicket but must have completely cleared the non-playing side before it can be played back through in the proper direction on a subsequent shot.

   b)   A ball may take croquet from another ball located in the jaws of a wicket and run that wicket, provided that no part of the striker's ball breaks the plane of the non-playing side and is running the wicket in the proper direction.

16. A ball that is dead on another ball resting in the jaws of its wicket (as determined by encroachment into either the playing or non-playing side) may not hit that ball in trying to make the wicket. See Part 9, Penalties, Rule 55 a. A player may use the jump shot to make a blocked wicket or blocked stake but must not hit the blocking ball at any time during the shot (except after hitting the stake when staking out).

17. A ball that is dead on another ball lying beyond (not intruding into) a wicket may hit that ball while attempting to run the wicket but must make a complete passage through the wicket in order to be clear and receive a continuation stroke. Should the striker fail to completely clear the wicket, see Rule 33. Part 9, Penalties, Rule 55 a applies.

18. A ball running a wicket other than the one in the proper sequence or direction shall not receive credit for that wicket nor receive an extra stroke, except if it is a rover. See Part 7, Rule 39.

19. A side (either ball) may block (stymie) a wicket once with a ball (or balls) upon which the opponent is dead. The side must leave the opponent a clear shot at the wicket by the beginning of the blocked ball's second turn. If the side does not do so, the stymied ball will be deemed alive on

the blocking ball (or balls), provided that the blocking side is responsible for the stymie. In order to be blocked, a player must have a possible shot at making the wicket until a ball encroaches on that direct path.

The term "clear shot" shall mean that no part of any ball on which the striker's ball is dead is intruding in the direct path the striker's ball would take to score the striker's wicket or hampers the normal backswing of the striker's mallet should the striker attempt to run the wicket the striker is for. The term "possible shot" shall mean a shot at the wicket which, in the opinion of the referee, would be considered to have any chance of running the wicket the striker is for.

20. At the beginning of the game all clips shall be placed on the first wicket and upon making a wicket the player shall remove his clip and place it on his next wicket at the conclusion of his turn. For the first six wickets the clip is placed on the top or crown of the wicket and for the back six wickets the clip is placed on either side of the wicket. As clips serve as an aid to the players and do not necessarily denote the official status of the game, each player, referee or official scorer shall call attention to a misplaced clip, giving the correct wicket placement if requested by the player in question and the clip shall then be properly placed. Notice of a misplaced clip shall be mentioned as soon as it is observed.

PART 4. WICKET POINTS, ROQUET, CROQUET AND ADDITIONAL STROKES

21. Wicket Points:
   a) When the striker's ball has scored a wicket point the striker shall be entitled to play one continuation stroke. If the striker's ball or any other ball it hits in running the wicket goes out of bounds, his turn ends and each ball off the court is replaced one mallet's head (nine inches) in from where it crossed the boundary line.
   b) When a ball other than the striker's is caused to score a wicket point, it is said to have been peeled through that wicket but does not receive a continuation stroke.

22. a) During a turn the striker is entitled to roquet any ball he is alive on and receive two extra strokes (EXCEPTION: Rule 47). Upon making his proper wicket the striker becomes alive on all balls and receives one extra stroke (EXCEPTION: Rule 21 a).
   b) The striker makes a roquet when his ball hits another ball it is alive on, either directly or by glancing off a wicket or stake.
   c) When hitting two or more balls upon which he is alive in the

same stroke, the roquet will be deemed to have been made on the first ball hit with the second ball being replaced. If two balls are roqueted simultaneously, the striker has the choice of which one to play from.

d) A ball that has made a roquet cannot thereafter in the same stroke make or score a wicket point for itself.

23. A striker who makes his wicket and then roquets another ball in the same stroke, or who hits another ball he is alive on lying beyond (not intruding into) his wicket while attempting to run the wicket, is deemed to have made the wicket, provided the striker's ball makes a complete passage through the wicket. The striker must roquet that or another ball in the continuation stroke in order to receive two additional strokes. The ball hit, in either case, is not replaced (EXCEPTION: Rule 21 a). If, however, the striker hits a ball he is alive on lying beyond (not intruding into) his wicket and, while attempting to run the wicket, the striker's ball fails to make a complete passage through the wicket, he is deemed to have not scored the wicket; rather, he has made a roquet and must take croquet from the roqueted ball.

24. The Croquet Stroke:

a) When a roquet is made the striker's ball becomes a ball in hand and shall be brought to and placed in contact with the roqueted ball. (EXCEPTION: Rule 32.)

b) To take croquet, the striker must place his ball on the ground in contact with the roqueted ball however he chooses, but may not have his ball touching any other ball except the roqueted ball.

c) Before playing his stroke, the striker may touch or steady the roqueted ball and may further apply such pressure by hand or foot, but not by mallet, as is reasonably necessary to make it hold its position. He may not move any ball except his own intentionally, but if he does so unintentionally, he shall replace it without penalty.

d) The ball hitherto known as the roqueted ball is in the croquet stroke known as the croqueted ball.

e) The striker now takes the croquet stroke with the balls placed as in (b) above and by hitting into the croqueted ball must move or shake the croqueted ball.

f) If a player feels an opponent has repeatedly committed striking faults such as pushing, double tapping or failing to move the roqueted ball on the croquet stroke, he may summon the referee to watch subsequent strokes. See Part 9, Penalties, Rule 55 a.

g) After the croquet stroke, the striker shall be entitled to play an additional stroke unless his turn has ended under Rule 46 or he has made another legal roquet, whereafter he takes croquet from that ball.

h) The striker may not place his foot or hand on his ball during the croquet stroke.

i) After each stroke any ball, except the striker's, less than nine inches off the boundary is replaced that length from the line. If that ball cannot be replaced directly in from the line from where it rests due to the presence of another ball, it may at the discretion of the striker be placed nine inches in from the line and up to nine inches in either direction from, but not in contact with, the ball. Should two balls be sent over the boundary the first ball out is replaced first. If two balls come to rest within nine inches from the boundary at the same place, the closest to the boundary is replaced first.

j) A ball may be placed in bounds by an adversary only if the adversary has the consent of the striker to do so.

25. Any player may handle any ball which is replaceable after contact, or may return any ball which has made a roquet to its player without penalty. A player may place a ball for his partner's croquet stroke to save time, and may give a temporary mark which must be removed before the stroke is taken. A player may lift his ball to clean it at any time during the game, but must advise his opponent before doing so. Any ball accidentally moved shall be replaced without penalty. (EXCEPTION: Rule 51 a.)

PART 5. BISQUES

26. A bisque is a handicap stroke wherein the striker is allowed to replay a shot from its original position on the court. A bisque may be taken only if the ball can be replaced accurately. The intention of taking a bisque need not be announced before the original shot is made, however, care shall be taken to mark the ball accurately when in a critical position.

27. A bisque may be taken only for the immediately preceding stroke.

28. A bisque may be taken on any infringement or fault except for a ball played out of turn. See Rule 47.

29. A player may take more than one bisque per turn.

30. a) In doubles matches, the averaging method will be used. This is done by averaging the partners' handicaps to determine the average strength of the partnership. For example, a 2 and a 4 will average 3. A 5 and a 7 will average 6. The difference between

each team's average handicap represents the difference in their strengths and the higher handicap team will receive bisques equivalent to this difference. In the example above, the difference would be 3 bisques. Where the difference between the average handicaps results in a one-half bisque this is moved up to the next full number (for example $2\frac{1}{2}$ bisques becomes 3 bisques).

b) Only the higher handicap player in the team receiving a bisque(s) may use the bisques. When both players on the side receiving a bisque(s) have the same handicap then either player may use the bisque(s). For example, a side receiving three bisques may decide that one player uses all three bisques or that one player uses two bisques and the other player one bisque, at their discretion.

31. In singles matches, a player may use his handicap quota between both balls. The two opponents will net out the difference in handicaps and where the handicaps are the same no bisques will be given. Where the handicaps differ, the lower handicap plays at zero while the higher handicap player receives the difference between the handicaps (example: player A has 2 bisques, player B has 4 bisques; therefore, player A plays at zero and player B plays at 2).

PART 6. DEAD BALL

32. When a striker's ball roquets another upon which it is alive, it is immediately ball in hand and dead on that ball until the player has made his next wicket in order, but he must play off it as in Rule 24 b. EXCEPTION: When the striker's ball roquets a ball out of bounds, his turn ends, but he remains alive on that ball, which is replaced one mallet's head (nine inches) from where it went out.

33. If a striker's ball hits a ball on which it is dead (except after a roquet), the striker's turn ends and all balls shall be replaced. EXCEPTION: During a croquet stroke, the ball being croqueted may be hit by the striker's ball more than once without penalty.

34. If the striker's ball roquets one it is alive on and thereafter during the same stroke hits another ball, whether alive or dead on it, the latter shall be replaced without penalty (i.e., no penalty if out of bounds, or credit for wicket or stake). The player must play off the first ball hit and is not dead on the second ball if originally alive on it.

35. If during a croquet stroke the striker's ball hits another ball upon which it is dead, the turn ends, and the ball just roqueted and the striker's ball are replaced with the croqueted ball remaining where it lies after the

stroke and given credit for any wicket or stake point made. If, however, in a croquet stroke, the striker's ball hits a ball on which it is alive, it has then made a roquet on that ball and must play off it as in Rule 24 b.

36. a) Any third or fourth ball struck (cannoned) by a roqueted or croqueted ball will be treated as having been played directly, with all balls remaining where they lie at the end of the stroke. The struck ball is given credit for wicket or stake points if made and no deadness is credited between the roqueted or croqueted ball and the cannoned ball. If no fault has occurred, the striker may then take his next stroke. If any ball (except the striker's on the roquet stroke) goes out of bounds, the striker's turn ends, all balls remain where they lie, and any out of bounds ball is replaced nine inches in from the boundary where it went out.

b) Special relief from deadness: When each ball of both sides passes through the 1-back wicket, the opposing side may (or may choose not to) clear the deadness from one of its balls. The side eligible to receive this relief must declare which ball it chooses to clear before playing the first shot of its next turn or no relief is given. However, this declaration may not be required to be given prior to that time.

c) Should the striker peel his opponent through the 1-back hoop, the striker will have an option to clear either his or his partner's ball. If the peel is accomplished on the roquet stroke, the striker may clear himself but must place his ball in contact with the roqueted ball and play his croquet stroke and is considered dead on the croqueted ball. If the peel is accomplished on the croquet stroke, the striker may clear himself on all balls and play his continuation stroke as if he had just scored a wicket. When a striker peels the opponent through the 1-back wicket he must clear one of his balls, if he so chooses, before the next stroke of his turn.

d) A rover ball may be cleared of deadness on 1, 2 or 3 balls when an opponent scores 1-back but may not be cleared of last deadness.

e) When a player declares which ball he is clearing of deadness after an opponent passes through the 1-back wicket (provided both of his balls have some deadness) the first color declared to be cleared shall be the one cleared and may not subsequently be changed.

37. A ball becomes alive on all balls upon being driven through its next wicket in order and in the proper direction.

PART 7. ROVER AND FINISHING THE GAME

38. A ball that has made all the wickets in the proper sequence becomes a rover and is considered alive on all balls upon making the rover wicket (red crown).

39. To become alive from a 2- or a 3-ball deadness, a rover may go through any wicket in any direction, receiving a continuation stroke. If the ball does not clear the wicket, it must, unless knocked out, continue through in the same direction in order to be considered clear. A rover may receive a continuation stroke for having made a wicket only if he was 2- or 3-balls dead.

40. a) A rover may roquet any other ball only once per turn. See Part 9, Penalties, Rule 55 a. Before clearing himself he must be dead on at least 2 balls, but nevertheless he remains dead on the ball last hit (last dead) until he hits another ball whereupon his temporary deadness disappears.

   b) A rover that runs a wicket in clearing its deadness and in the same stroke hits a ball upon which it was last dead incurs no penalty, and unless either ball is driven out of bounds, both balls remain where they lie and the striker is entitled to take his continuation stroke.

41. A rover ball may hit the stake itself or be driven into the stake by another rover, whereupon it will be considered to have finished the game, provided no fault occurred.

42. When one ball of a side has staked out of the game it is removed from the court immediately and play continues in proper rotation, without the staked out ball.

43. If, in a roquet shot, a striker's rover ball drives another rover ball into the stake, the roqueted ball is removed from play and the striker receives two strokes, the first taken nine inches in any direction from the stake.

44. The game is won by the side that finishes the game with both balls first, or in a time limit game by the side scoring the highest total of wicket and stake points.

PART 8. FAULTS AND PENALTIES FOR OUT OF BOUNDS, PLAYING OUT OF TURN, PLAYING THE WRONG BALL, ILLEGAL SHOTS AND CONDONED PLAY

45. A ball is out of bounds when its vertical axis crosses the boundary line (more than halfway over). It shall be replaced one mallet's head (nine inches) from where it first crossed the line, or, if in a corner, one mallet's head (nine inches) from both boundaries.

46. If the striker sends any ball out of bounds, his turn ends. See Part 9,

Penalties, Rule 55 b. (EXCEPTION: If, after a roquet, the striker's ball either goes out of bounds or caroms another ball out. See Rule 32.)

47. If a ball plays out of turn, all balls are replaced with no deadness incurred and proper play is resumed with the offending side losing its turn (example: if black plays when it was blue's turn, the balls are replaced and blue loses its turn; if black plays when it is the opponent's turn, the balls are replaced, the proper opponent plays and the next player for the blue/black side loses its turn).

48. If the striker plays a foot or hand shot his turn ends. See Part 9, Penalties, Rule 55 a.

49. If an opponent observes the striker playing a stroke with any ball (except the striker's, in his continuation or croquet stroke), not placed nine inches in from the boundary line, he may request that the shot be replayed from the proper position providing he does so before the next stroke of the turn. If he does not so request the replay, the shot will be deemed condoned.

50. If a player plays a ball other than the ball he started the game with, his turn ends. See Part 9, Penalties, Rule 55 a. In a singles game, a striker playing the wrong partner ball shall be considered to have played out of turn with the penalty as in Rule 47.

51. a) If a player, in attempting to strike his own ball, touches (with his foot or mallet) another ball, his turn ends and both balls are replaced.

   b) If, after striking his ball, the striker interferes with his ball in any way, his ball and all other balls affected by the stroke shall be replaced and the turn shall end.

   c) If a ball is interfered with by an outside agent, except weather, or accidentally by an opponent, in any way that materially affects the outcome of the stroke, that stroke shall be replayed. Otherwise, the ball shall be placed, as nearly as can be judged, where it would have come to rest, provided that no point or roquet can thereby be made.

52. If the striker plays his ball from a misplaced position, all balls are replaced to their correct position and the striker replays that stroke without penalty. Misplaced position refers to a striker taking croquet when not entitled to, taking croquet from a wrong ball, or lifting to an incorrect position. (This Rule does not supersede Rule 24 b.)

LIMIT OF CLAIMS

53. a) A fault or misplay shall be called by the striker or opponent as soon as it is discovered but must be called before the opponent

plays the first stroke of his next turn or the error is automatically condoned.

b) Any player, referee, or official shall bring attention to any misplacement error as soon as it is noticed. The limit of claims as in Rule 53 is in effect for unnoticed errors.

c) If an out-of-turn fault is discovered by either side after two or more turns have been played (and condoned), play shall continue in the new sequence with all wicket points, deadness, or faults incurred during any turn up to that turn in which the fault is discovered being deemed valid.

54. If a player makes any stroke or strokes as the result of any incorrect information concerning the state of the game supplied by the adversary or referee, he shall have the right to replay. This shall apply to the deadness board accuracy as well as accuracy of the placement of the clips provided the opponent or referee has confirmed this incorrect information beforehand.

PART 9. PENALTIES

55. The following penalties shall apply as noted in the preceding rules:
   a) All balls are replaced and the turn is over.
   b) All balls shall remain where they lie (balls out of bounds or less than nine inches in bounds being placed nine inches in from the boundary) and the turn is over.

PART 10. REFEREES

56. The role of the referee is to resolve disputes between players by referring to the Rule Book. Any situation that does not appear to be covered by these rules shall be decided by the best judgment of the referee.

57. A referee shall not intervene unless asked by the players except that the referee may correct clip placement, deadness board, misplacement of balls, and may make time announcements.

58. In the absence of an appointed referee, the players will act as their own joint referees, but there is an obligation on the adversary to watch the game, and if he fails to do so, the striker is, during such period, the sole referee. In doubles, all players share the rights and duties of a referee, and a reference to the striker includes his partner.

59. If, during a tournament match, a player fails to request that an adversary call a referee to observe a questionable stroke before it is taken, he may not appeal. Otherwise he may appeal as in Rule 66.

PART 11. TOURNAMENT PLAY

60. For each tournament there shall be a tournament director selected who shall be empowered to: administrate, interpret and enforce the Rules of the Game; appoint a committee to assist and provide referees, time-keepers and deadness board attendants; arrange the draw; assign handicaps; schedule matches; assign courts and otherwise direct all aspects of the competition, including the disposition of any appeal by players or teams not resolved by a referee.

61. In tournaments, game and shot time limits may be set by a tournament committee before the start of the first tournament game. These time limits may be increased or decreased by the committee at the conclusion of each full round (e.g., first, quarter, or semi-final rounds) as overall time and weather conditions dictate.

62. In a time limit game each player will be allowed 45 seconds to strike his ball following the completion of the last stroke by either side. The game clock continues, and the shot clock starts for the next stroke, at the conclusion of the previous stroke (see Part 1, Use of Mallet, Rule 3a) unless the next player to play requests the clocks be stopped until the balls off the court are replaced prior to his stroke. The timekeeper will announce when 15 seconds remain in the time allotted for the next stroke and will call "Time" when the 15 seconds has elapsed. Should the player not have struck his ball his turn ends and play resumes with the next player, after replacing balls displaced by the striker after time was called. Each side is entitled to receive two (2) one-minute time out periods to be taken only during that side's turn.

63. The timekeeper shall announce when fifteen minutes remain in the game, and again when one minute is remaining and declare "Match Time" when that minute has elapsed, taking particular care to note whether the striker's ball was in play when match time was called.

64. a) When "Match Time" is called, the player in play shall complete his turn (which is his last), and each remaining ball shall have one turn in rotation. The side that has scored the greatest number of wickets and stake points is declared the winner, but if there is a tie, play shall continue in full rounds until the tie is broken or both balls of one side stake out.

b) After "Match Time" has been called, a one-minute official's time-out may be requested by any player in his own turn to determine and announce the wicket score at that point. At the conclusion of that time-out, play shall resume under the 45 second per stroke limit until the tie is broken and the game has ended as in (a) above.

65. In doubles tournaments, where one player is absent at the beginning of play, that player's partner may place the absent player's ball in the starting area and waive that and any subsequent turn or, may wait for the shot time limit to expire.

66. a) If, during the course of a tournament, either the players or the referee are unable to resolve a question of fact or rule, they may appeal to the tournament director, who shall decide accordingly. If he, by coincidence, happens to have been a witness and is satisfied that he knows the answer, he shall inform the players that he is deciding the subject matter of appeal by observation, and give his decision accordingly. If he is not so satisfied, he should decide the dispute by investigation. He should hear what the parties have to say; at his discretion he may hear witnesses. He shall then give a decision to the best of his ability. If he is in doubt, he may, in the last resort, give a compromise decision, which may involve adjusting the clips arbitrarily and directing where the balls shall be placed. This includes the right to decide that the players shall replay the disputed play or begin the game again.

b) A referee or tournament official may call for a time-out or stop play at any time during a match to adjudicate any dispute, delay or postpone completion of a match due to inclement weather or court conditions. The time taken by these official actions will be added to the time left in the match when play resumes.

PART 12. WIRING

67. A ball is said to be wired from another ball if:

a) Any part of an upright of a wicket or the stake or another ball on which the striker is dead would impede the direct course of any part of the striker's ball toward any part of another ball upon which it is alive.

b) Any part of a wicket, stake or third ball so interferes with any part of the swing of the mallet prior to impact between mallet and ball that the striker, with his usual style of play, cannot, in order to make a roquet, drive his ball freely toward any part of another ball he is alive on when striking the center of his ball with any part of the face of his mallet.

c) Any part of the striker's ball is within the jaws of a wicket.

The mere interference of a wicket or stake or third ball with the stance of the striker does not constitute wiring.

68. If, at the beginning of a turn, the striker's ball (in rotation) is wired from all balls on which it is alive, and if the adversary is responsible for its position, then the striker may lift his ball and place it in contact with any ball on which it is alive and then play his croquet stroke. But if instead of lifting, the striker waives his turn then, unless the striker has lost a turn as a result of having played out of turn, he is deemed to be responsible for that ball's position.

69. If the next ball to play is dead on all three other balls, it may be left in any position on the court without being considered wired under this rule.

OPTIONAL RULES

The following rule is to be considered OPTIONAL by tournament directors and, if used, players MUST BE SO ADVISED ON THE ENTRY FORM:

REVISED WIRING RULE
OPTION TO RULE 68

If at the beginning of a turn the striker's ball (in rotation) is wired from all balls on which it is alive, and if the adversary is responsible for this position, then the striker may lift his ball and place it on any part of either baulk line and play from that location. But if instead of lifting, the striker waives his turn or elects not to lift, then he is deemed to be responsible for that ball's position.

Playing out of turn constitutes responsibility for a ball's position.

EXPERIMENTAL RULES

The following rules are to be considered experimental and are set forth here to permit testing by USCA players. Subsequent to a 12 month trial period, one or more of these rules (or some modification of them based on player input) may be considered for adoption as official rules of the USCA at such time as the USCA Rules and Referees Committee and USCA Management Committee have sufficient data on their impact on the game to make a decision as to their appropriateness. Until such rules are officially adopted and published as official rules in a supplement or future edition of this rule book, they may not be used in any USCA sanctioned events, unless notice of the intention to use one or more of these rules are provided to the participants on all player notification and entry forms prior to the tournament. However, players are actively encouraged to experiment with these rules in occasional, non-tournament play and provide the USCA with their comments and experiences.

STARTING THE GAME

Experimental Rule #1 (modification to Rule 12)

Any ball that has made #1 wicket may not block or impede the stroke of any ball that has not made the #1 wicket. Nor, conversely, may any ball that has not made #1 wicket block or impede the stroke of any ball that has made #1 wicket. If either occurs, the offending ball is marked and becomes ball-in-hand immediately preceding the turn of the blocked or impeded ball and is replaced immediately after the shot of the blocked or impeded ball. If, as a result of that shot, the marked space becomes occupied by another ball, the ball now occupying the space is lifted and placed in the #1 (blue) corner, in accord with Rule 24 i and Rule 45, and the originally lifted ball is then replaced on the marked space.

The term "block" as it relates to this rule only, means that any part of the offending ball intrudes in the direct path the striker's ball intends to take or lies beyond the striker's wicket less than a ball width from the playing side of the wicket if the striker's shot intends to be an attempt to make his wicket. The term "impede" means to hamper the normal backswing of the striker's mallet.

Experimental Rule #2

The game begins by each ball, in turn (beginning with blue), attempting to make the #1 wicket from the starting area. Any ball that fails to run (score) the #1 wicket, either intentionally or unintentionally, immediately becomes ball-in-hand until it is once again its turn in rotation. It is then again placed within the starting area and makes another attempt to run #1 wicket. This procedure continues until all balls are through the #1 wicket and in the game.

Experimental Rule #3

The game begins by each ball, in turn (beginning with blue), being placed within the starting area. As soon as a ball is placed within the starting area, it is in the game and live on all other balls which have already been placed in the starting area.

In using either Experimental Rule #2 or #3, players should assume that all other references in the rule book to balls "in the game" or balls "not in the game" be considered deleted.

Experimental Rule #4 (modification of Rule 26 and deletion of Rules 27, 28 and Section b of Rule 30)

A bisque is a handicap wherein the striker is allowed to replay a shot from its original position on the court or take an additional continuation stroke.

A replay bisque may be taken for any immediately preceding stroke except for an out of turn fault (see Rule 47). The intention to take a replay bisque need not be announced before the original shot is made, however, since a replay bisque may be taken only if the ball can be replaced accurately. The ball should be marked prior to taking the original shot if it is in a critical position.

A continuation bisque may be taken only following a continuation stroke earned as a result of a roquet.

THE 9-WICKET GAME

On the following pages are the rules for the 9-wicket, 2-stake croquet game as codified by the United States Croquet Association.

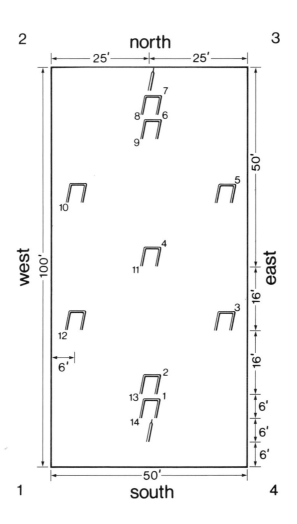

9-WICKET LAYOUT WITH MEASUREMENTS

The layout and direction of play on the official
United States Croquet Association 9-wicket court.

Many of the rules are the same in both the 9-wicket and 6-wicket game. To avoid unnecessary duplication, when the rules are the same, we have not spelled out the 9-wicket rule but, rather, have referred to the 6-wicket section. When the 9-wicket rule is different, the variation is spelled out in full.

THE STANDARD COURT

The standard court is a rectangle, with the length twice the width (50 by 100 feet is recommended). Its boundaries shall be marked out clearly, the inside edge of the definitive border being the actual boundary. (Nylon string stapled or otherwise affixed to the ground can be used for boundary lines.) The court may be scaled down proportionately, but smaller than 30 by 60 feet is not recommended.

THE STANDARD SETTING

Two stakes shall be set one at each end of the court, 6 feet from the adjacent end's boundary line, and equidistant from each side of the boundary line. The first and seventh wickets shall be 12 feet from the adjacent end line and equidistant from each sideline. The second and sixth wickets shall be 18 feet from the adjacent end line and equidistant from the two sidelines. The fourth wicket shall be set at the center of the court, equidistant from the side boundary lines. The far outside wickets (the third, fifth, tenth and twelfth) shall be set 34 feet from the adjacent end line and 6 feet from the adjacent boundary line. For smaller modified courts these dimensions may be reduced proportionately.

THE WICKETS

The wickets are the same as the 6-wicket game, except they are all painted white.

THE STAKE, THE BALLS AND THE MALLETS

The stake, the balls and the mallets remain the same as in the 6-wicket game.

THE COURT ACCESSORIES

Accessories are the same except clips are placed (as in Rule 20) on the top of the wicket for the first seven wickets and on the side for the last seven.

THE OBJECT OF THE GAME

SINGLES

The singles game is played between two players, of whom one plays the blue and black, the other the red and yellow balls. The object of the game is for a player to make both his balls score the 28 wicket points and 4 stake points, a total of 32 points, before his adversary.

DOUBLES

The doubles game is played between two sides, each side consisting of two players. One team plays the blue and black balls and the other the red and yellow balls. Each player plays only one ball throughout the game. As in singles, the object of the game is to have one team score the total of 32 points before its adversaries.

IN BOTH GAMES

A ball scores a wicket by passing through the wicket in the order and direction shown on a previous page. This is known as running a wicket. But a ball which has made a roquet cannot thereafter in the same stroke carom off that ball and score a point for itself. A ball which has scored all 14 wickets and the upper stake points is known as a rover. It can then score the stake point by hitting it.

HOW PLAY IS MADE

Play is made by striking a ball with a mallet. For the essentials of a fair stroke, see Part 1 of the 6-Wicket Game. The player so playing is called the striker, and the ball that he strikes, the striker's ball. The striker may never strike an adversary's ball. By striking his own ball, the striker may cause any other ball to move and to score a point.

THE TURN

The players play each turn in sequence (Blue, Red, Black and Yellow). A player is initially entitled to one stroke in a turn, after which his turn ends, unless in that stroke his striker's ball has scored a wicket or stake point or hit another ball. When the wicket or upper stake is scored, the striker is entitled to play one continuation stroke. When another ball is hit, the striker is said to have made a roquet on that ball. He becomes dead on that ball and is entitled to two extra strokes. The first of these two strokes is known as the croquet stroke, and is made after moving and placing the striker's ball in contact with or up to one mallet head away from the roqueted ball, which,

243

if in contact in the croquet stroke, is known as the croqueted ball. If in the croquet stroke the croqueted ball is sent off the court, or the striker's ball is sent off the court without first having made another roquet, the turn ends. During a turn the striker may roquet each ball he is alive on once, and he may make a further roquet on each ball provided that, since he has last roqueted it, his striker's ball has scored a wicket or upper stake point for itself and has thus cleared itself of its "deadness." Thus, by a series of strokes entitling him to continue, the striker may make one or more points, during one turn. Such a series is known as "making a break." But continuation strokes are not cumulative, so that a striker who:

a) scores a wicket or upper stake and hits another ball in the same stroke may take one continuation stroke or roquet the ball and take two;

b) makes a roquet in a croquet stroke, immediately takes croquet and continues accordingly;

c) scores a wicket or upper stake for his striker's ball in a croquet stroke, plays only one continuation stroke;

d) scores two wickets or one wicket and the upper stake for his striker's ball in one stroke, plays only one continuation stroke.

BALL IN HAND, BALL OFF THE COURT AND REPLACEMENT OF BALLS OFF THE COURT AND NEAR BOUNDARIES

All are the same as in the 6-wicket game.

STRATEGY

Along with the basic objective of scoring 32 points first, each team or player (in singles) should employ those offensive or defensive moves that will restrict the progress of the opponents as in the 6-wicket game.

This version should be played as diagrammed, and the exceptions of the American 6-wicket rules amended as noted.

PREFACE RULES

1. The Start: Each player must place his ball on a pre-designated spot between the first wicket and the lower stake (3 feet in front of the wicket). Upon striking a ball, the player is in the game and is considered "alive" on all other balls in the game. Play progresses in rotation. Various clubs rule that a ball struck through the first or upper two wickets in one shot is entitled to two extra strokes. This is an optional local rule with the preferred rule being only one extra stroke for making both wickets.

2. Upper Stake Rule: The upper stake, when hit in proper order, rewards the player one extra stroke, removes any prior deadness and counts as one point (i.e., is treated as having made a wicket).

3. Rover Rule: Only when a rover ball is caused to strike the final stake by a partner or its player is that ball considered to have completed the game and is removed from the field (NOTE: partner must also stake-out for the team to win.)

4. Should an opponent cause a rover ball to hit the final stake, the player so staked must remove his ball for his next two turns, and on his third turn (in rotation) must place his ball one mallet length or less from the final stake and hit up to the upper stake. In that shot, or subsequent turns, the player must hit the upper stake to return to the game as a rover (last deadness rule still stays in effect).

   a) Only one rover may be staked out by the opponent at any one time. There is no limit to the number of times an opponent can stake out a rover ball.

   b) A rover staked out by an opponent is not in the game until hitting the upper stake and shall be treated as if he did not exist (i.e., no one can play off him nor can he play off another) until hitting that upper stake, at which point he receives one extra stroke.

With the above as basic rule differences, the following are direct rule references to be used with the Standard American 6-Wicket Croquet Rules.

PART 1. USE OF THE MALLET
Rules 1 through 5 are consistent with those for the 6-wicket game.

PART 2. STARTING THE GAME
6. Same as the 6-wicket game.

7. All balls must start from the starting tee one yard in front of the first wicket in the order shown on the stake (blue, red, black and yellow) and must continue in that order throughout the game, or until put out of play. Upon striking the ball, a player is in the game and is considered "alive" on all other balls in the game.

8 and 9. These rules do not apply in 9-wicket croquet.

10. Rule 10 is the same, except a player is alive on all balls that have played into the game but have not made this wicket.

11 and 12. These rules do not apply in 9-wicket croquet.

PART 3. MAKING A WICKET

Rules 13 through 19 are exactly the same.

20. The placement of clips is as in the 6-wicket game but with the clips placed on the crown for the first seven wickets and on one of the uprights for the final seven wickets.

PART 4. WICKET POINTS, ROQUET, CROQUET AND ADDITIONAL STROKES

21. Same as in the 6-wicket game except that in 9-wicket play hitting the upper stake in proper order rewards the player one extra stroke, removes any prior deadness and counts as one point (i.e., is treated as having made a wicket).

22. Roquet: The same as in the 6-wicket game.

23. A player who makes his wicket, or hits the upper stake and hits a ball on the same play, must hit that ball again to receive two extra strokes from it. Unless he has driven either ball off the court in that same stroke, the striker may elect to take one continuation stroke and shall not be considered dead on the ball so hit. The hit ball is not replaced.

24. The Croquet Stroke: Optional rules for (A) Advanced (contact) or (B) Standard 9-wicket (mallet head) play are described below, and the choice of which is to be followed should be agreed upon by all players prior to a game.

SPECIAL NOTE: The USCA urges all serious players to opt for the contact version of the rule above as it will surely improve all other 2-ball (croquet) strokes with practice and better prepare you for Association level play anywhere in the world.

    A)   Advanced (9-wicket croquet stroke): This is identical with 6-wicket Rule 24 a through 24 i in that the striker's ball must be placed in contact with the roqueted ball and must then cause that ball to move or shake during the first (croquet stroke) of the two strokes it has earned for having made the roquet shot.

    B)   Standard (9-wicket croquet stroke):

        a) The same as in 6-wicket croquet.

        b) After roqueting a ball upon which it is alive a player must either:

            1) bring his own ball to a mallet head or part thereof from the roqueted ball and play two strokes from there, but he may not place his own ball through or under a wicket, or:

     2) place his ball in contact with a roqueted ball and play a croquet stroke and then his second stroke, or:

     3) place his ball against the one hit and hold it by foot or hand while driving the other away, and then play his second shot. Under no circumstances may a player, in taking any of the above shots, place his ball out of bounds.

  c) The same as in 6-wicket croquet.

  d) and e) The same if played in contact.

  f) Optional if playing contact.

  g) The same as in 6-wicket croquet.

  h) A foot or hand shot is optional for standard 9-wicket game but not recommended for the advanced version.

  i) The same as in 6-wicket croquet.

25. The same as in 6-wicket croquet.

PART 5. BISQUES

26 through 31, concerning bisques and bisque use in handicap play, are the same for both the 6-wicket and the 9-wicket game.

PART 6. DEAD BALL

32 to 35, concerning "deadness," are the same for both versions.

36. a) The same as in 6-wicket game.

  b) Optional rule for 9-wicket version provides relief of deadness for an opponent's ball when each ball hits the upper (or turning) stake (as occurs at the 1-back wicket in the 6-wicket game).

37. The same as in the 6-wicket game. The ball is considered alive when it is driven through a wicket or against the upper stake.

PART 7. ROVER AND FINISHING THE GAME

38. A player who has made all the wickets and the upper stake in proper sequence becomes a rover and is considered alive on all other balls.

39. To clear (or become alive) from two- or three-ball deadness, a rover may go through any wicket in any direction or hit the upper stake, receiving an extra stroke. If the ball does not clear the wicket, it must, unless knocked out, continue through in the same direction in order to be considered clean.

40. The same as in the 6-wicket game.

41. Only when a rover ball is caused to strike the final stake by a partner or its player is that ball considered to have completed the game and is removed from the field (NOTE: partner must also stake-out for the team to win). OPTIONAL RULE: Only a rover can stake out another rover (as in the 6-wicket rules).

42. Should an opponent cause a rover ball to hit the final stake, the player

so staked must remove his ball for the next two turns and, on his third turn (in rotation), must place his ball one mallet length or less from the final stake and hit up to the upper stake. In that shot or subsequent turns, the player must hit the upper stake to return to the game as a rover (last deadness rule still stays in effect).

43 and 44. When one ball of a side has staked itself out (or been staked out by a rover partner ball), it is removed from the court immediately, and play continues in proper rotation with the staked-out ball losing all subsequent turns.

PART 8. FAULTS

45 to 47. The same as in the 6-wicket game.

48. (See optional Rule 24B, h above.) If playing a foot- or hand-shot version and the player's foot or hand loses contact with his ball, his turn ends and both balls remain where they lie.

49 to 54. The same as in the 6-wicket game.

PART 9. PENALTIES

55. The same as in the 6-wicket game.

PART 10. REFEREES

56 to 59. The rules dealing with referees and their duties are the same for both versions of croquet.

PART 11. TOURNAMENT PLAY

60 to 66. The rules for tournaments apply to both the 6- and 9-wicket games.

RULES OF GOLF CROQUET

In the United States, as in the United Kingdom, golf croquet is played on a 6-wicket, 1-stake court layout as outlined below. It may, however, be played on a 9-wicket, 2-stake court by modifying the direction of play.

The rules relating to singles and doubles play apply subject to the following modifications:

1. The Course.
   a) Balls are played into the game from one mallet length from the center stake. In a short version, 7 points are contested; the first 6 wickets and number 1 wicket for a second time for the seventh point.
   b) When 13 points are contested, the first 12 points are as in croquet. The thirteenth point is the third wicket. When 19 points are contested, the wickets 1-back to the rover are contested twice before contesting the third wicket. The stake is not contested.

2. The Game.
   a) All balls are always for the same wicket in order. The point is scored for the side whose ball first runs the wicket.
   b) A short game is a contest for the best of 7 points, a middle length of 13 points and a long game for the best of 19 points. The game ends as soon as one side has scored a majority of the points to be played. It is customary to keep the tally of the score by declaring a side to be one or more points up or down or all square as the case may be.
   c) Each turn consists of one stroke. The rules relating to roquet, croquet and continuation strokes do not apply.
   d) The balls are played in the sequence blue, red, black, yellow. The opposing sides use blue and black, and red and yellow.

3. Running a Wicket. If a striker causes one of the balls of his side partly to run a wicket during a stroke, such a ball need not begin to run the wicket afresh before it can be scored by that ball in any subsequent stroke. If an adversary causes a ball partly to run a wicket during a stroke, such a ball may run that wicket in a subsequent stroke. If a ball runs two wickets in one stroke, it scores both wickets for its side. The wicket point is scored by a ball that is cannoned, peeled or roqueted through a wicket by an opponent or partner. (For advanced play, see Rule 8 below.)

4. Jump Shot. A player may not deliberately make his ball rise from the ground. If he does so accidentally or in ignorance of this rule, and in consequence runs a wicket for his striker's or partner's ball, the point shall

249

not be scored. Likewise, if in consequence thereof any ball is displaced, such a ball may be replaced at the option of the adversary side.

5. Advancing a Ball Prematurely for the Next Point. A player must play so as to contest the wicket in order rather than seek to gain an advantage for the next wicket in order. But a player bona fide contesting the wicket in order by, for example, attempting to cannon another ball, may legitimately play the stroke at the strength calculated to bring his ball to rest nearer the next wicket in order.

6. Playing Out of Turn or with a Wrong Ball. If the striker plays out of turn or with the wrong ball, that stroke and any subsequent strokes are null and void. All balls shall be replaced; the right ball shall be played by the correct player, and the other balls shall follow in due sequence. No points made during the period of error shall be scored. Any dispute should be settled by a referee.

7. Methods of Handicapping. Handicaps shall be allotted in the 13-point game according to USCA handicaps as follows:

USCA HANDICAP	GOLF CROQUET HANDICAP		
	7-Point Game	13-Point Game	19-Point Game
0	0	0	0
1 to 2	1	1	2
3 to 4	1	2	3
5 to 7	2	3	5
8 to 11	2	4	6
12 to 15	3	5	8
16 to 20	3	6	9

Notwithstanding the above provisions, special Golf Croquet handicaps may be given.

8. Advanced Play. In advanced play the foregoing rules apply except that Rule 3, Running a Wicket, is modified so that if a striker causes one of the balls of his side partly to run a wicket during a stroke, such a ball must begin to run such a wicket afresh before it can be scored by that ball in any subsequent stroke. However, the provision that if an adversary causes a ball partly to run a wicket during a stroke, such a ball may run that wicket in a subsequent stroke remains valid. A partner ball which has failed to clear the wicket on its own stroke may not be so driven through by his partner unless that ball was put into the wicket by an opponent.

A NOTE ON BRITISH AND AMERICAN RULES

Until the turn of the century all croquet-playing countries played the basic 4-ball game in a sequence of turns where blue would start, red would follow, then black and finally yellow would play; then the same rotation would be repeated until the game ended. England changed that law in 1920 in favor of the "either ball" or non-sequential game. This means that when it is the blue and black side's turn to play, either ball may be played no matter which had played during the player's turn. If a player wishes, he may continue to play the same ball each time it is his turn regardless of sequence.

The USCA rules retain the sequence rule.

Another key rule shared by all in 1900 was that involving the continuation of deadness by one ball on another. At that time, it was decided that a ball that was dead on another remained dead until that ball had made or cleared its next wicket in its proper order.

The British Association had changed this law by 1909, enabling all balls to be cleared of any deadness incurred previously at the start of each ball's next turn.

The USCA retains the rule that all deadness continues until the next wicket has been cleared.

Another differing rule has to do with roqueting (hitting) another ball off the court.

The British allow the striker to rush another ball out of bounds on his roquet stroke and continue to play after replacing that ball 36 inches into the court.

In the USCA rules, your turn ends if you knock another ball off the court on the roquet stroke. Both balls are brought in 9 inches—but you are not considered dead on that ball.

These three fundamental rules mark the primary difference in the British and U.S. Association games and call for strategies and tactics that, although we are at last playing on the same six wicket "pool table," are as different as 8-ball pool is from the rotation version of the game.

There are advantages and disadvantages to playing both games. On the surface, it would appear that the English game is easier and presumably faster. It gives you the freedom to hit balls off the court from any distance. It allows you not to be overly concerned about getting dead on other balls, because you will be clear on your next turn. And it gives you the choice of playing either of your side's balls at any time you choose.

In practice, however, English-rule games can and do run on for as many as five or six hours. Often it appears that the object of the game, that is, making wickets, has been forgotten altogether, as opponents jockey to pick up breaks and disdain shots at wickets unless they're only a foot away. The result is less than thrilling from the spectators' standpoint. But remember, Aunt Emma was born in England.

In International tournament play, a match consists of the best of three games so that in scheduling the event, provision is made for only one match a day.

In spite of our seemingly more complex needs to remember rotation and deadness, which compound the number of factors to be taken into consideration in planning tactics, the USCA game seems to race along. Because Americans *have* to make wickets to remove deadness, we shoot for them from dismaying distances. As a result, American games can and most often do end within an hour and a half, which is the time limit most often set in USCA tournament play. In fairness, the British Association rules tend to encourage better shot-making skills, owing to their forgiving nature.

The difference between the American (USCA) rules and the English (International) Laws as played today can be largely attributed to the psychological aspects of each countries' sporting upbringing. As explained to me by my old friend and competitor, Dr. William Ormerod, during our U.S. versus Great Britain tour in 1985, the national sport in England is not really soccer (or football, as it's known there) but Cricket. British Cricket match fans, he patiently explained, are quite accustomed to packing lunches for day long games. These matches occasionally extend, with the customary breaks for tea, for as many as five days and can end in a tie. No bother, the participants and fans alike seem perfectly content with the marathon contest, winner or not.

American spectators, by contrast, have cut their sporting teeth on contests that are resolved within predictable time limits along with shot clocks to insure a reasonable pace in the action and, with rare exception, do not end in a tie. Basketball and football's appeal to Americans is rooted in the interaction of their faster moving participants. Sport by our definition involves "torque" or the "give and take" between competitors. Our faster game under USCA rules, simply seems to better match our nation's sports psyche.

Understandably, a set of universally accepted rules would be most beneficial to the sport worldwide, but we see little likelihood of achieving this goal in the near future. Be it temperament or tempo, we Americans appear to favor the intellectual challenge of our more tactical version and enjoy playing it with a marvelous spirit and gusto.

Fortunately, for the sport worldwide, there are leading international players who have recognized some of the virtues of the American game, particularly those involving the reduction of the length of the matches so as to make the possibility of television coverage more likely. As a result, they have invented another version of their game appropriately named "Short Croquet." This new innovation, along with the USCA American Rules and golf croquet have been fully recognized by the new World Croquet Federation.

The USCA salutes the indomitable spirit of the English croquet player which has endured the invasion of lawn tennis in the late 1800s and World War II.

GLOSSARY

alive—a word for a ball that has cleared a wicket, and thus is said to be "alive"—able to play—on all other balls.

all-around break—a player running all the wickets in a single turn.

approach shot—a shot designed to place the ball into position to clear its next wicket or to roquet another ball.

Aunt Emma—an overly cautious, uninspired and altogether dull player whose aim is to clear not many wickets but one wicket per turn.

ball-in-hand—a ball that, after hitting another ball or going out of bounds, must be picked up and moved.

bisque—a handicap consisting of an extra stroke given to weaker players in order to equalize the game. It allows a player to replay a shot from the spot where it was originally taken. The bisque is sometimes called a "take-over."

break—an unbroken series of wickets run by a single ball in combination with another ball (a two-ball break), two other balls (a three-ball break) or all the balls in play (a four-ball break).

break down—make an unsuccessful shot or commit a fault, thus causing a turn to end.

bye—a position on a tournament ladder where the player is without an opponent. He then advances to the next round without playing.

cannon shot—a combination shot, in which 1) a roquet is made on the same stroke as the croquet stroke, or 2) the croqueted ball is driven into a third ball to displace it.

clearing (or cleaning)—becoming "undead" by running a wicket, or being relieved of deadness under the rules.

clips—markers made in the same colors as the balls which are placed on wickets to indicate which wickets the balls are going for next and in which direction on the court they are going.

condoning—failure of a player to claim a foul within the limit of claims.

contact—a move in which, after a roquet shot, the player places his ball in contact with the ball he has just roqueted and prepares to take croquet.

continuation shot—an extra shot, earned by clearing a wicket. Also, the shot taken after the croquet stroke.

corner—make a defensively shrewd shot into a corner.

Croquet Association, The—the British governing body founded as the All England Croquet Club.

croquet stroke (or shot)—the stroke in which, after a player roquets another ball, he places his ball next to the roqueted ball and, by striking his ball, moves both balls.

cross wire (or peg)—a leave in which the opponent's balls are left on each side of a wicket or peg, thus preventing them from hitting each other.

crush shot—an illegal shot used to knock a ball through a wicket so that during the stroke the mallet, ball and upright are all in contact at the same time.

cut rush—a single-ball shot that is played so that the roqueted ball (the "rushed" ball) goes off at a desired angle.

deadness—describing a player who has roqueted another ball. He is said to be "dead" on that ball—that is, he cannot play off that ball again—until his ball clears its next wicket.

deadness board—a board placed on the sidelines to aid the players and spectators in keeping track of which balls are "dead" on other balls.

double banking—playing two separate games on the same court at the same time with two sets of different-colored balls.

double elimination—a type of tournament in which a player must lose two matches in order to be eliminated.

double tap—a fault in which the striker's ball is accidentally hit twice in one stroke.

double target—two balls placed close together so that the target area is, in effect, doubled.

drive shot—a shot made by hitting squarely on the ball during the croquet stroke, causing the forward ball to go about three times farther than the striker's.

fault—an unacceptable stroke, or an action resulting in a penalty.

flags—visual aids to mark the corners of the croquet court.

foot shot—a croquet shot taken with the striker's foot on the ball, legal only in backyard croquet.

forestalling—claiming a misplay when a player observes that an opponent has committed or is about to commit a fault and stops him before his next stroke.

four-ball break—the mainstay of successful croquet, a break that uses all four balls to make a number of wickets, ideally allowing the striker to take his ball all the way around the court.

half-bisque—an extra shot used in handicap doubles and in some singles games, allowing the striker to re-take a shot but not allowing him to clear the wicket and score a point with the take-over shot.

hoop—used interchangeably with "wicket."

hoop-bound—describing a stroke or swing that is impeded by the wicket.

is for—the next wicket a ball must clear, as in "red 'is for' the second wicket."

jaws—entrance to the uprights of a wicket.

join up—play a ball to a spot near its partner ball.

jump shot—a shot in which the ball is struck so that it leaves the ground, thus avoiding an obstructing ball, wicket or stake.

laying a break—positioning balls at future wickets so that they can be used to set up breaks.

leave—the position on the court where a player leaves his and the opponents' balls at the end of his turn.

limit of claims—the time during which a fault may be called.

out of bounds—describing a ball whose vertical axis has crossed the boundary line.

pass—to waive or pass up a turn.

pass roll—a croquet stroke that sends the striker's ball farther than the croqueted ball.

peel—to cause a ball other than one's own to make its next wicket.

peg—the center stake.

peg-out—the final shot of a game, when a ball scores the peg or stake point.

penultimate—the next to last wicket.

pioneer ball—in a three-ball or four-ball break, the ball that is sent ahead to the wicket that is one beyond the wicket you are going for.

pivot ball—the middle ball in a four-ball break, usually left in the middle of the court.

pull—in the croquet shot, the tendency for a ball to curve in from its line of aim.

push—keeping the mallet head on the ball after hitting it, allowable only on the croquet shot, and then only if the mallet doesn't speed up after making contact.

questionable stroke—a play of doubtful legality, or one that has a large possibility of leading to a foul. When the striker anticipates such a play, he should call for the referee to observe the shot before he attempts it.

roll shots—a croquet shot in which both balls travel along the same line. Variations include the half roll, the three-quarter roll and full and pass rolls.

roquet—a shot in which the striker's ball hits another upon which it is alive. It is followed by a croquet shot and then a continuation stroke.

rover—a player whose ball has made the last wicket, or a ball that has cleared the final wicket but has not yet hit the peg.

running a wicket—hitting a ball through a wicket so that a mallet head run down the approach side of the wicket does not touch the ball.

rush—a roquet that sends the roqueted ball to a predetermined position.

rush line—a line extending between the ball about to be rushed and its intended target spot. A player imagines the rush line to assist him in determining a rush stroke.

scratch player—as in golf, a player who receives no handicap (bisque).

sight line—a line usually set lengthwise on top of the mallet head to aid the player in aiming the direction of his stroke.

smasher—a wooden hammer used to drive wickets into the ground.

split shot—a croquet shot that sends the two balls at divergent angles.

stalk—to stand behind the ball and walk toward it in order to be sure it is properly aimed.

sticky wicket—a particularly tight wicket that is difficult to clear without getting stuck in its jaws.

stop-shot—a croquet shot that sends the croqueted ball much farther than the striker's ball.

striker—the player whose turn it is to play.

stroke—a movement of the mallet in the process of striking a ball, whether the ball is successfully struck or not.

stymie—a ball blocking the intended path of the striker's ball when the striker's ball is dead on it.

take-off shot—a croquet stroke in which the croqueted ball moves very little and the striker's ball moves a greater distance.

take-over—see "bisque."

tice—a shot that places the striker's ball in a position where the opponent is tempted to shoot at it and miss (from "entice").

time limit—in USCA tournament play, usually $1^1/_2$ to 2 hours, but may vary depending on the number of courts and entrants.

waive—to pass up a turn. The ball is then considered to have been placed where it lies.

wicket—a straight- or curved-topped arch, usually made of iron, through which a ball must be driven (synonymous with "hoop" in England).

winter wickets—bent iron wickets often used when the ground is hard or frozen.

wired ball—a ball behind a wicket or peg which can't be hit by the striker's ball because of the obstruction.

UNITED STATES CROQUET ASSOCIATION
RECORDS 1977-1988

USCA NATIONAL CHAMPIONS
SINGLES – USCA RULES

Year	Winners	Runner-Up
1977	J. Archie Peck, Palm Beach	Jack R. Osborn, NY
1978	Richard Pearman, Bermuda	Jack R. Osborn, NY
1979	J. Archie Peck, Palm Beach	Richard Pearman, Bermuda
1980	J. Archie Peck, Palm Beach	Arthur Bohner, NY
1981	Richard Pearman, Bermuda	Jack R. Osborn, NY
1982	J. Archie Peck, Palm Beach	Richard Pearman, Bermuda
1983	Ted Prentis, Florida & NY	Richard Pearman, Bermuda
1984	James Bast, Phoenix	Kiley Jones, NY
1985	Ray Bell, Arizona	John C. Osborn, NY
1986	Reid Fleming, Puget Sound	Debbie Prentis, Palm Beach
1987	John C. Osborn, NY	Ray Bell, Arizona
1988	Reid Fleming, Puget Sound	Dana Dribben, FL

DOUBLES – USCA RULES

Year	Winners	Runner-Up
1977	Jack Osborn & Archie Peck	Nelga & John Young
1978	Ted Prentis & Art Bohner	Jack Osborn & Archie Peck
1979	Jack Osborn & Archie Peck	Ted Prentis & Art Bohner
1980	Ted & Ned Prentis	Dick Pearman & John Young
1981	Ted & Ned Prentis	Dick Pearman & John Young
1982	Archie & Mark Burchfield	Jack Osborn & Archie Peck
1983	Kiley Jones & R. Illingworth	Archie Peck & Dana Dribben
1984	James Bast & Ray Bell	Dick Pearman & John Young
1985	Dana Dribben & Ray Bell	Jack & John Osborn
1986	Dana Dribben & Ray Bell	Reid Fleming & Tremaine Arkley
1987	A. Burchfield & Damon Bidencope	John C. Osborn & Kiley Jones
1988	Ted Prentis & Bart Richardson	Lisle Guernsey & Carl Behnke

SINGLES – INTERNATIONAL RULES

Year	Winners	Runner-Up
1987	Bob Kroeger, Boston	Reid Fleming, Puget Sound
1988	Damon Bidencope, California	Kiley Jones, New York

DOUBLES – INTERNATIONAL RULES

Year	Winners	Runner-Up
1987	Tremaine Arkley & Reid Fleming	Ray Bell & Damon Bidencope
1988	Kiley Jones & Ted Prentis	E. McClatchy & D. Bidencope

USCA NATIONAL CLUB TEAM CHAMPIONSHIPS

Year	Winners	Runner-Up
1980	New York Croquet Club	Westhampton Mallet Club
	Jack Osborn & Ted Prentis	Al Heath & Ned Prentis
1981	New York Croquet Club	Aulander Croquet Club
	Jack Osborn & Ted Prentis	Francis Taylor & Mac Penwell
1982	New York Croquet Club	Arizona Croquet Club
	Jack Osborn & Ted Prentis	James Bast & Stanley Patmor
1983	New York Croquet Club	Palm Beach Polo & Country Club
	Jack Osborn & John Osborn	Dana Dribben & Ted Prentis
1984	Arizona Croquet Club	New York Croquet Club
	Ray Bell & Ed Cline	Richard Illingworth & Kiley Jones
1985	Arizona Croquet Club	New York Croquet Club
	Ren Kraft & Don Stallings	Jack Osborn & John Osborn
1986	New York Croquet Club	Palm Beach Polo & Country Club
	Jack Osborn & John Osborn	Dana Dribben & Ted Prentis
1987	Stamping Ground Croquet Club	Palm Beach Croquet Club
	Archie Burchfield & Ren Kraft	Ellery McClatchy & Dan Shepherd
1988	New York Croquet Club	Willamette Croquet Club
	John Osborn & Kiley Jones	Tremaine Arkley & Reid Fleming
1989	Bald Head Island	The Croquet Club at PGA National
	Harper Peterson & Reid Fleming	Chuck Reif & Jim Rule

US/INTERNATIONAL CHALLENGE CUP

1981	USA – 1	ENGLAND – 15
1982	USA – 8	SOUTH AFRICA – 10
	USA – 7	SCOTLAND – 7
1983	USA – 11	BERMUDA – 5
	USA – 15	CANADA – 1
1984	USA – 8	AUSTRALIA – 16
1985	USA – 11	IRELAND – 13
1986	USA – 17	*INTERNATIONAL CHAMPIONS – 13
1987	USA – 7	GREAT BRITAIN – 23
1988	USA – 39	**INTERNATIONAL CHAMPIONS – 33

*Great Britain, Scotland, South Africa, Canada and Bermuda
**Great Britain, Scotland, South Africa, Ireland, Canada and Bermuda

SOLOMON TROPHY MATCHES – International Rules

1988	GREAT BRITAIN – 20	USA – 1
1989	GREAT BRITAIN – 15	USA – 5

PRESIDENT'S MATCHES – USCA (American) Rules

1988	GREAT BRITAIN – 5	USA – 4
1989	GREAT BRITAIN – 6	USA – 3

USCA NATIONAL GRAND PRIX RANKINGS

These ratings are based on the final standings of all individual competitors entered in major USCA Sanctioned events, including:

USCA National Singles Championships
USCA National Doubles Championships
USCA National Club Team Championships

Five USCA Regional Championships,

USCA State/Sectional/District Championships
USCA Club Invitationals
USCA Club Championships

Regions: S=Southern M=Mid Atlantic N=New England
C=Central W=Western I=International

1983 USCA Grand Prix Rankings

RANK	PLAYER	REGION	DOUBLES	SINGLES	TOTAL
1	Prentis, T	S	155.18	253.30	408.48
2	Osborn, J C	M	177.43	153.20	330.63
3	Arnett, R B	C	120.32	202.40	322.72
4	Burchfield, A	C	116.45	176.60	293.05
5	Jones, K	M	156.13	138.00	294.13
6	Osborn, J R	M	181.91	93.50	275.41
7	Dribben, D	S	180.23	93.20	273.43
8	Pearman, R	I	57.72	213.40	271.12
9	Peck, A	S	146.73	108.30	255.03
10	Bell, R	W	76.26	174.40	250.66

1984 USCA Grand Prix Rankings

RANK	PLAYER	REGION	DOUBLES	SINGLES	TOTAL
1	Osborn, J C	M	1,352.12	1,023.65	2,375.77
2	Jones, K	M	1,359.10	973.04	2,368.14
3	Bell, R	W	1,546.14	611.63	2,157.77
4	Bast, J	W	943.69	1,025.31	1,969.00
5	Young, J	I	946.41	.894.37	1,840.78
6	Osborn, J R	M	1,321.66	469.51	1,791.17
7	Pearman, R	I	826.15	684.16	1,510.31
8	Dribben, D	S	853.59	536.83	1,390.32
9	Illingworth, R	M	1,141.00	244.99	1,385.99
10	Peck, A	S	729.40	447.99	1,177.39

1985 USCA Grand Prix Rankings

RANK	PLAYER	REGION	DOUBLES	SINGLES	TOTAL
1	Osborn, J C	M	4,957.13	5,260.95	10,218.08
2	Osborn, J R	M	4,622.89	3,526.62	8,149.51
3	Bell, R	W	2,927.45	4,630.33	7,557.78
4	Erwin, J	M	3,258.86	3,270.42	6,529.28
5	Young, J	I	3,316.71	2,454.28	5,770.99
6	Degnan, D	M	2,174.16	3,483.12	5,657.28
7	Dribben, D	S	3,860.23	1,559.34	5,419.57
8	Prentis, D	S	2,813.12	1,806.37	4,619.37
9	Burchfield, A	C	554.02	3,862.19	4,416.21
10	Young, N	I	2,251.67	2,157.93	4,409.60

1986 USCA Grand Prix Rankings

RANK	PLAYER	REGION	DOUBLES	SINGLES	TOTAL
1	Osborn, J C	M	5,934.07	5,010.92	10,944.98
2	Prentis, D	S	5,895.98	4,893.33	10,789.32
3	Erwin, J	M	6,681.17	3,564.25	10,245.42
4	Dribben, D	S	6,963.83	2,042.72	9,006.55
5	Young, J	I	5,009.11	3,934.80	8,943.91
6	Bell, R	W	4,901.86	3,963.35	8,865.21
7	Fleming, R	W	3,801.18	4,695.49	8,496.67
8	Osborn, J R	M	5,775.31	2,221.59	7,996.90
9	Hiltz, W	M	3,914.08	1,850.41	5,764.50
10	Arkley, T	W	3,801.18	1,733.18	5,534.36

1987 USCA Grand Prix Rankings

RANK	PLAYER	REGION	DOUBLES	SINGLES	TOTAL
1	Osborn, J C	M	7,641.21	7,653.73	15,294.93
2	Burchfield, A	C	8,043.92	3,927.43	11,971.36
3	Jones, K	M	5,999.48	5,724.98	11,724.46
4	Bidencope, D	W	7,221.52	3,992.95	11,214.47
5	Osborn, J R	S	6,586.69	4,170.97	10,757.66
6	Bell, R	W	4,516.16	6,233.62	10,749.77
7	Young, J	I	5,777.20	4,910.30	10,687.49
8	Pearman, R	I	5,260.82	4,792.26	10,053.09
9	Arkley, T	W	5,816.05	4,189.74	10,005.80
10	Prentis, D	N	5,644.61	4,310.62	9,955.24

1988 USCA Grand Prix Rankings

RANK	PLAYER	REGION	DOUBLES	SINGLES	TOTAL
1	Fleming, R	W	5.873.04	12,834.84	18,707.89
2	Prentis, T	S	11,685.54	5,792.55	17,478.10
3	Jones, K	M	9,958.60	6,264.37	16,222.97
4	Bidencope, D	W	9,532.99	6,449.61	15,981.91
5	Osborn, J C	M	11,366.84	3,637.28	15,004.12
6	Gibbons, M	M	8,403.82	5,447.34	13,851.17
7	Spooner, N	W	8,034.08	5,770.19	13,804.28
8	Young, J	I	7,219.40	5,115.63	12,335.03
9	Kroeger, R	N	4,771.29	7,380.74	12,152.03
10	Osborn, J R	S	8,2250.85	3,563.31	11,814.16

1988 USCA SANCTIONED TOURNAMENTS INCLUDED IN GRAND PRIX RATING

USCA NATIONALS:
USCA National Club Team Championships, Palm Beach Gardens, FL
USCA National Singles and Doubles Championships, Palm Beach Gardens, FL
International Rules Championship, Bourbonnais, Illinois

USCA NATIONALS:
Western: St. Helena, California
Central: Bourbonnais, Illinois
Mid-Atlantic: Long Island, New York
New England: Newport, Rhode Island
Southern: Boca Grande, Florida

USCA STATE CHAMPIONSHIPS:
California: Sonoma
Florida: Palm Beach Gardens
Georgia: Greensboro
Maine: Kennebunkport
Massachusetts: Bolton
Minnesota: Brainerd
New York: New York City
North Carolina: Bald Head Island
Oregon: Independence

INVITATIONALS:
Addison Hill Invitational, GA
Arizona Open, AZ
Austin Mallet Invitational, TX
Bald Head Island Invitational, NC
Beach Club Invitational, FL

Blossom Cove Invitational, MA
Delaware Invitational, DE
Edgartown Mallet Club, MA
Everglades Invitational, FL
Green Gables Invitational, NJ
Madden's Resort Invitational, MN
Meadowood Domaine Mumm Classic, CA
Pine Mallet Invitational, NC
Palm Beach Invitational, FL
Port Royal Invitational, SC
San Francisco Open, CA
Sky Farm Invitational, NH
Southern California Invitational, CA
Stark Lane Invitational, NH
Texas Croquet Classic, TX

CLUB CHAMPIONSHIPS:
Arizona Croquet Club, AZ
Bald Head Island, NC
Beach Club, FL
Bombay Mallet & Wicket Club, USVI
Greenbrier Croquet Club, WV
New York Croquet Club, NY
Palm Beach Croquet Club, FL
Perrysburg Croquet Club, OH
Croquet Club at PGA National, FL
Roxbury Croquet Club, NJ
San Francisco Croquet Club, CA
Quantuck Bay Croquet Group, NY
Westhampton Mallet Club, NY

1988 USCA GRAND PRIX RANKINGS (TOP 500)

1988 Rank	1987 Rank	Player's Name	Region	Singles Points	Doubles Points	Total Points	Events Used
1	11	FLEMING, REID	W	12834848	5873046	18707894	5
2	78	PRENTIS, TED	S	5792553	11685547	17478100	7
3	3	JONES, KILEY	M	6264371	9958604	16222976	5
4	4	BIDENCOPE, DAMON	W	6449617	9532298	15981915	5
5	1	OSBORN, JOHN C	M	3637283	11366842	15004125	7
6	21	GIBBONS, MIKE	M	5447343	8403827	13851171	9
7	127	SPOONER, NEIL	W	5770199	8034086	13804285	6
8	7	YOUNG, JOHN	I	5115634	7219402	12335036	9
9	26	KROEGER, ROBERT	N	7380744	4771290	12152033	7
10	5	OSBORN, JACK R	S	3563310	8250853	11814163	9
11	20	GUERNSEY, LISLE	W	2525237	8727416	11252653	6
12	137	RICHARDSON, BART	S	2041920	9058532	11100452	9
13	16	DEGNAN, DON	M	2901069	8149385	11050454	9
14	12	DRIBBEN, DANA	S	6227276	4729986	10957261	3
15	2	BURCHFIELD, A	C	3113638	7841539	10955177	3
16	28	BEHNKE, C	W	1868183	8341097	10209280	3
17	9	ARKLEY, T	W	3173111	6872162	10045273	5
18	194	ESTRADA, FRANK	W	2223130	7332889	9556019	6
19	81	PETERSON, HANS	W	3709442	5801822	9511264	6
20	138	ESQUIVEL, SAL	W	2753435	5801822	8555258	6
21	18	REEDY, RICHARD	C	2281755	5867364	8149119	5
22	19	KARLOCK, MERLIN	C	1762182	5867364	7629546	6
23	79	SMITH, C B	W	3927038	3605404	7532442	6
24	128	WATKINS, MIKE	S	856692	6511420	7368112	5
25	25	YOUNG, NELGA	I	2225010	5043840	7268851	9
26	31	BAITSCHOVA, LILA	M	2258419	4612897	6871316	9
27	36	COOPER, TOM	M	2227502	4558579	6786081	7
28	13	PENWELL, MAC	S	3312224	3434606	6746830	5
29	48	HUGHES, JIM SR.	M	2426343	4266567	6692911	6
30	63	KRAFT, R	W	985914	5630324	6616238	4
31	14	MYER, ALBERT	N	2616545	3945945	6562490	5
32	34	PEARCE, ELSTON	S	1606638	4869150	6475788	9
33	24	HULL, DAVE	N	3308301	2958420	6266721	6
34	45	McCLATCHY, E	S	751785	5505024	6256809	9
35	76	MILES, JIM	S	2660422	3561092	6221514	9
36	97	RULE, JIM	S	1397772	4752465	6150237	9
37	66	HOY, WILLIAM	S	2987598	3053603	6041201	7
38	88	REIF, CHUCK	S	1221271	4717645	5938916	9
39	30	KAYDEN, XANDRA	N	2062845	3781830	5844675	7
40	80	DOLE, PATTY	W	453537	5381026	5834564	6
41	27	BESSETTE, BUTCH	S	1359378	4464160	5823538	5
42	96	HUGHES, TOM	M	2147254	3657186	5804440	6
43	17	JANITZ, WALT	C	1363619	3909235	5272854	4
44	910	HULL, PETER	N	2211074	3054854	5265929	4
45	683	STARK, J	W	845069	4300539	5145608	4
46	69	ARRINGTON, J	N	1626270	3373992	5000262	8
47	93	RHEAULT, GERRY	N	2337691	2547809	4885500	6
48	67	BARKER, K	C	2668156	2151731	4819886	3
49	89	COLES, TOM	M	2194903	2619226	4814129	4
50	484	LONG, LARRY	C	740891	3963071	4703963	4
51	15	BALLENGER, P	W	1106702	3561466	4668168	5
52	43	ERWIN, JIM	M	1971735	2598505	4570240	4
53	82	GUTHERIE, T	S	194137	4368384	4562521	6
54	813	MABEE, CARLTON	N	1292353	2974076	4266430	5
55	71	YOUNT, ROBERT	S	603997	3639571	4243568	8
56	272	WEIMERSKIRCH, MIKE	C	1599946	2420912	4020858	4
57	107	LAWFORD, BETTY	M	2699469	1317907	4017376	8
58	62	CARTER, FOXY	N	753474	3175628	3929102	5
59	65	SCHMID, HANK	S	570796	3253644	3824440	5
60	10	PRENTIS, D	N	1261799	2340577	3602376	5
61	59	SIMONTON, JEFF	M	1742570	1802108	3544677	6
62	689	TAYLOR, JOHN	W	771237	2617341	3388578	8
63	640	MAHONEY, D	S	611490	2714946	3326795	7
64	288	BERNE, BILL	S	931292	2373572	3304864	7
65	61	HILTZ, WILL	M	1503820	1799635	3303455	4
66	333	McGONAGLE, T	C	879120	2420912	3300032	4
67	135	BERNSTEIN, D	N	850352	2401530	3251882	4
68	38	LESEUR, HEIDI	I	1161545	2061566	3223111	5
69	8	PEARMAN, R	I	1197379	1974278	3171657	3
70	266	COTE, JON, SR.	N	731369	2394493	3125862	6
71	267	COTE, JONATHON	N	606958	2394493	3001450	6
72	70	GIBBONS, CYNTHIA	W	489349	2489225	2978574	9
73	195	LAYTON, CHRIS	W	854173	2079064	2933238	7
74	22	SHEPHERD, DAN	S	1474161	1362675	2836836	6
75	115	CAMPBELL, WILLIAM	W	688327	2087018	2775345	8
76	281	PETERSON, HARPER	S	433559	2276276	2709835	7
77	56	HEATH, AL	M	1129550	1567387	2696937	7
78	90	CLAYTON, ROBERT	M	848806	1840983	2689788	8
79	111	RIPLEY, FRANKLIN	S	1292353	1388642	2680995	4
80	122	HUGHES, JIM JR.(JAY)	M	966346	1397593	2363939	3
81	819	CHAMBERS, BARRIE	I	0	2337323	2337323	1
82	39	KELLEY, RORY	W	0	2335251	2335251	2
83	110	TANKOOS, CATHY	S	328653	1911190	2239842	5
84	167	MAHONEY, W	M	1207933	967043	2174976	2
85	620	KARLOCK, KENT	M	1004706	1080481	2085187	4
86	60	GRUELICH, RICHARD	M	860326	1153749	2014075	4
87	170	WOOD, CORT	M	24384	1980280	2004664	5
88	49	PRENTIS, NED	M	985385	967355	1952739	7
89	42	KARBO, LEN	W	140845	1779271	1920116	3
90	58	ROCHE, BIFF	W	813400	990936	1804336	4
91	53	BROWN, HAROLD	S	355498	1447481	1802979	4
92	148	HAMLIN, JIM	S	220979	1563221	1784200	5
93	55	SCHOTT, JOHN	N	535701	1243282	1778983	3
94	353	MEISNER, L	C	211273	1542160	1753433	4
95	132	MYER, A	N	1401999	324081	1726080	3
96	52	THOMPSON, GREG	N	951366	714875	1666241	4
97	95	COLLINS, DAVE	W	462002	1186814	1648815	5
98	102	ORGILL, MIKE	W	210088	1417828	1627916	4
99	144	CURTIS, RICH	M	656243	967032	1623274	6
100	758	BRODSKY, JANE	C	0	1621573	1621573	4
101	47	WATERS, JOY	I	241587	1363509	1605095	3
102	86	ROSSBACH, JAY	S	522736	1047548	1570284	5
103	84	MARTEL, L	N	803551	714875	1518426	3
104	619	JUVINALL, DREW	W	516209	990936	1507145	4
105	92	SMITH, BEN	N	438308	1057827	1496135	6
106	106	NEWELL, LIBBY	S	171525	1307700	1479225	8
107	33	CARTER, STEVEN	M	671267	798258	1469525	4
108	85	LUFKIN, JANE	W	462002	971665	1433667	4
109	672	ROWE, JEFF	W	231001	1111373	1342374	5
110	108	HUNTER, JOHN	N	848095	483054	1331148	4
111	23	MARSAC, MAURICE	W	416924	894356	1311280	4
112	561	BAST, J	W	1267604	0	1267604	1
113	6	BELL, R	W	1126759	119287	1246046	2
114	143	FINSNESS, JOSI	I	449017	773526	1222543	2
115	100	ALMAN, R	W	361047	805543	1166590	6
116	51	PAYNE, DOUG	M	578673	569556	1148230	6
117	114	KELLOGG, HOWARD	W	156346	990936	1147282	4
118	83	LANYON, GEN	M	581835	565101	1146936	7
119	623	KILBORNE, BRIGGS	S	0	1143768	1143768	1
120	50	SPRAGUE, STEVEN	W	803551	335699	1139250	2
121	581	CLINE, E	W	704224	430415	1134640	3
122	566	BREUER, ED	W	362775	769925	1132700	6
123	264	JANITZ, SANDY	C	211273	878752	1090025	4
124	449	MOODY, WILLIAM	C	304383	771080	1075462	3
125	99	ELIASSEN, GARTH	W	138051	934929	1072980	3
126	246	MAXWELL, M	M	483173	587353	1070526	4
127	159	McCAMPBELL, D	W	663027	397374	1060400	6
128	282	GUTHERIE, L	S	208186	843717	1051903	7
129	29	McREYNOLDS, DREW	I	0	1036896	1036896	2
130	238	DEGNAN, C	W	18245	970835	989081	5
131	230	OLSEN, LEE	S	105989	870397	976386	8
132	64	PAYNE, BETTY	M	127598	834718	962316	6
133	87	BAYARD, RUFUS	M	576931	367620	944551	4
134	601	ERIKSON, G	W	0	934929	934929	1
135	444	STAUFFER, JOHN	W	120428	807237	927665	5
136	57	FITZPATRICK, JACQUE	W	449017	464116	913133	2
137	133	HOY, REBECCA	S	152191	717244	869435	2
138	311	KETCHAM, RUSS	W	56255	810184	866434	3
139	774	SMITH, CHARLIE	W	247297	602699	849995	4
140	75	COBB, TY	W	263065	579426	842491	4
141	622	KEMPER, JIM	W	140845	701197	842042	2
	73	LUFKIN, TOM	W	140845	701197	842042	2
143	103	MARTIN, MAL	I	175575	622257	797832	3
144	660	PETERSON, VANGIE	W	146187	647777	793964	4
145	179	THOMPSON, A	N	429555	348986	778542	4
146	32	FITZPATRICK, BARRY	W	299345	464116	763461	2
147	98	PASSARELLI, O	S	285011	476784	761795	4
148	187	CUTTER, JOHN	W	377337	382569	759906	4
149	739	LYNCH, ALYSON	W	111454	647777	759230	4
150	109	McMILLAN, JACK	W	185435	571868	757303	4
151	772	REBUSCHATIS, R	W	478921	270468	749389	3
152	820	HARLAN, BILL	W	24808	721043	745851	2
153	54	BERGEN, CHRISTOPHE	N	401775	335699	737475	2
154	140	GORSLINE, J	M	724760	0	724760	1
155	634	LINDBLOM, DAN	W	0	701197	701197	1
156	161	HANNER, MICHAEL	W	334189	330312	664501	4
157	157	PHANEUF, JOHN	N	267850	396078	663928	3
158	37	JACOB, MERRITT	N	133925	503549	637474	2
159	155	HART, MIKE	C	295409	323017	618414	2
160	592	DODT, MIKE	W	563379	47715	611094	2
161	184	PEARCE, JULIE	W	5341	603591	608933	5
162	141	MARRON, AL	M	139304	465564	604868	4
163	151	McREYNOLDS, KEN	I	267850	335699	603549	2
164	200	DENNEY, MURIEL	W	404487	153353	557840	3
165	235	BRANDT, P	C	177245	376854	554099	2
166	795	BRODSKY, STUART	C	236327	311653	547981	3
167	280	HEATH, VAL	M	0	509929	509929	3
168	745	CROWLEY, KIT	S	64285	439899	504184	3
169	857	DANOVA, CESARE	M	271133	221032	492165	2
170	94	SIMPSON, RANDI	S	31832	442243	474076	7

1988 USCA GRAND PRIX RANKINGS (Continued)

1988 Rank	1987 Rank	Player's Name	Region	Singles Points	Doubles Points	Total Points	Events Used
171	392	CURTAIN, P	W	3651	467465	471116	2
172	120	FORMENTO, BRIAN	M	0	462888	462888	1
173	186	CROWLEY, A	M	107142	355161	462302	3
174	382	MOSSBROOK, S	W	319029	138835	457864	4
175	805	CURTIS, DAVID	M	36286	402987	439272	4
176	101	CAULKINS, DAVE	N	267850	167850	435700	2
177	249	RYDER, WILLIAM	S	77752	351427	429179	4
178	560	BASSFORD, G	W	422535	0	422535	1
179	203	BARNES, GEORGE	S	103495	295784	399279	4
180	111	LANGSTROTH, W	I	144574	253880	398454	5
181	207	MARSELLUS, RICHARD	W	0	390816	390816	1
182	118	WOOD, LEE		58616	328761	387376	4
183	35	LOENING, BROOKE	N	67783	317558	385341	3
184	242	DIX, NORMAN	M	21312	363970	385282	4
185	844	IMHOF, MARY	M	0	381323	381323	1
186	208	RINE, JUDY	S	39077	341233	380310	4
187	216	MIHLON, M	M	76431	303690	380120	7
188	231	HINDS, J	M	171426	195474	366901	2
189	498	MITSINIKOS, C	N	61110	305551	366661	2
190	136	WATERER, TONY	S	204222	155461	359684	4
191	147	SEXTON, CHARLES	W	120428	235415	355843	4
192	105	SUPPER, FRED	N	102689	244179	346868	4
193	126	HIGHT, JACK	N	121168	221727	342895	2
194	196	FENTON, V	M	0	338954	338954	1
195	150	HOWARD, F	M	43954	283592	327546	6
196	139	KANELOS, GEORGE	S	157440	161434	318873	3
197	183	FENNELL, V	M	206996	108641	315636	4
198	638	LIVINGSTON, CARL	W	90156	225390	315546	2
199	145	HANNER, SUSIE	W	167095	139573	306668	4
200	225	DIX, ELINOR	M	26640	279231	305871	4
201	104	BROWN, SANDY	N	133925	167850	301775	2
202	227	HARNETT, JOE	I	93449	208291	301740	3
203	665	RENAHAN, JEAN	M	0	296584	296584	1
204	173	SHANKLAND, SID	W	126765	167493	294258	2
205	362	CHATHAM, MARGARET	M	212555	79274	291829	6
206	755	VANCE, WILLIAM	C	59082	221836	280918	3
207	174	HART, M/JR.	C	118164	161509	279672	2
208	197	TORIAN, JIM	W	109024	167493	276517	2
209	303	VERWAY, ADRIAN	M	159425	114612	274037	4
210	189	LAWSON, MICKEY	S	128584	139410	267994	2
211	567	BROGAN, M	M	0	254215	254215	1
212	190	REDDING, S	S	144476	107074	251550	4
213	171	ROWAND, F	W	96841	151144	247985	7
214	466	KNOLL, DOLCIE	S	0	243771	243771	3
215	279	TUBRIDY, DON	S	186967	50693	237659	3
216	241	MARSAC, MELANIE	W	66376	167780	234155	4
217	570	BURCH, MIKE	W	0	233732	233732	1
	414	DANIELS, J	W	0	233732	233732	1
219	335	HILTON, E	M	123126	108641	231766	4
220	166	HOEGBERG, C	I	128736	98544	227281	4
221	212	COOPER, LORETTA	M	46697	175069	221766	5
222	113	BROOKS, M F	S	0	221727	221727	1
223	239	HINDS, G	M	21428	195474	216902	2
224	845	O'CONNOR, L	M	0	211846	211846	1
225	218	MARGULIES, HARRIETT	M	8012	201302	209314	3
226	383	McNEIL, G	M	149882	54519	204401	3
227	243	MILES, ROGER	W	99259	99616	198875	4
228	156	SHORT, A	S	113478	83464	196942	2
229	180	WOODALL, J	S	163882	32103	195984	2
230	779	DEVEREUX, READ	S	0	194750	194750	1
231	201	PURCELL, P	S	138442	53292	191734	4
232	261	CUTTER, SYBIL	M	0	191285	191285	2
233	234	MARRON, A	M	551	190166	190717	3
234	594	DONDERO, DAVE	W	169021	20729	189750	2
235	757	DICK, JOANNE	C	0	186778	186778	3
236	424	CHATHAM, H	W	63334	120339	183673	5
237	199	MIHLON, F	M	16024	165089	181112	5
238	206	HERMANN, JIM	W	175576	4962	180537	3
239	904	PETERSON, ERVAND	W	45078	135234	180312	2
240	190	CAMPAGNA, S	M	48185	130316	178501	3
241	733	COOLEY, WILLIAM	S	2005	174096	176102	3
242	240	FORELLE, C	M	90427	83549	173975	5
243	633	LEMBO, G	M	0	169477	169477	1
244	780	BELL, PAUL	S	0	166929	166929	1
245	134	SWOPE, HERBERT	S	58525	107622	166148	2
246	429	DORSEY, MAUREEN	M	0	164619	164619	2
247	482	HEBERT, P	N	6945	150947	157892	2
248	415	SMITH, WANDA LEE	W	56825	98430	155255	6
249	321	HOLLENDER, A	M	1872	150314	152187	6
250	259	VAN WINKLE, ART	N	0	152079	152079	1
251	217	COLEMAN, G	M	19538	131283	150821	4
252	761	ABOUZOID, SANDY	S	43222	104207	147430	5
253	149	JOHNSTONE, NANCY	M	10656	136528	147184	3
254	121	NOON, PAUL	C	140845	0	140845	1
255	781	COLVIN, KRIS	S	0	139107	139107	1
256	357	WATKINS, W	S	355	135434	135789	4
257	488	LORENZE, E	M	1412	133548	134960	4
258	846	SCNELL, INA	M	0	127108	127108	1
259	861	HATHAWAY, TYLER	M	87908	36027	123935	4
260	255	LOEW, R	S	15760	105427	121187	2
261	405	PARK, J	W	37207	83271	120478	5
262	682	STALLINGS, DON	W	0	119287	119287	1
263	366	BERNE, BJ	S	14318	102105	116423	6
264	811	TIMONEY, LAUREN	N	0	114244	114244	1
265	371	HAYES, RUSSELL	M	80269	32579	112848	3
266	338	GARDINER, C	S	221	111287	111507	2
267	252	BESSETTE, A	S	0	111286	111286	1
268	865	SALLOUM, CHARLES	M	43405	66882	110287	4
269	247	HOEGBERG, A	I	11476	98544	110021	4
270	808	TRACY, BERNADETTE	M	43405	66020	109425	4
271	142	BAXTER, F	I	46725	62099	108824	2
272	379	MEISNER, B	C	0	107672	107672	1
273	456	SHERRY, M	S	0	105427	105427	1
274	215	McMARTIN, H	I	0	102235	102235	1
275	301	BESSETTE, E	S	0	102235	102235	1
276	220	THORNBROUGH, ALT	S	0	101386	101386	1
277	853	KLINE, KIETH	M	37503	62930	100433	2
278	77	COBB, R	W	41507	57928	99435	4
279	393	McDERMOTT, A	M	0	97870	97870	1
280	299	COTE, M	N	6945	90568	97513	2
281	330	FISH, BOB	S	245	94710	94955	3
282	501	DEIBEL, MC	N	18586	74842	93427	4
283	248	SACK, A	I	62300	31049	93349	2
284	182	HARNETT, N	I	62300	30865	93165	3
285	41	THOMAS, BYRON	S	24384	67541	91926	2
286	812	SCHMIDT, B	M	0	91395	91395	1
287	300	COTE, PAULINE	N	0	90568	90568	1
288	202	RHEAULT, J	N	0	90568	90568	1
289	290	RHEAULT, GENE	M	0	90568	90568	1
290	881	DEL SIMONE, AL	W	45276	45078	90354	3
291	903	CHESTELSON, CLAUDIA	W	45078	45078	90156	2
292	381	ROGERS, L	S	0	88095	88095	1
293	165	DENNEY, ART	M	0	87289	87289	1
294	158	TORIAN, A	W	31150	55831	86981	2
295	284	WATKINS, J	S	473	86399	86872	4
296	324	JAMES, M	M	21428	65158	86586	2
297	928	KLEIN, K	M	85713	0	85713	1
298	345	HALMAN, MIA	M	2192	83308	85499	3
299	237	BOAK, G	M	0	84738	84738	1
	224	D'ELIA, W	M	0	84738	84738	1
	274	LINDEN, S	M	0	84738	84738	1
	674	SCHNELL, EUGENE	M	0	84738	84738	1
303	278	DYER, T	S	0	83464	83464	1
	782	ROSE, BENNETT	S	0	83464	83464	1
305	408	HILTON, W	M	5328	76327	81655	2
306	372	MITCHELL, BARBARA	W	51793	29769	81562	3
307	403	SCHNEDL, D	W	118	79148	79267	3
308	130	MIRANDA, AL	S	78154	0	78154	1
309	799	SINCLAIR, PEGGY	I	46725	31049	77774	2
310	306	HUHN, L	S	3342	73164	76506	4
311	305	BECKERS, J	C	3734	71271	75005	4
312	443	NOBORI, J	W	46921	27580	74501	6
313	752	DICK, BILLY	C	0	73309	73309	2
314	391	GARRETT, J	W	29769	41617	71386	3
315	191	WITTLER, LARRY	W	71293	0	71293	1
316	175	BLACK, J	S	19538	49107	68645	3
317	283	BUSH, LORE	S	0	68310	68310	2
318	285	ROWAND, R	S	8810	58766	67576	3
319	786	MURRIE, RICHARD	M	0	65423	65423	1
320	347	HUNT, T	M	44686	20092	64778	4
321	512	JOHNSON, J	S	38311	26181	64492	5
322	223	TABOADA, T	S	26742	37485	64228	2
323	162	KNOLL, DON	S	0	64206	64206	1
324	605	GOODE, BUD	S	7048	56746	63794	3
325	743	HYDE, B	S	0	63351	63351	1
326	800	SINCLAIR, ANDREW	I	31150	31049	62199	2
327	339	LAMONTAGNE, ROGER	N	0	60379	60379	4
	340	LAMONTAGNE, OVIDE	N	0	60379	60379	1
	276	SANDERS, CENTER	N	0	60379	60379	1
	814	PHANEUF, PAULA	N	0	60379	60379	1
	815	COTE, SYLVIA	N	0	60379	60379	1
332	756	WHITLOW, CHARLES	C	0	60327	60327	2
333	503	LEVY, L	S	5328	54519	59847	2
334	402	CAWLEY, A	W	14885	42393	57278	3
335	573	CAHILL, D	W	46831	9923	56754	3
336	436	ROBERTS, E	S	56739	0	56739	1
337	710	FEENEY, W	S	0	56285	56285	1
	759	WITKOWSKI, M	C	0	56285	56285	1
339	153	FLANAGAN, DAVID	W	0	55831	55831	1
340	798	HOFFMAN, WILL	M	0	55643	55643	1

1988 USCA GRAND PRIX RANKINGS (Continued)

1988 Rank	1987 Rank	Player's Name	Region	Singles Points	Doubles Points	Total Points	Events Used
341	154	STEFFY, J	M	8767	45408	54175	4
342	929	KANE, M	M	21428	32579	54007	2
343	948	BROWNLEE	C	0	53836	53836	1
	949	SCHMIDLAPP	C	0	53836	53836	1
345	789	O'DEA, JULIE	C	0	53742	53742	1
346	748	GALLO, C	S	0	52714	52714	1
	749	YORK, TY	S	0	52714	52714	1
	767	BEALE, J	I	0	52714	52714	1
349	409	STANTON, P	N	3734	48761	52495	3
350	277	FRIDAY, M	C	40515	11946	52462	4
351	163	WOOD, RODNEY	M	0	51118	51118	1
352	160	FORWOOD, A	M	18752	31465	50216	2
353	222	GRUELICH, DONNA	M	43405	4865	48270	4
354	747	BARBER, WILLIAM	W	0	47715	47715	1
355	245	SACK, S	I	15575	31049	46624	2
356	213	LEVERING, W	S	0	46470	46470	1
357	367	UPTON, J	N		45698	45698	1
358	911	BIDENCOPE, MICHAEL	I	24808	19846	44654	2
359	204	LAND, L	S	6575	37874	44449	4
360	522	RESSLER, B	M	807	43616	44422	2
361	327	YOUNT, U	S	10507	33718	44224	3
362	777	WASYLYK, BRIAN	I	27148	15870	43018	4
363	146	SEXTON, A	W	21497	21497	42993	2
364	776	HERRMANN, JOHN	W	12471	30183	42654	4
365	847	BOAK, M	M	0	42369	42369	1
366	833	MYER, CARL	N	26136	14935	41070	2
367	304	BECKERS, C	C	18668	21193	39862	3
368	232	CASSADY, C	S	0	38166	38166	2
	485	CASSADY, T	S	0	38166	38166	1
370	817	CURRIER, PHIL	M	6945	30189	37134	2
371	741	DEFALCO, AUDREY	W	10649	25964	36613	2
372	192	BOGOUNOFF, B	M	22526	13196	35722	3
373	669	ROCHE, BILL	M	20572	14885	35457	3
374	658	PALMER, HARVARD	W	4962	29769	34731	2
375	152	BELL, A	W	10649	23857	34506	2
376	762	KUHASZ, M	S		34386	34386	2
377	763	KUHASZ, G	S	0	34078	34078	2
378	517	RESSLER, D	M	1009	32712	33720	2
379	178	BURRUSS, W	S	32776	0	32776	1
380	930	WRAGOFF, M	M	0	32579	32579	1
381	312	THOMPSON, D	S	0	32103	32103	1
382	297	SARGENT, J	S	123	31638	31761	3
383	719	FISH, POLLY	M	0	31679	31679	2
384	737	SWITZ, OLIVIA	M	0	31675	31675	1
385	452	KUENSELL, S	M	0	31465	31465	1
	457	FRANCIS, W	M	0	31465	31465	1
	542	DEGAS, A	M	0	31465	31465	1
388	309	SUPPER, P	N	31150	0	31150	1
389	123	MAST, G	W	24033	6910	30942	2
390	764	KURELIC, MARY	M	0	30431	30431	1
391	349	SWARTZ, M	S	0	30213	30213	1
392	384	RICHMOND, DORRY	N	0	30189	30189	1
	385	RICHMOND, CHARLIE	N	0	30189	30189	1
	818	CURRIER, JUNE	N	0	30189	30189	1
395	728	PAYSON, S	S	5380	24640	30020	5
396	291	WILLIAMS, A	C	13441	15001	28442	4
397	437	BROWN, W	S	28369	0	28369	1
398	263	MERRILL, W	S	0	27821	27821	1
399	289	QUAST, L	S	652	25964	26616	2
400	834	MCGILL, JAKE	N	22402	3734	26136	2
401	574	CAHILL, M	W	25896	0	25896	2
402	329	REIF, IVA	S	2740	22676	25416	4
403	125	SILLS, LEONARD	S	23925	0	23925	2
404	307	SCHOTT, S	N	0	22849	22849	1
405	328	RULE, MARILYN	S	0	22514	22514	1
406	219	COLBERT, N	M	11536	10615	22151	4
407	775	WYRO, JOHN	W	14605	7272	21877	2
408	738	BARBER, MADELINE	W	21298	0	21298	1
409	476	YOUNG, J III	M	6575	13675	20250	2
410	751	GLOVER, FOREST	C	0	20242	20242	2
411	913	LAIL, ROBIN	W	4962	14885	19846	2
412	315	DONNELL, J	C	0	19473	19473	1
413	696	VONESH, R	S	165	18743	18908	2
	835	MAGEE, SASHA	N	7467	11201	18668	2
	836	KILDALL, SCOTT	N	7467	11201	18668	2
416	765	SUMWALT, BOB	S	3524	14283	17807	3
417	257	THOMAS, BARRY	S	15814	1132	16947	4
418	787	O'DEA, JOHN	C	9613	6910	16523	2
419	268	YOUNG, R	N	15973	0	15973	1
420	313	MITCHELL, K	S	0	15758	15758	1
421	269	LARKIN, CARL	N	11201	3788	14989	3
422	214	GOLDBERG, E	S	0	14683	14683	1
	348	SAWDON, F	S	0	14683	14683	1
424	778	BAIRD, MATT	W	3651	10908	14560	2
425	256	FRIDAY, F	C	5324	9166	14490	2
426	590	DANZ, C	W	10649	3636	14285	2
427	468	PINKARD, N	S	0	13828	13828	2
428	210	BRODIE, D	C	0	13820	13820	1
	253	CRAWFORD, R	C	0	13820	13820	1
430	346	BEURY, M	S	0	12982	12982	1
	617	HYDE, A	S	0	12982	12982	1
	370	McKIEVER, CHUCK	S	0	12982	12982	1
	418	MANKIN, H	M	0	12982	12982	1
	419	MANKIN, R	M	0	12982	12982	1
	753	WITKOWSKI, D	S	0	12982	12982	1
	754	ALBAN, JIM	S	0	12982	12982	1
437	905	SCELFO, RON	S	4679	8278	12958	2
438	421	WRAGG, PETER	M	5481	7144	12625	4
439	724	HUHN, TOM	S	1337	11038	12375	2
440	390	KELLY, WILLIAM	M	0	12356	12356	2
441	788	FOGLE, MARY ANN	C	0	12221	12221	1
442	655	McLAUGHLIN, T	N	4965	7195	12159	2
443	441	FENNELL, G	M	1210	10904	12114	2
444	531	TANNEN, S	M	605	11250	11855	2
445	766	SUMWALT, BARBARA	S	0	11257	11257	1
446	838	BRACKETT, DICK	S	3734	7467	11201	2
447	354	McGONAGLE, L	C	5788	5372	11160	4
448	181	KANELOS, A	S	9769	1263	11032	2
449	783	COLE, BILLY	S	8807	1854	10661	3
450	821	HAYES, MARY KANE	M	10656	0	10656	1
451	740	LINDEN, NAT	W	10649	0	10649	1
	742	MUREAU, CH.	W	10649	0	10649	1
453	496	KELLY, M	M	0	10557	10557	1
454	344	SCHRIBER, T	S	5286	5198	10484	3
455	725	LARKIN, TOM	S	2005	8278	10284	2
456	912	BLANTON, BILL	W	9923	0	9923	1
	914	HOUSTON, BEN	W	4962	4962	9923	2
	915	SMITH, C	W	9923	0	9923	1
459	400	KERR, M	M	1097	8006	9103	3
460	425	O'DEA, D	W	2781	6110	8891	2
461	919	STOCK, A	N	2482	6295	8778	2
462	308	MORAN, J	S	669	7575	8244	2
463	855	PRICKETT, LINDA	M	0	7918	7918	1
464	918	SPRAGUE, K	N	3310	4497	7806	2
465	399	YODER, J	W	0	7663	7663	1
466	921	WILSON, R	M	0	7195	7195	1
467	373	SCHRIBER, H	S	1762	5351	7113	3
468	807	BRYSON, DAVID	M	2743	4310	7053	2
469	864	TAHTA, RIKKI	M	4389	2586	6975	2
470	316	ALEXANDER, P	M	0	6837	6837	1
471	858	CHARRIER, MICHAEL	M	1646	5172	6818	2
472	423	GUTHERIE, TOM JR.	S	6080	692	6772	3
473	732	WITRY, SHARON	S	0	6491	6491	1
474	244	GUTHERIE, P	S	5253	1133	6386	2
475	497	MOSS, T	M	732	5278	6010	2
476	427	FINKLEA, W	W	0	5903	5903	1
	193	UPDEGRAFF, KURT	W	0	5903	5903	1
478	863	HOLCOMBE, ED (BUD)	M	3292	2586	5878	2
479	131	BOYD, JOHN	W	0	5747	5747	1
480	368	ETHERINGTON, S	N	5324	0	5324	1
	352	YOUNG, A	N	5324	0	5324	1
482	547	GRIFFIN, S	M	0	5278	5278	1
483	685	SULLIVAN, M	N	1655	3597	5252	2
484	810	MARTIN, BILL	S	0	5172	5172	1
485	507	SHEELY, RICK	C	2781	2317	5098	2
486	271	CAMPBELL, M	N	0	5050	5050	1
487	768	HINZE, BOB	W	0	4919	4919	1
488	874	CURRIER, PAULINE	N	1655	2698	4353	2
489	860	MEJIA, LUIS	M	0	4310	4310	1
490	481	PINKARD, B	S	0	4229	4229	1
	832	SPURLOCK, CATHERINE	S	0	4229	4229	1
492	458	HALE, B	W	0	3935	3935	1
	461	SLATAPER, L	W	0	3935	3935	1
494	916	KETCHAM, SALLIE	S	3520	378	3898	2
	917	LEVERING, LOUISE	S	3520	378	3898	2
496	355	LAMM, RICHARD	W	0	3831	3831	1
	119	WHALEY, ROB	W	0	3831	3831	1
	890	TOAL, JAMES	W	0	3831	3831	1
499	859	MEAD, BILL	M	0	3448	3448	1
	862	THOMAS, NATALIE	M	0	3448	3448	1
501	467	DAVIS,O	S	0	3383	3383	1
	455	SPURLOCK, S.	M	0	3383	3383	1
503	871	SALLOUM, JR.	M	1646	1724	3370	2
504	422	COREY, E	S	2627	692	3318	2
505	236	BARMORE, B	C	0	3055	3055	1
506	854	CUNNINGHAM, TERRY	M	366	2639	3005	2
507	785	MORGAN, CHARLES	S	2627	327	2953	3
508	469	DEATON, M	W	0	2951	2951	1
	470	FLOWERS, C	W	0	2951	2951	1
	460	RANNEY, J	W	0	2951	2951	1

UNITED STATES CROQUET ASSOCIATION MEMBER CLUBS

As of October 1989

SOUTHERN REGION

ALABAMA
Choccolocco Croquet Club	Anniston
Montgomery Mallet Club	Montgomery
Pond House Croquet Club	Pell City

ARKANSAS
Royal Knights of Croquet	Arkadelphia
Little Rock Croquet Club	Little Rock
Trigger Gap Croquet Club	Eureka Springs

BAHAMAS
Lyford Cay Club	Nassau

FLORIDA
Associated Marine Institute	Tampa
The Beach Club	Palm Beach
Bentley Village Croquet Club	Naples
Boca Raton Hotel & Club	Boca Raton
The Breakers Hotel	Palm Beach
Card Sound Croquet Club	Key Largo
Carlouel Yacht Club	Clearwater
Crossed Mallet Club	Stuart
Dogwood Croquet Club	Brooksville
East Hammock Croquet Club	Safety Harbor
The Everglades Club	Palm Beach
First Coast Croquet Club	Jacksonville
Fountainview	West Palm Beach
Gasparilla Inn	Boca Grande
Hamilton Croquet Club	Plantation
Indian Creek Country Club	Miami
Key Biscayne Mallet Club	Key Biscayne
Key Largo Anglers Club	Key Largo
Marriott At Sawgrass	Ponte Vedra Beach
Ocean Ridge Croquet Club	Ocean Ridge
Old Harbour Croquet Club	N. Palm Beach
Palm Beach Croquet Club	Palm Beach
Palm Beach Polo & CC	West Palm Beach
PGA Sheraton Hotel	Palm Beach Gardens
Croquet Club at PGA National	Palm Beach Gardens
PGA Mallet Club	Palm Beach Gardens
Quail's Nest Mallet Club	Naples
Royal Palm Yacht & CC	Boca Raton
Seaside Croquet Club	Seaside
SeaWatch of Boca Grande	Boca Grande
St. John's Croquet Club	Jacksonville
Sun Air Country Club	Haines City
Tampa Bay Croquet Club	Tampa
Useppa Island Croquet Club	Bokeelia
The Villas of Grand Cypress	Orlando
Winter Park Croquet Club	Winter Park

GEORGIA
Addison Hill Croquet Club	Greensboro
Atlanta Mallet Club	Atlanta
Brookstone Golf & CC	Atlanta
Croquet Club of the South	Atlanta
Frogmore Continental Croquet Club	Statesboro
Georgia Croquet Club	Williamson
Glen Oak Croquet Club	Camilla
Hampton Court Croquet Club	Hampton
Inn on the Green at Port Armor	Greensboro
Jekyll Island Croquet Club	Jekyll Island
Jekyll Island Resort	Jekyll Island
Okefenokee Mallet Club	Waycross
Olde Towne Mallet Club	Marietta
Oxford Lawn Club	Oxford
Smokerise Plantation	Peachtree City

LOUISIANA
Acadiana Croquet Club	Lafayette
Baton Rouge Croquet and Crawfish Club	Baton Rouge

MISSISSIPPI At Large Members

NORTH CAROLINA
Biltmore Croquet Club	Asheville
Bald Head Island Croquet Club	Bald Head Island
Chatooga Club	Chatooga
Grandfather Golf & CC	Linville
Lake Winnekeag Croquet Club	Morrisville
Lake Toxaway Croquet Club	Lake Toxaway
Pine Mallet Club	Southern Pines
Pinehurst Croquet Club	Pinehurst
Stoneridge Croquet Club	Chapel Hill
Treyburn Country Club	Durham

SOUTH CAROLINA
Columbia Croquet Club	Columbia
Hilton Head Croquet Club	Hilton Head Island
The Melrose Club	Hilton Head Island
Pine Lakes Croquet Club	Myrtle Beach
Port Royal Croquet Club	Hilton Head Island
Turnbridge Plantation	Hardeeville
Wexford Croquet Club	Hilton Head Island
Victoria Croquet Club	Irmo

TENNESSEE
Cottonwood Bocce and Croquet Club	Franklin
Indian Hills Golf & Athletic Club	Murfreesboro

UNITED STATES CROQUET ASSOCIATION
MEMBER CLUBS (Continued)

Knoxville Croquet Club	Knoxville
Willow Spring Mallet Club	Athens
US VIRGIN ISLANDS	
Bombay Mallet & Wicket Club	St. Croix
Tennis Club of St. Croix	St. Croix
WEST INDIES	
Jumby Bay	Antigua

CENTRAL REGION

INDIANA	At Large Members
ILLINOIS	
Bon Vivant Country Club	Bourbonnais
Croquet & Racquet Club	Chicago
Croquetoberfest	Chicago
Chicago Croquet Club	Chicago
Wester Croquet Club	Rockford
IOWA	At Large Members
KANSAS	
Split Rail Croquet Club	Howard
Topeka Country Club	Topeka
KENTUCKY	
Blue Flag Croquet Club	Bowling Green
Lexington Croquet Club	Lexington
Stamping Ground Croquet Club	Stamping Ground
West of England Croquet Club	Mayfield
MICHIGAN	
Harbor Balls & Mallet Club	Harbor Point
Kalamazoo Country Club	Kalamazoo
Salisbury Croquet Club	Owosso
MINNESOTA	
Gull Lake Croquet Club	Nisswa
Madden's Croquet Club	Brainerd
St. Paul Croquet Club	St. Paul
Westwood Croquet Club	Wayzata
MISSOURI	
Bellerive Country Club	St. Louis
Quimper Croquet Club	Kansas City
Spendthrift Circle Croquet Club	Kansas City
St. Louis Croquet Club	St. Louis
NEBRASKA	At Large Members
NORTH DAKOTA	At Large Members
OHIO	
Central Ohio Croquet Club	Worthington
Chagrin Valley Hunt Club	Gates Mills
Maumee River Mallet Club	Rossford
The Polo Club	Springfield
River Rooste Croquet Club	Piqua
Perrysburg Croquet Club	Perrysburg
Western Reserve Croquet Club	Shaker Heights

OKLAHOMA	
The Gardens Croquet Club	Tulsa
Tulsa Croquet Club	Tulsa
SOUTH DAKOTA	At Large Members
WISCONSIN	
The Birches Spa & Croquet Club	Ridgeway
Oconomowoc Croquet & Racquet Club	Milwaukee

SOUTHWESTERN REGION

ARIZONA	
Arizona Croquet Club	Scottsdale
Enchantment	Sedona
The Phoenician	Scottsdale
The Wigwam	Litchfield Park
CALIFORNIA	
Beverly Hills Croquet Club	Beverly Hills
Calabasas Croquet Club	Calabasas
Casa Woodfin Croquet	Indian Wells
Erawan Garden Hotel	Indian Wells
Fairbanks Ranch Country Club	Rancho Santa Fe
La Mancha Villas & Court Club	Palm Springs
Las Palmas Rancho Croquet Club	Santa Ana
Morningside Croquet Club	Rancho Mirage
Newport Beach Croquet Club	Newport Beach
Rancho Santa Fe Croquet Club	Rancho Santa Fe
Santa Barbara Croquet Club	Santa Barbara
Tennis Club at PGA West	La Quinta
The Sherwood Club	Thousand Oaks
COLORADO	
Castle Pines Croquet Club	Castle Rock
Denver Croquet Club	Denver
COSTA RICA	
The Croquet and Cricket Club of Costa Rica	San Jose
HAWAII	At Large Members
NEVADA	At Large Members
TEXAS	
Aerie Croquet Club	Amarillo
Austin Mallet Club	Austin
Columbia Lakes Croquet Club	West Columbia
Dallas Croquet Association	Dallas
Dallas Wicket & Mallet Club	Dallas
Ft. Worth Croquet Club	Ft. Worth
Ft. Worth Mallet Club	Ft. Worth
Hat Creek Croquet Club	Houston
Houston Mallet Club	Houston

UNITED STATES CROQUET ASSOCIATION
MEMBER CLUBS (Continued)

Northgate Country Club	Houston
Seventeen Acres Mallet Club	Arlington
Weston Lakes Country Club	Fulshear

NORTHWESTERN REGION

ALASKA	At Large Members
CANADA	
Vancouver Croquet Club	Vancouver
CALIFORNIA	
Foxhollow Croquet Club	Sacramento
Ink Grade Group	Pope Valley
Los Altos Croquet Club	Los Altos
Marlborough Court Croquet Club	Oakland
Meadowood Mallet Club	St. Helena
Newton Croquet Club	St. Helena
The Plough and the Stars Country Inn & Croquet Club	Arcata
Rancho Valencia Croquet Club	Rancho Santa Fe
San Francisco Croquet Club	San Francisco
Shalako Mallet Club	Sacramento
Sonoma-Cutrer Croquet Club	Santa Rosa
Sunnyside Croquet Club	Tahoe City
University of California	Berkeley
IDAHO	At Large Members
MONTANA	At Large Members
NEVADA	At Large Members
OREGON	
Cherry Blossom Cottage	Portland
Forest Lawn Mallet Club	Creswell
Portland Croquet Club	Portland
Willamette Croquet Club	Independence
WASHINGTON	
Puget Sound Croquet Club	Bellevue
Seattle Croquet Club	Seattle
WYOMING	
Teton Pines Mallet Club	Jackson

NEW ENGLAND REGION

CANADA	
Grenadier Island	Thousand Islands
Pugwash Mallet Club	Nova Scotia
Toronto Cricket, Skating & Curling Club	Toronto, Ontario
The Royal St. Catharines Croquet Club	St. Catharines, Ontario

CONNECTICUT	
Bayberry Mallet Club	Greenwich
Compo Beach Mallet Club	Westport
Conroy Croquet Club	Greenwich
Greenwich Croquet Club	Greenwich
Madison Croquet Club	Madison
Minerva Mallet Club	Old Greenwich
Money Point Mallet Club	Mystic
Peken Mallet Club	Washington
Ridge Acres Mallet Club	Darien
Ridgefield Croquet Club	Ridgefield
Round Island Croquet Club	Greenwich
Second Step Croquet Club	Easton
ENGLAND	
Lloyds Croquet Society	London
MAINE	
Gorges Grant Resort	Ogonquit
Kennebunkport Croquet Club	Kennebunkport
MASSACHUSETTS	
Ballymeade Country Club	Falmouth
Beverly Historical Society	Beverly
Blantyre Croquet Club	Lenox
Boston Croquet Club	Boston
Cape Cod Mallet Club	Cape Cod
Clark Hill Croquet Club	Belmont
Edgartown Croquet Club	Edgartown
Lenox Club	Lenox
Pheasant Hill Croquet Club	South Hamilton
Richmond Mallet Club	Richmond
Sconset Croquet Club	Siasconset
Smith College Croquet Team	Northhampton
The Wauwinet Inn	Nantucket
NEW HAMPSHIRE	
Freedom Mallet Club	Freedom
Hampstead Croquet Association	Hampstead
Spalding Inn & Club	Whitefield
Stark Lane Croquet Association	Manchester
Strawberry Banke Croquet Club	Portsmouth
RHODE ISLAND	
Agawam Hunt	East Providence
The Atlantic Inn	Block Island
Block Island Croquet Club	Block Island
Dead of the Winter Croquet Society	Providence
Newport Casino Croquet Club	Newport
Newport Croquet Club	Newport
Point Judith Country Club	Pawcatuck
VERMONT	
Croquet Club of Vermont	Woodstock

UNITED STATES CROQUET ASSOCIATION
MEMBER CLUBS (Continued)

MID ATLANTIC REGION

BERMUDA

Lantana Colony Club	Somerset
Sommers Isle Croquet Club	Hamilton
Croquet Club of Bermuda	Somerset

DELAWARE

Delaware Croquet Club	Wilmington
Vicmead Mallet Club	Wilmington

DISTRICT OF COLUMBIA

Capital City Croquet Club	Washington

MARYLAND

Annapolis Croquet Club	Annapolis
Carroll Creek Croquet Club	Clarksburg
Gay Willows Croquet Club	Oxford
Harbor Court Hotel	Baltimore

NEW JERSEY

Basking Ridge Croquet Club	Basking Ridge
Blossom Cove Mallet Club	Redbank
Broadlawn Wicket Club	Sussex
Green Gables Croquet Club	Spring Lake
Hunterdon Hall Farm Croquet Club	Whitehouse Station
Roxbury Croquet Club	Roxbury
Short Hills Mallet Club	Short Hills
Short Hills Croquet Club	Short Hills

NEW YORK

Alderbrook Croquet Club	Katonah
Champagne Croquet Club	Rochester
Crooked Wicket	Fredonia
Eastman House Croquet Team	Rochester
Gipsy Trail Croquet Club	Carmel
Glens Falls Country Club	Queensbury
Meadow Club of Southampton	Southampton
Millbrook Mallets	Millbrook
Naples Croquet Club	Naples
New York Croquet Club	New York
Palladian Wickets	Bridgehampton
Pine Court	Tuxedo Park
Quantuck Bay Croquet Group	Quogue
Saratoga Croquet Club	Saratoga
Silver Fox Inn	Milbrook
Tuxedo Croquet Club	Tuxedo
Westhampton Mallet Club	Westhampton

PENNSYLANIA

Argyle Croquet Club	Glenside
Merion Cricket Club	Haverford
Nemacolin Woodlands	Farmington
Walnut Green Mallet Club	West Grove
The Wickets	Rosemont

VIRGINIA

Burton Point Croquet Club	Charlottesville
Hampton Croquet Club	Hampton
Lake James Croquet Club	Virginia Beach
Meadow Lane Lodge	Warm Springs
Sandy Fields Croquet Club	Richmond
University of Virginia	Charlottesville
Wheatland Croquet Club	Purcellville
Windsor Croquet Club	Windsor

WEST VIRGINIA

Buckingham Court	Lewisburg
The Greenbrier	White Sulpher Springs
Greenbrier Croquet Club	White Sulphur Springs

In addition to these USCA Clubs there are over 700 At Large Members' including some in the states of Indiana, Idaho, Iowa, Kansas, Montana, Nevada and North Dakota.

Photo and Drawing Credits

Photos

Lucien Capehart – 63, 77, 83 thru 92, 109, 111, 127 thru 135, 178, 210; William Powers – 58, 68, 69, 96, 104, 114 thru 125, 136 thru 139; Robert Phillips – 176, 182, 202(1), 203, 206(1); Jack R. Osborn – 28, 29, 31, 40, 183, 196, 197, 199, 204; USCA – 47, 50, 93, 94, 165, 167, 193, 205 thru 207; Croquet International Ltd. – 54, 60, 61, 65 thru 72, 79; Roy deFilippis – 42, 169, 180, 215, back cover; Ron Nelson – Cover and CIL product shots; Richard Carver Wood – 24, 25, 212 (3 & 4); Davidoff Studios – 30, 78; Croquet Foundation of America 212 thru 215; Jacque Cappella – 214, 216; Lee Olsen – 48, 199; Bill Hickey – 177; Jean Negulesco – 27; UPI – 80 / Tom Salyer – 200; Jean Pearman – 76; Luke Majorki – 194, 195

Drawing/Diagrams

Alan Scheuch – 56, 57, 107, 112 thru 117, 124; Jack R. Osborn – 143 thru 161; Bill Hoy – 185; Linda West (NYCC) – 188.

What Members Receive When Joining the USCA

Basic USCA Membership privileges for individuals joining as either club or non-club affiliated At Large Members.

Annual membership dues provide each individual (or couple) with the following:

1. A subscription to the US Croquet Gazette magazine.
2. USCA Bulletins which feature tournament results and news of upcoming events.
3. USCA Rule Books as they are updated.
4. A USCA Membership Card
   a) Which is required to earn Grand Prix points in all USCA sanctioned tournaments and discounts for USCA schools and clinics.
   b) Entitles each member to guest playing privileges at those USCA member clubs whose policies and/or facilities permit guests (i.e., private country clubs may have guest restrictions or family clubs, limited space and time available).
5. USCA blazer badge and tie that are available for purchase by members only.

USCA Club Privileges

All USCA member clubs are provided with the following benefits for their annual dues:

1. Four individual memberships.
2. Reduced annual dues for additional individual members.
3. Sanctioning of Club tournaments which enables Club members to participate in USCA recognized intra-club and invitational competitions and thus establish Regional and National Grand Prix rankings and handicaps.
4. USCA Bulletins providing organizational assistance for croquet activities, publicity and promotional aids.
5. Tournament and instructional information and formats.
6. Frameable 9" x 12" certificate of club membership.

USCA Dues Structure

Annual Dues for USCA At-large Member (not affiliated with USCA Clubs)
Individual – $25.00, Couples – $40.00, Junior (under 18) – $15.00

1989 USCA Dues Structure For USCA Croquet Club **Club Type**	**Basic Annual** **Club Dues**
Family and Private Clubs	$125.00*
Country, Tennis & Sports Clubs	175.00*
Resorts, Hotels & Inns:	
a) Accommodations for less than 25 guests	150.00*
b) Accommodations for 26-50 guests	200.00*
c) Accommodations for over 51 guests	250.00*
Real Estate Developments	$175.00 to $250.00*

   * BASIC ANNUAL DUES INCLUDES FOUR (4) MEMBERS' DUES
(i.e.: President, Vice President, Secretary and Treasurer of the Club or Club Committee Members)
ALL ADDITIONAL CLUB MEMBERS:
$30.00 per couple / $20.00 per adult / $10.00 per junior (under 18)

Schools, Colleges, Universities, Retirement Groups $75.00**
and Communities. Historical, Charitable or Church Facilities, Municipal Parks & Recreation Departments.

   ** BASIC ANNUAL DUES INCLUDES TWO (2) MEMBERS' DUES
ALL ADDITIONAL CLUB MEMBERS:
$25.00 per couple / $15.00 per adult / $10.00 per junior (under 18)

USCA Informational Offerings

Publications

The United States Croquet Association publishes the Official Rules for American 6-Wicket and 9-Wicket Croquet as well as Golf Croquet. Literally pocket-sized (4 x 6 inches), the rule book is invaluable for ending disputes on the greensward. The cost of the Rule Book is $5.00 including postage.

The USCA also carries copies of the English (or International) Rule Book available at $8.00 including postage. John Solomon's "CROQUET" provides knowledgeable insights to the English Rules game and its 1988 up dated paperback edition is available for $25.00 including postage.

"CROQUET: How to Play the Perfect Game" by American star Bob Kroeger, published by the Croquet Foundation of America, combines an audio cassette and book with colored diagrams and is available from the USCA for $34.95 plus $3.00 postage and handling.

This book, "CROQUET/The Sport," will also be obtainable from the USCA at $24.95 for hardcover and $15.95 paperback plus $3.00 postage and handling.

The "U.S. CROQUET GAZETTE," the official quarterly magazine of the USCA, is also available at $4.00 per issue plus $1.25 postage or yearly subscriptions can be ordered directly from the publisher (Farsight Communications, Inc.) at $17.00 including delivery. (See next page)

Videotapes

In 1981 the Croquet Foundation of America produced a 40 minute videotape. Starting with a tour of the court, the video, **"Croquet: A Primer,"** shows top U.S. players demonstrating the various grips, stances, swings and shots. Because it was filmed at the USA vs England matches, it features English greats John Solomon, Bernard Neal and Nigel Aspinall executing two-ball, three-ball and four-ball breaks. As a visual teaching aid, this tape is without peer. It is available in $^1/_2$ inch videotape cassettes in either the VHS or Beta II formats at a cost of $35.00 including postage.

Also available is a 20 minute videotape titled **"Introduction to USCA Croquet, America's Most Misunderstood Sport,"** which serves as an entertaining overview of the USCA game and its various competitive and social attractions. It is available in either the VHS or Beta II formats for $25.00 including postage, or it can be ordered in combination with **"Croquet: A Primer"** for $50.00 including postage.

"The Fundamentals of Croquet Shotmaking" is a 50 minute video featuring Nigel Aspinall and narrated by Teddy Prentis, available for $50.00 including postage.

Additional instructional tapes are produced on an ongoing basis. For a listing of new tapes, or to order those named above, contact the United States Croquet Association, 500 Avenue of Champions, Palm Beach Gardens, Florida 33418 (phone: 407-627-3999).

CROQUET EQUIPMENT AND SERVICES

ANGLO/AMERICAN SPORTS, INC.

In his pre-croquet life, Jack R. Osborn headed his own New York Design and Marketing Consultant firm from 1958 through the early 1970's, and in 1975 he formed Farsight Communications, Inc.

After founding the United States Croquet Association in 1976, Jack served as its President and Executive Director until early 1989. Throughout this period, Jack applied his earlier experience in public relations, design, advertising and marketing to the creation of the USCA's key communications efforts including the U.S. Croquet Gazette, advertising and sponsorship sales, development of instructional materials, video tapes, rule books, equipment standarization and logo merchandise. Since 1984, Farsight Communications, Inc. and Jack have provided these management services to the USCA under a contract which, in order to provide for their continuation, was extended and expanded when Jack retired from his offices. While he will also serve on the USCA Management Committee until 1991, Jack's focus, through Farsight, Croquet International Ltd. and his newly formed Anglo/American Sports, Inc., is providing services to the USCA, as well as toward fulfilling the sports growing needs which cannot be provided by a sports association.

Anglo/American Sports, Inc. has become the corporate holding company of Farsight (FCI), Croquet International (CIL) , and more recently , American Croquet Enterprises (ACE) headed by William Hoy.

Each of these subsidiaries provide specialized services and/ or products for existing and potential USCA members, clubs, advertisers, sponsors and others interested in furthering the sport of croquet.

CROQUET INTERNATIONAL LTD. (CIL)

Since 1978, Croquet International Ltd. has been the exclusive United States importer, distributor and marketer of John Jaques & Son Ltd. croquet equipment. Over these years Croquet International has provided the United States Croquet Association with close to $250,000 in royalty, sponsorship and overhead support.

CIL distributes Jaques English made equipment and American made ACE products through select retailers, pro shops and via direct mail. For a catalog, price information and list of retailers carrying this croquet equipment, contact: **Croquet International Ltd.**
7100-23 Fairway Drive, Palm Beach Gardens, FL 33418
or by calling (407) 627-4009 or by FAX (407) 624-3040.